Praise for *Your Edible*

Millions of people are waking up and realizing that our grassy lawns
no longer make sense when we can instead be producing our own healthy,
organic food right at home. But many of those millions just don't know how
to take the practical steps forward. In *Your Edible Yard*, Crystal lays out the
path for us to turn our bland yards into the gardens of our dreams, full of
healthy food, while saving us money at the grocery store and precious
environmental resources. This book has the potential to change
the landscaping of our nation and the design of our lives.
— Rob Greenfield, author, *Dude Making a Difference*

A beautiful synthesis of organic, regenerative, and permaculture
practices for an abundant yard anywhere.
— Matt Powers, author and educator at ThePermacultureStudent.com

Too many people, even in the overdeveloped world, find themselves in food
deserts, deprived of good, nutritious, fresh food on a daily basis. Crystal Stevens
shows us that food insecurity is completely unnecessary. All the food we could
ever want lies just outside our doorstep and gathering and preserving it the
permaculture way can be carefree and delightful.
— Albert Bates, author, *The Post Petroleum Survival Guide and Cookbook*
and *The Biochar Solution*

We are at a turning point in our society. Increasing climate changes are creating
global food shortages, which are predicted to become more widespread in the
very near future. Pending power outages will soon leave neighborhoods without
much food ...unless we get creative and take action. *Your Edible Yard* is a timely,
clear, inspiring, and valuable resource for anyone interested in the why and
how of getting started in transitioning your yard from lawn to edible garden.
Now is the time to create local food security, health, and the community
connections that help us to thrive....through organic, locally grown food.
— Zen Honeycutt, founding executive director of Moms Across America,
and author, *Unstoppable*

Crystal provides the tools, knowledge, and confidence for homeowners to transform their property into productive edible gardens. Her book is filled with gardening tips to assist small scale farming practices that can be practiced in any back yard or front yard setting.

— Jere Gettle, founder and owner of Baker Creek Heirloom Seed Company

This thorough and well-illustrated manual is a rich source of information for anyone looking for ways to incorporate permaculture practices into their gardens. With the emphasis on working with nature to grow diverse plantings that support a thriving community of living things, building healthy soil, and recycling waste, this will be a useful resource for any gardener.

— Linda Gilkeson, author, *Backyard Bounty*

Growing food changes who you are; you'll eat better, feel better, and live better. Give yourself to this book; it's the omen you've been waiting for.

— MaryJane Butters, farmer, author, and editor, *MaryJanesFarm* magazine

your Edible yard

landscaping with fruits and vegetables

Crystal Stevens

new society
PUBLISHERS

Cover design by Diane McIntosh. Cover Image ©Kaitie Adams.
All images ©Crystal Stevens unless otherwise noted.

Printed in Canada. First printing January 2020.

Inquiries regarding requests to reprint all or part of *Your Edible Yard* should be addressed to New Society Publishers at the address below. To order directly from the publishers, please call toll-free (North America) 1-800-567-6772, or order online at www.newsociety.com

Any other inquiries can be directed by mail to:
New Society Publishers
P.O. Box 189, Gabriola Island, BC V0R 1X0, Canada
(250) 247-9737

LIBRARY AND ARCHIVES CANADA CATALOGUING IN PUBLICATION

Title: Your edible yard : landscaping with fruits and vegetables / Crystal Stevens. Names: Stevens, Crystal, author.
Description: Includes index.
Identifiers: Canadiana (print) 20190214406 | Canadiana (ebook) 20190214414 | ISBN 9780865719224
   (softcover) | ISBN 9781550927153 (PDF) | ISBN 9781771423113 (EPUB)
Subjects: LCSH: Edible landscaping. | LCSH: Natural landscaping. | LCSH: Gardens—Design. | LCSH:
   Plants, Edible. | LCSH: Vegetable gardening. | LCSH: Fruit-culture.
Classification: LCC SB475.9.E35 S74 2020 | DDC 712.6—dc23

Funded by the Government of Canada
Financé par le gouvernement du Canada

New Society Publishers' mission is to publish books that contribute in fundamental ways to building an ecologically sustainable and just society, and to do so with the least possible impact on the environment, in a manner that models this vision.

Contents

Dedication and Acknowledgments

THIS BOOK IS DEDICATED to my loving father, Carl V. Moore, from whom I inherited my love for nature and the great outdoors, the spirit of adventure, a strong work ethic, endless ambition, and his giant stack of *Mother Earth News* magazines.

This book is dedicated to my family, friends, and mentors.

To my children, Cay and Iris, for the infinite love, joy, and inspiration they bring to my life daily. I am grateful and honored to be their mother.

To my husband, Eric Stevens, for his love, patience, support, and encouragement. His altruistic spirit and desire to make the world a better place inspires me greatly. This book would not have been possible without him.

To my mother, Cathy Moore, and her husband, Steven McGehee, who continue to encourage and support our family in all of our endeavors and for their generosity, dedication to family, and unconditional support. To my sister, Candice Pyle, and her husband, Dustin, for endless support and filling my heart with joy. To my niece, Cali Moore, for her humor, love, support, and all her hard work. Her strength and resilience are inspiring. To my nephews, Tysen and Mason, for the love and humor. To

my brother, Jason Crawford, for being a pillar of strength in our lives and for giving me loving support and encouragement. To my niece, Kaya Crawford, who lights up our lives. To my in-laws, Ann and Barry Stevens, for the wonderful support throughout the years and for raising such an amazing, thoughtful, creative, and loving son. To the entire Stevens family: for the unconditional love and support.

To all my dearest friends, mentors, and teachers: for sculpting my path, filling my life with purpose, and direction, and the endless inspiration you bring to this world.

To the entire team at New Society Publishers: for their continued support and for believing in the work that I do.

To everyone at La Vista Farm, EarthDance Organic Farm School, Slow Food St. Louis, Tower Grove Farmers Market, Permaculture Design Course, and all of our wonderful farmer friends: for their dedication to the good food movement. A special thanks to Robert Riley, Ingrid Witovet, Tradd Cotter, Meredith Leigh, and the *Mother Earth News* family: for the inspiration and humor.

A special thanks to JB Lester of the *Healthy Planet* magazine, *Feast* magazine family, Daniel Romano, Jean Ponzi, Byron Clemens, Beatrice

Buder, Ray Feick, Rich Rodriguez, Jim Scheff, Stephen Brooks, Serene Bardol, Brandy and Joe Heller, Elnora Martinez, Erica Cunningham, Katie Canale, Chelsea Burdge, Kelley Powers, Heather Barth, Carolyn Crews, Pandora Thomas, Jason Gerhardt, Gibron Jones, David Bohlen, Molly Rockamann, Rachel Levi, Monica Pless, Michael Neu, Matt Lebon, Jessi Bloom, Sydney Woodward, John VanDeusen Edwards, Aur Beck, Terry Winkleman, Jere Gettle, Vandana Shiva, Winona LaDuke, Wil Allen, Rosemary Gladstar, and Lupe Grios for opening my eyes and sculpting my path.

A special thanks to Kaitie Adams for her friendship and the book cover photo.

A special thanks to Heather Jo Flores and everyone at the Permaculture Women's Guild for their dedication to the Earth.

A special thanks to Molly Hayden and Jeremy Buddemeir, my dear friends who happen to be editors.

A huge shout-out to my editor and friend, Elena Makansi, for her insight throughout the book. Check out ElenaMakansi.com

Introduction:
Building Resilient Communities Through Food

RESILIENT COMMUNITIES begin with food; they begin with seeds of change.

Imagine a world where no one is starving, where tree-lined streets are filled with mulberries, peaches, and juneberries in the summer, and apples, pears, persimmons, and pawpaws in the fall; where every neighborhood has a thriving community garden; where children collect and trade seeds; and where edible landscaping and bountiful gardens replace lawns.

Imagine a surplus of food, and that children could have access to healthy fresh foods in their schools through school gardens and edible landscaping programs. Imagine if every home could have a front and backyard thriving with edibles and medicinals. What if you were able to walk a few feet out your front door to harvest your favorite seasonal fruits, vegetables, flowers, and herbs. Think of the possibilities if every apartment building had balcony gardens and rooftop gardens. Picture community garden spaces at churches, homeless shelters, and prisons.

Individuals around the world are rising to the occasion of a food revolution as a way of building resilient communities and uniting around the common thread that connects us. We all need food to exist and to thrive. We see the positive impacts from guerilla plantings in inner cities, urban farms, rooftop gardens, edible food forests in city parks, and neighborhood community gardens. The good food movement is on the rise. This vision is not just one of the future but a fragment of the past that has smoldered in the ashes of the industrialization of the food system — one that is significantly broken, but not beyond repair. There is hope if we take action steps to change the future of food.

Communities, neighborhoods, towns, and cities need advocates, leaders, pioneers, and visionaries all working toward the common mission: growing for the greater good. It doesn't stop at food. We need trees and native plants for the future, as well. Luckily, groups are sprouting up all over with the vision to plant as many trees as possible in their lifetime.

While this may be viewed as a utopian fantasy, it is one practical solution to so many of the threats facing our world today. In permaculture, the problem is the solution.

Let's not forget about the devastation already done. There are ceaseless areas of soil, air, and water contamination from oil spills, radiation, toxic waste, natural gas fracking, groundwater contamination, just to name a few. Fortuitously, individuals like Paul Stamets are bringing their visionary ideas to life through mycoremediation — the process of using mycelium to remediate the environment following the aftermath of deadly environmental catastrophes caused by man.

If we examine a few continents around the globe, we see an unwavering passion for growing gardens using permaculture principles, planting trees and adding mycelium for mycoremediation as a solution to issues of not only hunger but also social justice, environmental issues, poverty, food accessibility, and as a way to bring inclusivity to the community.

North America: a cauldron of biodiversity. From the Pacific to the Atlantic, North America is home to beautiful old-growth forests, prairies, savannas, glades, woodlands, and riparian ecosystems, all of which have an abundance of wild food. From the stunning old-growth trees of the California redwoods to the breathtaking beauty of the mountainous ranges of Colorado and Wyoming, there are individuals and communities planting seeds for the future. From the gorgeous river valleys of the mighty Mississippi to the hauntingly beautiful rolling fog-covered hills of Appalachia, spirited individuals are taking on the role of caretakers for these regions while brainstorming solutions to meet human needs and stewarding the land.

The Gulf Islands of Canada have one of the last remaining Garry oak ecosystems, home to dozens of dwindling species. These islands are rich in biodiversity, especially in the provincial parks and protected areas, as well as local culture — home to farms, fromageries, wineries, artist communities.

Africa: Home to savannas, deserts, and evergreen, deciduous, and temperate forests. It is rich in biodiversity in flora and fauna but is in danger of habitat loss due to deforestation. According to research done by the University of Pennsylvania African Studies Center in 2011, "Thirty-one percent of Africa's pasture lands and nineteen percent of its forests and woodlands are classified as degraded. Africa is losing over four million hectares of forest every year, which is twice the average deforestation rate compared to the rest of the world."[1]

Luckily groups are putting solution-based ideas into practice. Gorongosa National Park is one of the world's most amazing wildlife restoration projects. Over the last two decades, over 4,000 square kilometers have been restored to promote habitat for wildlife and biodiversity.

Australia: Home to permaculture and, according to the Australian Department of Environment and Energy,

home to between 600,000 and 700,000 species, many of which are endemic, that is they are found nowhere else in the world. These include, for example, 84% of our plant species, 83% of mammals, and 45% of birds. Australia's biodiversity — the plants, animals, micro-organisms and their ecosystems — is threatened from the impacts of human activities. Since European settlement, more than 50 species of Australian animals and over 60 species of Australian plants are known to have become extinct.[2]

Europe has been leading the way in banning GMOs, promoting backyard gardens and slow foods for decades. South America continues to transform the land into tropical preserves. We see a rise in the ambition to promote healthy food and clean living.

Carl Sagan once said, "Anything else you're interested in is not going to happen if you can't breathe the air and drink the water. Don't sit this one out. Do something. You are by accident of fate alive at an absolutely critical moment in the history of our planet."

People in the know are doing their part and inspiring their friends and families. They are causing ripples of change via social media. But unless each of us honestly acknowledges and assesses the negative impact we have on the Earth and actually puts solution-based thinking into practice, we cannot change the future of our home, planet Earth.

Understanding that the soil is a living organism covering the Earth, we then can examine and implement simple solutions in the ways we eat and live that everyone can take part in. It could be as simple as planting more trees, planting an organic garden with native pollinator-attracting plants. It could be as simple as removing a few items from your diet that contribute to soil degradation. It could be as simple as shopping locally or joining a local CSA (community supported agriculture) farm. It could be as simple as taking public transportation. It

could be as simple as buying less. It is up to the individual to be the solution.

Gardening and self-sufficiency are making a comeback, and we are, in essence, getting back to our roots. While local foods may be slightly more expensive, it helps to think of it in terms of spending a few extra dollars per week to reduce our overall healthcare costs and to improve the well-being of the environment. Local foods grown without pesticides help to improve our health and are a viable form of preventative healthcare. Additionally, purchasing sustainably grown food contributes to the future of the planet. Localized food systems significantly reduce the carbon footprint by cutting back on the number of miles that food travels. They also circulate funds back into the local economy. Plenty of farmers markets around the country accept SNAP (Supplemental Nutrition Assistance Program) benefits or food stamps, expanding access for low-income families. Locavores on a budget can join CSA farms and supplement with their own backyard gardens. The rise of food awareness is paramount for our growth as a healthy, sustainable community. Seeing the world from the potato's-eye view makes us firm believers in the local foods movement as a remedy for the global food crisis.

By teaching and empowering others, especially youth, to grow their own food, we provide them with a sense of purpose, accomplishment, and responsibility. By encouraging them to source food locally, we instill in them a sense of community that fosters respect and commitment, and provides a stepping-stone for them to tackle other pressing environmental concerns, such as deforestation, global climate change, air and water quality, natural gas fracking, and exploitative extractive industries.

Your Edible Yard will empower each of us to foster a better future, one that can begin with the simple act of growing food in our own yard. By grasping the basic concept of the vital importance of food for humans around the globe, we can begin to understand how to change the world, one small seedling at a time.

Beyond the theoretical, this book will cover basic gardening tips, permaculture projects, and small-scale sustainable farming practices. The book also provides dozens of creative suggestions for encouraging friends, family, and community members in this work. Community gardening, crop sharing, plant sales, seed swaps, guerilla gardening, workshops, and sustainable backyard tours can bond and unite us in achieving these goals.

This book will focus on the importance of ecological growing methods. Organic is better for the environment! Humans had been growing organically up until the 20th century, when chemicals developed in the wake of the two world wars led to the Green Revolution. The Green Revolution was not actually very green, and unfortunately these new growing methods, which quickly became the norm in industrialized nations worldwide, led to a devastating loss of healthy topsoil that had been built up over millennia. Pesticides, herbicides, and fungicides (etc.) contaminate our groundwater with toxins that are harmful to the soil, the water, and our bodies, especially for children who are particularly vulnerable to toxic exposures.

The Earth's surface is composed of approximately 30% land and 70% water. Soil forms on the land surface and plays a crucial role in supporting life on Earth. Think of the soil as a blanket covering the Earth's land surface, home to billions of organisms, all part of a symphony orchestra that gives rise to life. These tiny unseen organisms assist in soil formation that allows forests to grow and provide structure and nutrients for shrubs, grasses, wildflowers, fungi, lichens, and moss to grow.

The soil is the foundation for life on Earth. It is here that life forms, where flora and fauna thrive, where complex interdependent relationships occur. Soil provides the framework to the mycelium sheath, the network of mycelium that allows for plant communication, nutrient uptake, and soil, and ultimately new soil formation. It takes 500 years for 1.5 centimeters of topsoil to form.

While there are thousands of different soils in the world, their existence is dwindling due to development, monoculture, erosion, clear-cutting, and fracking, among other processes. Monoculture is the production of single crops over large amounts of acreage that leads to the increased usage of pesticides and herbicides. Farmers who grow these crops are often subject to signing a contract to purchase genetically modified (GMO) seed and the chemicals that accompany them. This leads to various major problems, including contamination of soil and water, erosion, a decrease in soil life, a decrease in biodiversity on that land, and over time, complete degradation of the once fertile land, and the flora and fauna.

Unfortunately, the damage done by these types of farms has already caused a great deal of irreversible destruction to the environment. Fortunately, many large-scale farmers are transitioning to no-till methods, more humane treatment of animals, pesticide-free growing methods, and smaller-scale operations. Joel Salatin has been planting the way by offering practical advice for farmers who wish to make the transition from conventional farming to no-till farming.

The idea of "local foods" began nearly one million years ago with the first hunters and gatherers who ate only what they could find in a 100-mile radius. It is only through the globalization of trade and the development of food industry technologies that the concept of local foods was lost to most of us. The modern local foods movement peaked during the victory garden days of World War I and II when canning and preserving fruits and vegetables was the citizen's duty to reduce pressure on the public food supply during wartime. It took a long hiatus postwar through the industrialization of mass food production prompted by the modernization of large-scale farming and the introduction of chemical fertilizers and pesticides and inevitably the growth of grocery store chains in the 1950s. Coincidently, the so-called Green Revolution spawned from the development and production of war chemicals.

Good food requires good soil. Good soil requires worms and a variety of other soil-dwelling organisms and microorganisms to sprout life from the soil. Soil has been labeled as a nonrenewable resource by many scientists, and therefore, measures must be taken to ensure that the soil that is left on Earth will be preserved and held with reverence. In an article in *TIME* magazine, John Crawford of the University of Sydney estimates that in 60 years the topsoil will be depleted:

> Some forty percent of soil used for agriculture around the world is classed as either degraded or seriously degraded, meaning that seventy percent of the topsoil, the layer allowing plants to grow, is gone. Because of various farming methods that strip the soil of carbon and make it less robust as well as weaker in nutrients, soil is being lost between 10 and 40 times the rate at which it can be naturally replenished.[3]

Further, he concludes that "microbes need carbon for food, but carbon is being lost from the soil in a number of ways — over-ploughing, the misuse of certain fertilizers, and overgrazing."[4]

If these problems are not immediately addressed, Crawford says two major issues of concern will arise. First, he predicts the loss of soil productivity will result in a 30% decrease in food production over the next 20 to 50 years. Second, he fears water will reach a crisis point, an issue that is causing worldwide conflict.

Citizen gardeners can help build soils and add organic matter back to the Earth through sheet mulching, composting, and no-till methods of gardening.

The best efforts the human race can make are to:

- Stop relying on big agriculture for our food supply. This means altering our diets to eat with the seasons.
- Grow your own fruits, vegetables, and herbs and practice soil-building techniques in the process.
- Leave the soil better than you found it.
- Educate others in your community about the importance of soil building — for the health of the environment, air and water quality, for the health of all life on Earth, from the tiny microscopic organisms beneath our feet to insects, reptiles, amphibians, birds, mammals, and humans.
- Support your local farmers. Join a CSA. Shop at the local grocer or farmers markets. Join a co-op or buying club to source local meats, fruits, veggies, eggs, dairy, etc.
- Become an advocate in your community. Get involved in ways to prevent the depletion of nonrenewable resources.
- Participate in river and litter cleanups.

Another resource-intensive issue is that of manicured lawns. Unfortunately, most landscape companies are not practicing sustainable techniques. With billions of homes in the United States alone, unsustainable front and backyards can truly leave a negative carbon footprint. Pesticide and herbicide residue from lawn applications can be found not only in the soil but also in the water supply and even the air long after these chemicals have been applied to lawns.

Overexposure to these chemicals has been linked to many life-threatening illnesses, including cancer. It is estimated that there are 40 million acres of lawns in the US and that 30,000 tons of pesticides are sprayed on them annually.

There is no need for chemical applications in your home. Beautiful lawns can certainly be achieved sustainably. Remember that the idea of using chemicals to grow plants is a recent one and came from the ironically named Green Revolution. Transitioning to a more sustainable lawn is a wonderful way to make a green contribution to the future of the planet. Native landscaping will attract pollinators and will make a significant difference in your region's ecosystem.

Numerous sustainable landscaping businesses are popping up across the globe that provide a diverse array of services including, but not limited to, native garden installation, small-scale prairie restoration, rain garden installation, edible landscaping, vegetable garden installation, compost bin installation and education.

Sustainable landscaping services typically landscape with native plants, putting an emphasis on perennial flowers, shrubs, and trees instead of annuals. These companies often follow organic practices and provide invasive plant species removal.

Edible landscaping incorporates fruits and vegetables into the landscape in an aesthetically pleasing way. Landscapers choose the perfect fruits and vegetables for full sun, partial sun, and shady spots throughout a front or backyard and artistically arrange them in a functional and creative way. Edible landscaping brings sustainability and functionality to life.

A good way to ease into gardening is to start with the landscape. Sustainable, native, and edible landscaping are a few great methods to adopt to get your thumbs green.

In my hometown in Missouri, Terry Winkleman founded a very cool project. The Sustainable Backyard Tour, a St. Louis organization that aims to showcase local sustainable backyards, sets an example for anyone wanting to go green. They focus on those who have replaced invasive and energy-intensive plants with native flowers, shrubs, and trees. They have great ideas for backyard chicken coops, rainwater catchment systems, compost bins, and other urban gardening projects. Visit sustainablebackyardtour.com.

Transitioning to a more sustainable lawn is a wonderful way to make a green contribution to the future of the planet. Native landscaping attracts pollinators and will make a huge difference in your region's ecosystem. Get out and be inspired by individuals in your own neighborhood who have taken a stance to avoid chemicals on their lawn and use sustainable landscaping methods.

Another of my favorite local companies is an inspirational model founded by Joseph Heller after he noticed "a need for sustainable landscape solutions in the St. Louis area." Simply Sustainable Landscaping, owned by Heller and his wife, Brandy McClure-Heller, is solution-focused, based on individual needs and desires. Their services include native garden installation, small-scale prairie restoration, rain garden installation,

edible landscaping, vegetable garden installation, and compost bin installation and education. They landscape with native plants, emphasizing perennial flowers, shrubs, and trees instead of annuals; they follow organic practices, and they remove invasive plant species. Brandy's approach focuses on artistic landscape design and integrating medicinal herbs and edibles into landscapes.

In their collaborative creative process, Joe chooses the plant material and draws a rough sketch of his vision, and Brandy brings the landscape to life in a beautiful artistic rendition. They enjoy creating gardens that are both aesthetically pleasing and functional.

Their top ten favorite full-sun native plant varieties for the Midwest are:

- Missouri evening primrose
- rattlesnake master
- compass plant
- purple coneflower
- Baptisia
- Eastern blazing star
- prickly pear
- smooth hydrangea
- white fringe tree
- bur oak

Their top ten favorite shade-loving plant varieties are:

- Virginia bluebells
- trillium
- May apple

- Solomon's seal
- columbine
- Jacob's ladder
- witch hazel
- flowering dogwood
- sassafras
- pawpaw

Sustainable landscape designers and architects are changing the world one lawn at a time.

Be inspired by the artists, environmentalists, and plant lovers who make this profession their passion. Landscape design is a vast field, with practitioners that focus on many different aspects, including edible landscaping, native/heritage gardens, and pollination gardens. You can incorporate the basic principles of good landscape design into your own home projects, as well as call upon these professionals to help you out.

Chapter 1

The Detriment of the Lawn Obsession

I CAN'T HELP BUT FEEL SHOCKED and a little dismayed when I travel by airplane. While I look forward to getting a window seat and watching the landscape glide by, I often feel an array of conflicting emotions when flying, especially over the US Corn Belt. The patchwork quilt of monoculture corn and soy leaves me deeply unsettled and hopeless. The altitude of the plane provides a big-picture perspective that is hard to capture on land. I begin to contemplate all of the issues surrounding our modern food system. I think about soil erosion and the degradation of our precious topsoil. I think about chemical runoff and subsequent groundwater contamination. I think about the displaced wildlife whose habitats are being destroyed to create ever more farmland and human development. I think about the huge amounts of fossil fuels required to run these industrial machines, all the pollutants released into the air, and the rising numbers of children who struggle with asthma. I look into the clouds and think about the damage done to the ozone layer and the buildup of greenhouse gases in the atmosphere that are causing steadily rising global temperatures.

As the plane descends into the city, I watch as the subdivisions come into focus and am dismayed to see those smooth carpets of non-native, unproductive, high-maintenance green lawns that so encapsulate the average American experience. As a recent UC Santa Barbara (UCSB) study reveals, the lawn is actually the largest irrigated crop in the United States![1] UCSB's Bill Norrington summarizes the troubling issue with lawns:

> Each year, we drench our lawns with enough water to fill the Chesapeake Bay! That makes grass — not corn — America's largest irrigated crop. Our nation's lawns now cover an area larger than New York State, and each year, we use about 2.4 million metric tons of fertilizer just to maintain them. When there is too much fertilizer on our lawns, essential nutrients are easily washed away by sprinklers and rainstorms. When these nutrients enter storm drains and water bodies, they often become one of the most harmful sources of water pollution in the United States.[2]

But then I start to think: *this* is where we can make an impact! While changing the practices of the industrial agriculture giants is like turning around a massive cruise ship, we all have the power to change our immediate surroundings. Those green lawns may be an apotheosis of our culture's distorted relationship to our land, but they also represent a huge opportunity for change. By transitioning our yards from lawn to edible landscapes, we can create positive ecological impacts while building momentum on the local and regional levels for a larger movement toward a truly sustainable and compassionate food system.

I am just one person, and I cannot personally stop this billion-dollar industry. However, I can commit to transitioning to a more ecologically sound way of life by producing food for my family and my community, by building healthy soils and planting polycultures for future generations, and by teaching others everything I've learned in the process. Together, as empowered citizens equipped with the right knowledge, we *can* change the system.

So, what gives? How did this obsession with the perfect lawn and our dependence on industrial agricultural methods come to be? Part one of this chapter explores the history of that exalted green carpet, the unnatural means by which these lawns are pursued and maintained, and the health and environmental consequences of such an obsession. While we've seen a much-needed outpouring of books and articles detailing the negative consequences of chemically sprayed lawns and a cultural shift toward a more natural garden aesthetic emphasizing local ecology and edible food production, chemically sprayed lawns are nevertheless still the norm. The 2018 *Lawn & Landscape State of the Industry Report*[3] shows continued overall growth, with lawn care/chemical application as the most popular service for lawn and landscape contractors surveyed. Unfortunately, this very necessary cultural shift is actually inhibited by outdated municipal regulations that favor precisely trimmed green grass over more ecologically healthy and productive gardens. Cultural resistance and status quo attitudes around what a yard "should" look like also play a significant role.

Part two of this chapter provides a brief treatment of these laws, promising stories of grassroots action leading to legislative and cultural changes, and ways we can beat this outdated and unhealthy system through individual and collective action.

A BRIEF HISTORY: THE (NOT-SO) GREEN REVOLUTION

Would you believe me if I said that lawn grasses are not native to this continent? The mowed grass lawn may be a uniquely American preference, iconic of suburbia, but is only made possible with grass species imported from Europe coupled with technological tricks such as the lawn mower, the rubber hose and sprinkler system, and commercially available fertilizers, pesticides, and herbicides. All these are necessary to keep these non-native grasses alive, thriving, and weed-free from sea to shining sea. In fact, the native grasses of the East Coast, which dominated the landscape when European settler-colonialists arrived, were mostly annuals such as broom straw, wild rye, and marsh grass, all of which were considered by the newcomers to be markedly inferior to pasture grasses of Northwestern Europe. Settlers' animals quickly destroyed most of the native grasses, and European and African grasses slowly replaced them. Most people began to assume the new grasses were indigenous. Even Kentucky bluegrass finds its origins not in Kentucky at all, but Europe or the Middle East![4]

Lawns first appeared in residential gardens in England and France but were quickly imported by wealthy American landowners who learned about European landscape trends through reading or travel. Those without the funds to travel also saw the expansive green turf lawns through imported English landscape paintings depicting picturesque garden estates. This fashion of trimmed lawns, combined with the 19th century pastoral notion that good health and moral character, often religious in essence, was cultivated by open space, fresh air, and tasteful greenery, led to an anti-urban attitude that was more about order and social status than it was ever about going back to the land or preserving nature.

As Virginia Jenkins puts it, "Single-family houses set in their own gardens were seen as moral bastions of the nation in opposition to the corruption of the cities."[5] Over time, the front lawn became cemented into American society as a symbol of social status and moral character. "Lawns," notes *Atlantic* journalist Megan Garber, "originally designed to connect homes even as they enforced the distance between them, are shared domestic spaces. They are also socially regulated spaces. Lawns … have doubled as sweeping, sodded outgrowths of the Protestant ethic."[6] Not to mention a form of highly conspicuous consumption, as lawn maintenance was expensive and time-consuming. Lawns owe their widespread existence to a number of factors, but their cultural significance can be attributed to aesthetic movements promoted by the Garden Club of America and early influential landscape theorists and designers such as Frederick Law Olmsted and Andrew Jackson Downing whose landscape theories were modeled on the English country estate. Through this lens, the disproportionate energy and effort families have put into their front lawns begins to make more — or less — sense.

But the American lawn as we know it today couldn't spread to every subdivision in America without socioeconomic factors as well: the growth of the middle class, suburban migration patterns like white flight, and the development of a mass-produced lawn care industry made possible by developments in chemical and mechanical engineering.

Many of the pesticides, herbicides, and fungicides in use today were developed in a period misleadingly referred to as the Green Revolution. It's difficult to overstate how important the period during and after the two world wars was to the rapid rise in practically all areas of the US economy: manufacturing, agricultural technology, weapons development, and so forth. A great sense of pride in nation and the forward-thinking optimism of modernity suffused the era's considerable developments. The US military, as part of postwar science funding programs, sponsored much of the research that led to the development of pesticides, herbicides, fungicides, etc. At the time, these developments were thought to be harbingers of a great new era of progress and equity. The efficiencies created by electric and gas-powered machinery, breeding technologies aimed at improving crop resilience and yields through genetic engineering, and the production of synthetic nitrogen fertilizers and targeted chemicals that allowed yields to flourish led to a faith in the inherent goodness of these developments. Part of this faith was, of course, due to heavy lobbying by the newly profiting chemical engineering and industrial agriculture industry.

Just think! More variety would improve the nation's health and standard of living. Higher yields of staple crops at lower costs could end world hunger. Everyone could go to the supermarket and get whatever they fancied whether it was in season or not. A good life for all!

Unfortunately, the reality is not quite so simple — nor so good. The ecological effects of the Green Revolution very quickly caught up to us, and it was only seventeen years after World War II that Rachel Carson shook the nation with the publication of *Silent Spring*, giving birth to the modern environmental movement and leading to the creation of the Environmental Protection Agency. With her thoroughly researched exposé on the effects of indiscriminate pesticide use, a national consciousness about the devastating and counter-productive effects of these chemicals was born. Unfortunately, industrial agriculture only grew, and now, as Carson predicted, we are dealing with far worse and far more widespread problems.

While the Green Revolution may have begun as a way to help feed the world, it evolved into something very different. Wouldn't it have been easier to pass laws requiring people nationwide to have space to grow their own food? For over five decades, junk food, convenience foods, and prepackaged meals made their way onto kitchen tables around the world, and unfortunately that trend only grows as people get busier. Gardens were replaced with lawns. Real fruit was replaced with artificially flavored vacuum-packed fruit cups swimming in syrup. Home-cooked meals were replaced with Hamburger Helper or a stop at the drive-thru. Commercials targeted women in the workforce, advertising promises of affordable and convenient meals for busy families.

Below I will summarize the major issues relating to the environmental and human health effects of industrial agricultural methods used in residential lawn and garden care. However, I strongly recommend following up with some more research of your own. Knowledge is power, and this is life-or-death stuff! Empowered, knowledgeable citizens taking political action in their communities and inspiring others is our best way forward.

ENERGY REQUIREMENTS FOR LAWN AND LANDSCAPE MAINTENANCE

A tidy lawn requires frequent mowing, often from a gasoline-powered mower. If you use a push mower, you can avoid the nearly 400 pounds of CO_2 emissions per year for a quarter-acre yard, a typical American lawn size,[7] while also getting exercise. Of course, using a push mower on a large yard would quickly become a tiresome effort, so it's no surprise that many people opt for riding lawn mowers. Many people are practically driving minicars to keep their expansive lawns in order! In fact, in the 1950s, riding mowers were promoted as sports cars for the lawn.[8] Electric lawn mowers, often used for small to medium-sized lawns, will cut greenhouse gas emissions and are a cleaner choice overall. Many Americans also use power trimmers, edgers, and leaf blowers, which can be fueled by gas, battery, or electricity. Today, lawn mowers account for approximately 5% of the nation's air pollution![9]

All of these power tools appeal to consumers for the perceived convenience and were created out of a culture that looks at short-term efficiency and ease over long-term distributed effects. Examine the big picture, and you'll see it is vastly more efficient to opt for a low-maintenance or, better yet, a productive edible yard instead of the expanse of flawless green lawn in the first place! Plus, letting yourself sweat a little by gardening improves physical *and* mental health.[10]

ECOLOGICAL EFFECTS OF AGRICULTURAL CHEMICALS

Typical features of a residential lawn care regimen are pesticides and fertilizers (from here on "pesticides" will refer generally to pesticides, herbicides, fungicides, and insecticides unless otherwise noted). Think about it: Pesticides are literally meant to kill living things! Though they are developed to target particular species (weeds and pests) while preserving what we want (usually turf grass on lawns or genetically modified soy, wheat, corn, and cotton on industrial farms), their harmful effects are typically not limited to its target. Pesticides range in toxicity, and organic pesticides are a less harmful option for organic garden care. But without adequate knowledge, most Americans still rely on conventional means of keeping their lawns green and tidy, so much so that 30 thousand tons of pesticides are sprayed on roughly 40 million acres of lawns in the United States alone every single year.[11] And this is tiny compared to the load carried by commercial farms. Between 1987 and 2016, annual US farm use of glyphosate alone grew from less than 11 million pounds to nearly 300 million pounds.[12]

When you spray a lawn with pesticides, you might rightly think it will just, you know, stay on the lawn. Unfortunately, that's rarely true, and small amounts will leak into the larger environment. Plus, most homeowners lack the finesse of agricultural specialists and vastly overuse pesticides due to bad timing and lack of knowledge about proper application. Pesticides and synthetic fertilizers contaminate our groundwater, expose our skin and sensitive organs to short- and long-term health risks (of which children and the elderly are particularly vulnerable), pollute the air, and affect local and regional ecologies by upsetting nutrient balances and harming wildlife. Many Americans are unaware of these harmful effects because the burdens of these toxic exposures are unequally borne by those who cannot choose to live or work far from these toxic industrial farms. Another major issue is a lack of government funding or resources to assess the actual environmental and health effects of pesticides in the environment, meaning much is unknown about the risks of widely used chemicals such as glyphosate, sold commercially under the Monsanto brand as Roundup. You might even have Roundup in your garage, as it is the second most widely used US lawn and gardens weed killer.[13]

The environment is an open system of nutrient and water cycles. All of the nutrients, minerals, and human pollutants in the air, soil, and water flow in and out of different ecological systems. Agricultural inputs are difficult to contain within the confines of a farm or residence. They move through the soil into the groundwater and into streams and rivers. They are carried by the wind and pollute the air with greenhouse gas emissions or toxic particles that get into our lungs as we breathe. They build up in the environment across the food chain in a process called bioaccumulation. If you take nothing else away from this chapter but that everything is ecologically interconnected, I will be satisfied!

The 2018 USGS National Water-Quality Assessment Project Report sums it up quite nicely: "Most historical and current water-quantity and water-quality impacts from agriculture are the result of the modification of the natural water flowpaths and (or) the use of chemicals."[14]

Agricultural effects on water quality can occur at local, regional, and national scales. For example, increased levels of nutrients from agricultural fertilizers can stimulate algal blooms and affect the ecology of local streams. Nitrate and some herbicides can move through the soil to groundwater and, eventually, to local streams. Farther downstream, these elevated nutrients can increase costs associated with treating the water so that it is suitable for drinking. Ultimately, chemicals associated with agricultural activities (such as nutrients, pesticides, antimicrobials, and trace elements) and sediment (eroded soil) empty into our estuaries and can harm valuable commercial and recreational fisheries. Elevated nutrient inputs stimulate harmful algal blooms along the Nation's coasts causing negative economic impacts.[15]

How agricultural chemicals specifically affect and contaminate local water systems is highly dependent on the local hydrology, which is the structure and flow dynamics of the water features. Take some time to learn about your local hydrology, both directly on your property as well as in your city and region as a whole, to better understand how agricultural chemicals interact with the water table.

HUMAN HEALTH EFFECTS OF AGRICULTURAL CHEMICALS

The chemicals in many EPA-approved pesticides have been linked to cancer and other diseases. According to the Pesticide-Induced Diseases Database created by the Beyond Pesticides organization: "The common diseases affecting the public's health are all too well-known in the 21st century: asthma, autism and learning disabilities, birth defects and reproductive dysfunction, diabetes, Parkinson's and Alzheimer's diseases, and several types of cancer. Their connection to pesticide exposure continues to strengthen despite efforts to restrict individual chemical exposure, or mitigate chemical risks, using risk assessment-based policy."[16] Some of the same chemicals that were used to defoliate forest and farmland under the Herbicidal Warfare Program during the Vietnam War were later used in herbicides and pesticides and sold to consumers.

In March 2015, the World Health Organization's International Agency for Research on Cancer declared glyphosate, the primary ingredient in the popular weed killer Roundup, a "probable human carcinogen."[17] Glyphosate's widespread use on genetically modified seeds — nearly all US-grown corn, soy, and cotton are treated with glyphosate — has been linked to antibiotics resistance[18] and hormone disruption.[19] Despite our high exposure levels from lawn care, living near farms, or eating/wearing crops treated with glyphosate, the chemical is not included in US government testing for pesticide residues on food crops or human bioaccumulation in blood and tissues, and there isn't much comprehensive information about its effects on human health. Industry representatives, such as Monsanto, the American Soybean Association, and the National Corn Growers Association, have tended to decry the research that has been done as inconsistent with their own safety assessments.

According to research summaries from Beyond Pesticides, a Washington, D.C. based nonprofit,

Of the 30 most commonly used lawn pesticides, 17 are possible and/or known carcinogens, 18 have the potential to disrupt the endocrine (hormonal) system, 19 are linked to reproductive effects and sexual dysfunction, 11 have been linked to birth defects, 14 are neurotoxic, 24 can cause kidney or liver damage, and 25 are sensitizers and/or irritants. Of those same 30 lawn pesticides, 19 are detected in groundwater, 20 have the ability to leach into drinking water sources, 30 are toxic to fish and other aquatic organisms vital to our ecosystem, 29 are toxic to bees, 14 are toxic to mammals, and 22 are toxic to birds.[20]

The big unanswered question is the potential health effect of low levels over extended periods of time. Despite a lack of comprehensive research, we would do well to remember a fundamental tenet of environmental policy: the precautionary principle. As defined by the authors of a paper published in *Environmental Health Perspectives* in 2001, the precautionary principle "has four central components: taking preventive action in the face of uncertainty; shifting the burden of proof to the proponents of an activity; exploring a wide range of alternatives to possibly harmful actions; and increasing public participation in decision making."[21] Sounds like sound advice!

POLLINATORS AT RISK

Bees, birds, bats, butterflies, beetles, and other pollinator animals sustain our ecosystem and food supply by helping plants reproduce. Pollinators are thought to be responsible for one third of our total food supply. Pollinators bring us fruits, vegetables, nuts, oils, fibers, and other raw materials. They help prevent soil erosion and increase carbon sequestration. Between 75% and 95% of all flowering plants on Earth need pollinators.[22] Thus, we need pollinators. It's as simple as that.

Pollinator populations are at risk or in decline, mostly due to habitat loss and fragmentation. Pollution, pesticide poisoning, and climate change are also significant factors in population loss. We have seen severe honeybee hive losses known as colony collapse disorder (CCD) across the United States. Many point to pesticide regulations that fail to take into account sublethal effects of these agricultural chemicals on nonhuman species such as insects as a major cause of CCD. Toxicity of chemicals is relative, and it would make sense that a small animal such as a bee would experience pesticides in the environment differently than large animals like humans do. While it remains somewhat of a mystery exactly what is going on with CCD, ecologists do have very clear recommendations for helping our pollinator friends. Plant a pollinator garden, stop using toxic pesticides, include the birds and bees in any land use plan from residential to commercial, support local beekeeping operations or start a small honey operation in your own backyard, and get involved in public awareness campaigns around pollinator issues.

WASTING WATER

Just as most Americans overuse pesticides, they also overuse water. The average American family devotes about 30% of their total water consumption, approximately 320 gallons a day or 100 gallons per person, to residential outdoor uses, mostly for landscape irrigation, as well as washing cars, swimming pools, and cleaning sidewalks and driveways. Turfgrass receives the highest percentage of irrigation water. Planting natives, mulching regularly, installing rain gardens, and composting to create healthy soils all reduce typical water requirements. According to the EPA, some researchers estimate that more than half of commercial and residential water use is actually wasted due to overwatering, leaks, and evaporation/wind.[23]

ERODING TOPSOIL

I've saved perhaps the scariest issue for last. The topsoil is not just *dirt* — it is a fertile, living thing, and it is an important part of what makes vegetation possible. Alive with trillions of microorganisms, mycorhizzal fungal networks, and crawlies like worms, the topsoil provides essential nutrients to plants. Not just agricultural crops, but all plants! The Earth is covered with an average of three feet of topsoil, but that quantity is rapidly declining due to soil erosion, which is caused largely by industrial agricultural methods. Topsoil erosion decreases crop yields and crop health. It also increases water requirements as the soil cannot store as much water. Compound this with decreasing access to freshwater and a rapidly increasing human population, and Houston, we have a problem! How much topsoil is eroded is dependent on weather, surface topography (the steepness of the slope), and what plants are growing on the soil.

Soil does erode and replenish naturally. However, the rate of replenishment is approximately one to two inches every several hundred years, and the rate of erosion is far outpacing the rate of replenishing. A Cornell University study compiling statistics from more than 125 sources warns of "slow, insidious" soil erosion that "nickels and dimes" us to death. Here are some of its troubling statistics as reported by *Cornell Chronicle*'s Susan Lang:

- The United States is losing soil 10 times faster — and China and India are losing soil 30 to 40 times faster — than the natural replenishment rate.
- The economic impact of soil erosion in the United States costs the nation about $37.6 billion each year in productivity losses. Damage from soil erosion worldwide is estimated to be $400 billion per year.

- As a result of erosion over the past 40 years, 30 percent of the world's arable land has become unproductive.
- About 60 percent of soil that is washed away ends up in rivers, streams, and lakes, making waterways more prone to flooding and to contamination from soil's fertilizers and pesticides.
- Soil erosion also reduces the ability of soil to store water and support plant growth, thereby reducing its ability to support biodiversity.
- Erosion promotes critical losses of water, nutrients, soil organic matter, and soil biota, harming forests, rangeland, and natural ecosystems.
- Erosion increases the amount of dust carried by wind, which not only acts as an abrasive and air pollutant but also carries about 20 human infectious disease organisms, including anthrax and tuberculosis.[24]

We all have a role to play in changing the future of our planet, and we all need to keep pushing ourselves to do more. Though the majority of impacts, like from industrial farm operations, may feel beyond our control, what we *can* control is what we do in our own homes. Get rid of that lawn, go organic, and grow some food!

Chapter 2

It Shouldn't Be a Crime to Grow Vegetables!

WHILE IT SOUNDS SIMPLE, growing your own food on your own property is made a bit more complicated by outdated municipal regulations that seek to govern how our yards look. There are numerous laws restricting vegetable gardens and fruit orchards, as well as practices such as keeping chickens, bees, or other livestock. Zoning laws may regulate the height of your plants. Food safety laws regulate the sale and distribution of homegrown food products. Even if you are a homeowner, you are obliged to follow rules laid out by your neighborhood association and local zoning regulations, especially in areas with higher property values with "more to lose" from seemingly unkempt gardens. These zoning restrictions are generally about protecting property values and defining community aesthetics according to what is considered neat and proper. Thus, there are generally way more rules about growing food in public-facing front yards. Flowers and manicured bushes, and of course mowed lawns, are generally acceptable, while useful plants that might not look as beautiful to the average American, such as herbs or food crops, are considered unsightly. While the scope of laws governing gardens may be intimidating to the beginning gardener, planting seeds for the future is incredibly important. Changing the laws to promote urban ecosystems and food accessibility are important issues to put into motion now for future generations.

A quick internet search on "laws and edible gardens" will yield a distasteful crop of news stories about people facing fines and jail time just for trying to grow food. In some cases, local governments have even ripped up food-bearing plants without permission from residents. In a somewhat extreme and controversial case in 2012, local officials invaded Denise Morrison's front yard in Tulsa, Oklahoma, for violating a city ordinance that regulated the height of plants. Her case was dismissed by two federal courts.[1]

One year earlier, Julie Bass of Oak Park, Michigan, was charged with a misdemeanor, arguing that her edible plants were not suitable live plant material.[2] The City eventually dropped the charges, possibly due to a language dispute in the code.

In one high-profile case in Miami Shores, Florida, couple Hermine Ricketts and Tom Carroll were forced to uproot their highly productive garden when the City changed the local code to prohibit growing vegetables in front yards in 2013 and threatened them with $50/day fines.[3] The couple still have an active petition going on change.org, and are fighting to pass SB 1776, a Senate bill that would prohibit Florida cities from banning vegetable gardens on private property, no matter where they're located.

It is clear from these cases that the manicured lawn and flower bed aesthetic still reigns supreme in many American cities. Fortunately, people are fighting back and laws are changing. The best thing we can do to accelerate this cultural and policy shift is plant an edible garden ourselves and actively participate in local environmental politics. The rest of this book gives you the tools, knowledge, and confidence necessary to turn your property into a productive edible garden. Your edible yard will improve your health at all levels, from exercise to better nutrition to reducing depression and anxiety. It will save water and reduce water bills every month. It will improve the soil and provide habitat for pollinators. And most importantly, it may spark inspiration for your neighbors to transform their outmoded green carpet into an edible oasis.

In St. Louis, the Missouri Coalition for the Environment put together *A Guide to Urban Agriculture and Farming in St. Louis*, published under the direction of Melissa Vatterott, Food and Farm Director at Missouri Coalition for the Environment, and Chair of the St. Louis Food Policy Coalition. This guide is a free comprehensive booklet that includes information on starting various types of gardens and farms. The guide covers neighborhood involvement, finding a location for a garden or farm, soil testing, water resources, regulations and laws for community gardens and urban farms, farm animals, composting, zoning regulations, produce sales, as well as urban agriculture policy. Check your local environmental or food and farming advocacy groups or extension agency for a list of local regulations.

The following information was adapted from the guide.

COMPLIANCE CHECKLIST

- If you live in the US, you need to call Dig Rite before planting trees or deep tilling. Dig Rite will come out and flag all of the buried utilities so that you don't accidently break an underground line. The cost to repair damaged utilities is astronomical.

- If you live in a subdivision, you may need to check with your local Homeowners Association to find out what regulations they may have for edible landscapes.

- Check the laws and guidelines for gardens with your local municipality. These may vary by neighborhood, city, county, and state.

- Be sure your gardens don't break codes such as fire hazards, zoning laws, or safety hazards.

- Contact your local chapter of Sierra Club, Environmental Coalition, Master Gardener Program, University Extension Office, or Food Policy Coalition to find out if they have either resources to point your toward or agents to assist you.

- If you are fined for a garden, contact your local legal services providers.

- Show up at City Council meetings to address your concerns. Offer a list of benefits to front yard gardens to local residents.
- Contact your local alderman to discuss garden regulations and guidelines in your community.

KEEP YOUR NEIGHBORS HAPPY

- Share the harvest. Send baskets of the bounty over to your neighbors. Invite them over for a garden tour.
- Plant a pollinator garden and integrate food producing crops into it. Paint a sign that says Pollinator Garden. As long as it is kept tidy, the neighbors shouldn't complain.
- Install a rain garden integrating perennial edible plants. In my community, the Metropolitan Sewer District awards grants to those who plant rain gardens to mitigate stormwater runoff. Check your local sewer district to find out if they have a similar program.

Chapter 3

Building Healthy Soils with Compost and Vermicompost

Each of us can play a role in building healthy soils. Whether through backyard gardening, composting, vermicomposting, permaculture, adding mycelium to the soil, adding soil amendments, practicing regenerative soil building techniques — every bit helps. On a larger scale, adding cover crops, practicing polyculture and biodynamic farming techniques, and implementing large-scale permaculture methods are good places to start.

For nearly a decade, my husband, Eric Stevens, and I have been growing food for our community, always using organic methods. For smaller gardens that we have installed, we have used no-till methods. From 2010 to 2016, we co-managed a CSA farm, operating on a shoestring budget that forced us to find creative solutions to issues such as soil fertility, plant health, and increasing crop yields.

We built the vermicompost bins upon our arrival at La Vista. While we did use tillers and tractor implements, we tried to remediate the soil by practicing crop rotation, planting cover crops, and applying compost, straw, leaf mulch, and other organic materials. We used vermicompost (often with worms still in it) to fertilize our crops with living microbes and nutrients, side-dressing each plant in the field with a scoop to give them a jumpstart and facilitate growth and plant vitality.

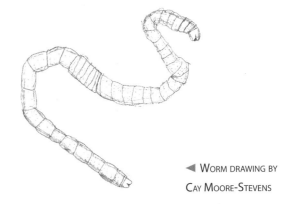

◀ Worm drawing by Cay Moore-Stevens

▲ *Compost bin system.*

Fastening three pallets together, we started with a single compost bin under a shade tree. We filled it with straw, fallen leaves, grass clippings, food scraps, shredded cardboard, torn strips of newspaper, as well as small branches and twigs to provide air spaces. We turned the compost a few times and let it sit for a few days. We then purchased a bag of mail-order red wriggler worms from Uncle Jim's Worm Farm after seeing an ad in *Mother Earth News.* When the package came, we told our son we had a gift for him. You can imagine the look on his face when discovering it wasn't a new toy, but 1,000 red wriggler worms! After making a

▲ *Cayan holding worms.*

little indentation in the compost, we added the worms. Our son got to help, and boy, was that such a neat experience to watch a young little lad holding a hundred worms in his hands. His eyes lit up, and he didn't want to put them in the bin. He wanted to bring them home. But we told him the vital role that worms play and how much they will love their new home, which made it a little easier to say farewell to the worms for now, with the promise that he could visit them each day.

After adding the worms nearly a decade ago, we have seen them multiply by the thousands. We have been separating them out and adding them to new piles or giving them away at talks ever since. We have been teaching Vermiculture 101 workshops since 2010, specifically at Mother Earth News Fairs across the country. Please know that everyone approaches vermicomposting a little bit differently, but in this chapter, I will share methods that worked for us. Our passion for Earth stewardship fuels our drive to want to share the knowledge.

Avid gardeners are fully aware of the importance of compost. We have seen the enormous difference that it makes on crops such as tomatoes, eggplant, and peppers. We have done experiments planting two rows of the same crops: one row with vermicompost added and one without. The crop with vermicompost doubled in size within just a few short weeks. Most gardeners will talk as long as you let them about their prized compost pile. It is often life-altering when newbie gardeners come to the exciting realization that over half of their waste can simply be thrown into a bin in a corner of the yard and over time breaks down into the most nutrient-rich soil. They usually throw all of the veggie ends and recycled brown paper bags in the compost bin and forgets about it for months. When they return, they discover the "black gold."

Ideally, all of our garden beds would be exactly like a compost bin, alive with various layers gently breaking down with no compaction. Building healthy soil is the key to having optimal health in any garden setting. It can be thought of in terms of building the soil's immune system to help fight off unwanted diseases or pests. The soil is a living organism covering the Earth's surface. Like all living things, it needs to be fed proper nutrients to thrive. Feed your soil by planting cover crops. Add organic matter, or continuously add compost to help build healthy soil and also yield abundant and healthy crops.

NITROGEN FIXATION AND CARBON SEQUESTERING

Christine Jones, in a *Permaculture News* article, stated:

> Nitrogen is a component of protein and DNA and, as such, is essential to all living things. Prior to the Industrial Revolution, around 97% of the nitrogen supporting life on Earth was fixed biologically. Over the last century, intensification of farming, coupled with a lack of understanding of soil microbial communities,

has resulted in reduced biological activity and an increased application of industrially produced forms of nitrogen to agricultural land. Despite its abundance in the atmosphere, nitrogen is frequently the most limiting element for plants. There is a *reason* for this. Carbon, essential to photosynthesis and soil function, occurs as a trace gas, carbon dioxide, currently comprising 0.04% of the atmosphere. The most efficient way to transform carbon dioxide to stable organic soil complexes (containing both C and N) is via the liquid carbon pathway. The requirement for biologically fixed nitrogen drives this process. If plants were able to access nitrogen directly from the atmosphere, their growth would be impeded by the absence of carbon-rich topsoil. We are witnessing an analogous situation in agriculture today. When inorganic nitrogen is provided, the supply of carbon to associative nitrogen-fixing microbes is inhibited, resulting in carbon-depleted soils. Aggregation is the key. Aggregates are the small "lumps" in soil that provide tilth, porosity and water-holding capacity. Unless soils are actively aggregating, they will not be fixing significant amounts of atmospheric N or sequestering stable forms of carbon. All three functions (aggregation, biological N-fixation, and stable C-sequestration) are interdependent. The microbes involved in the formation of soil aggregates require an energy source. This energy initially comes from the sun. In the miracle of photosynthesis, green plants transform light energy, water, and carbon dioxide into biochemical energy, which is transferred to soil as liquid carbon via an intricate network of mycorrhizal fungi and associated bacteria. Biological nitrogen fixation is the key driver of the nitrogen and carbon cycles in all natural ecosystems, both on land and in water. When managed appropriately, biological nitrogen fixation can also be the major determinant of the productivity of agricultural land. Many farmers around the world are discovering first-hand how the change from bare fallows to biodiverse year-long green, coupled with appropriate livestock management and reduced applications of inorganic nitrogen, can restore natural topsoil fertility. Improving soil function delivers benefits both on-farm and to the wider environment.[1]

▲ *Up-close image of forest floor.*

Here are some actions that each of us can take in our own yards:

- Do not use synthetic fertilizers, pesticides, herbicides, fungicides, insecticides, or other inorganic sprays.
- Reduce the size of your lawn by planting native species and participating in ecological restoration.
- Over-seed lawns with Dutch white clover.
- Don't rake leaves: allow them to decompose, help build soil, and store carbon.
- Use regenerative farming and gardening practices.
- Plant nitrogen-fixing leguminous living mulches between vegetable rows.

NATURE IS A GOOD MODEL TO FOLLOW

We like to encourage individuals to look at nature, to *really* look:

- Observe the forest floor up close.
- Notice the layers of leaves, twigs, moss, fungi, and detritus all decaying at various rates.
- You will notice the top layer has the appearance of basic mulch.
- Scratch the surface and you will notice the layers below get broken down inch by inch into perfect soil.
- We strive to obtain those rich qualities in the soil by mimicking those natural layers in the substances we add to our own garden soil.

Ideally, all of our garden beds would be exactly like a compost bin, alive with various layers gently breaking down with no compaction.

Good garden soil is essentially a larger version of a compost pile, preferably composed of ongoing layers of the following:

- Small stems and twigs
- Fallen leaves
- Grass clippings
- Compost
- Worm castings
- Aged sawdust (untreated)
- Living organisms
- Fruit and vegetable scraps
- Decomposing materials
- Straw
- A nice mix of sand, silt, and clay

Vermiculture is the term given to worm farming, or the use of worms to break down organic material. *Vermicompost*, the by-product, is a nutrient-rich natural fertilizer, called worm castings, and is similar to compost, but it uses worms such as red wigglers and earthworms to help break down organic material. Red wigglers can be purchased at a bait shop, online, or through mail order.

Vermicompost, which is rich in nitrogen, phosphorus, and potassium, also contains macronutrients and micronutrients; all benefit plant health and stimulate growth. It also adds nutrient-rich minerals back into the soil. Vermicompost can be made into a nutrient-rich tea to water garden plants. We use one part vermicompost to ten parts water. Simply fill a

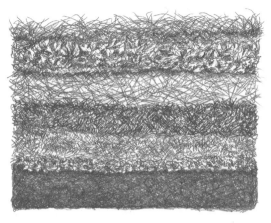

▲ *Layers in the compost pile.*

▲ *Side-by-side vermicompost bin.*

burlap sack, potato sack, or mesh bag with vermicompost. Place the sack in a large bin, such as a Rubbermaid container or 55-gallon drum. Fill with water. Steep the bag for a minimum of one day and a maximum of one week.

Worm castings are the final by-product of vermicompost; essentially, they are the aggregate, dark-brown rich soil medium found at the bottom of the vermicompost bin. Add them to a seed-starting soil mixture or use to top-dress seedlings in pots and to side-dress larger transplants in a garden bed or field. Worm castings can also be sprinkled on top of small garden beds.

A GOOD GARDEN BEGINS WITH HEALTHY SOIL

Building healthy soil is the key to having optimal health in any garden setting. Building the soil structure is crucial in the role of fighting off diseases or pests.

While there are thousands of different soils worldwide, their existence is dwindling due to development, monoculture, erosion, the overuse of herbicides and pesticides, and the overall mistreatment of soils. Because soil is a nonrenewable resource, it must be held with reverence. If we don't try our best to preserve the soil we have left, we will see more and more of the devastating effects of soil degradation in our lifetime.

▲ *A good garden begins with healthy soil.*

We need the soil. Soil provides the framework for life on land. It provides structure for forests and a growing medium for food production. Some of the best ways that each of us can contribute to solutions to healthier soil begin with food. Grow your own by practicing backyard permaculture. Localize food systems by supporting area farmers who practice regenerative growing practices. Buy less. Support renewable energy. Plant native flowers, shrubs, and trees. There are so many things we can be doing for the Earth during our short time here to ensure that our children and grandchildren have access to clean air, clean water, and fertile soil to grow their food.

- Soil-building techniques can be easily implemented in backyard gardens.
- Ditch the pesticides and herbicides.
- Consider backyard chickens or other livestock.
- Each of us can play a role in building healthy soils.

SOIL QUALITY

Quality soil is the most vital aspect of growing organically! A healthy living soil is the key to vibrant and healthy plants. Compost, vermicompost, and other organic soil add nutrients to your soil, improving plant vitality.

All soils are different. A soil analysis or test is a good starting point to determine what nutrients might be lacking and to understand better the composition and personality of your soil. Soil agronomists offer soil analyses. Typically, they collect and analyze samples from multiple quadrants of your field or farm to determine

PREPARED FOR: ERIC STEVENS GODFREY IL

Sample ID	Analysis Date	Organic Matter %	Cation Exchange Capacity CEC meq/100g	% K (+)	% Mg (+)	% Ca (+)	% H (+)	% Na (+)	Soil pH	K (+) ppm	Mg (+) ppm	Ca (+) ppm	Na (+) ppm	P1 (WEAK BRAY 1:7) (-) ppm	P2 (STRONG BRAY 1:7) (-) ppm	Bicarb (Olsen) (-) ppm	S (ICAP) (-) ppm	Zn (+) ppm	Mn (+) ppm	Fe (+) ppm	Cu (+) ppm	B (-) ppm
1 FRONT	02-16-12	1.6	7.4	3.9	14.5	80.7		0.9	7.2	112	129	1190	15	30	39	-	8	3.1	15	34	0.8	0.4
Desired Level				3-5	12-16	70-75			6.8	87-144	107-142	1036-1110		25-50	50-100	33	50	5.0	20	20	5.0	2.0
1 BACK	02-16-12	1.7	8.9	5.2	17.0	77.1		0.7	7.4	181	182	1366	14	42	76	-	9	3.4	14	29	0.9	0.4
Desired Level				3-5	12-16	70-75			6.8	104-174	128-171	1246-1335		25-50	50-100	33	50	5.0	20	20	5.0	2.0
GR HOUSE	02-16-12	4.3	19.1	5.1	24.7	67.6		2.6	7.4	383	565	2579	113	159	160	-	170	7.7	11	52	1.4	1.4
Desired Level				3-5	12-16	70-75			6.8	223-572	275-367	2674-2865		25-50	50-100	33	50	5.0	20	20	5.0	2.0
SM GARDEN	02-16-12	2.4	14.7	5.1	18.3	76.0		0.6	7.7	290	322	2233	21	109	116	-	9	9.0	7	42	1.3	0.9
Desired Level				3-5	12-16	70-75			6.8	172-287	212-282	2056-2205		25-50	50-100	33	50	5.0	20	20	5.0	2.0
2 BACKLEFT	02-16-12	1.7	10.2	2.8	17.3	79.1		0.8	7.5	110	212	1621	18	37	56	-	7	4.1	6	31	0.9	0.6
Desired Level				3-5	12-16	70-75			6.8	119-199	147-196	1428-1530		25-50	50-100	33	50	5.0	20	20	5.0	2.0
2 BACKRIGH	02-16-12	1.6	8.9	3.5	17.7	78.2		0.6	7.5	122	189	1392	12	43	57	-	7	3.4	6	30	0.8	0.5
Desired Level				3-5	12-16	70-75			6.8	104-174	128-171	1246-1335		25-50	50-100	33	50	5.0	20	20	5.0	2.0
2 FRONT	02-16-12	1.6	8.7	4.1	16.2	79.1		0.6	7.4	140	169	1374	12	49	98	-	6	4.3	7	29	0.9	0.5
Desired Level				3-5	12-16	70-75			6.8	102-170	125-167	1218-1305		25-50	50-100	33	50	5.0	20	20	5.0	2.0

10955 Blackhawk Drive ▪ Blue Mounds, WI 53517
(608) 437-4994 ▪ FAX (608) 437-4441

Soil Analysis Report
from Midwest Laboratories
13611 B St Omaha, NE 68144
(402) 334-7770

Submitted by:
D SIEGENTHALER

Date: February 2, 2015
Samples: 7
Page: 1
Report Number: 12-045-0087

▲ *An example of soil test results.*

your soil types and which minerals and trace minerals are abundant or lacking. Most soil agronomists also offer custom natural fertilizers that are OMRI (Organic Materials Review Institute) certified, based on test results.

THE ESSENTIALITY OF WORMS

Worms are essential, for the following reasons:

- Often referred to as ecosystem engineers, worms — especially earthworms — play crucial roles in ecosystem functions. Earthworms improve soil structure by opening small channels or pores within the soil structure, which let air and water through, allowing plants to penetrate their roots deeper into the various layers of soil.

- They break down and recycle organic matter into useable growing medium.

- They create space in the soil for bacteria and fungi, which help make nutrients available to plants.

▲ *Worms are essential.*

- They increase nutrient availability by adding and incorporating organic matter into the various levels of soil and also by unlocking the nutrients contained within dead and decaying flora and fauna, making nitrogen, phosphorus, trace minerals, and other nutrients available to microorganisms and the roots of plants.

• As part of the food web, they are eaten by predators.

According to vermiculturists and educators Joel and Kathy Adams:

> 78% of the Earth's atmosphere is nitrogen. The role of worms in nitrogen fixation is in their symbiotic relationship with the whole soil food web. The bacterial strains that do the heavy lifting of fixation benefit from the worms' cast egestion (poop), mucus production, and decomposition of matter — providing nutrients for nitrifying bacteria and other feeders in the soil food web. The ingestion, digestion, and egestion of organic matter by worms helps break biology down into microbiology, including the important nitrogen fixing bacteria.

During the 19th century, only natural fertilizers were used. Between 1840–1906 Anhydrous ammonia was created and farming was never the same.

We are growing our food with the same chemicals used to level buildings in the Oklahoma City bombings. With artificial fertilizer, worms get driven out or killed by the toxins. This is a problem for the soil structure as worms serve a significant purpose. In chapter 24 of *Teaming with Microbes* by Jeff Lowenfels and Wayne Lewis, they make a strong point — no one ever fertilized an old growth forest. There are roughly 2 million worms per acre in an old growth forest.[2]

Research scientist Dr. Julia Stevens stated:

> Four examples of how microorganisms shape the ecosystems around them, often leading to benefits that can be felt at an observable scale. These examples include: The hyphae — branches — of fungi coil through the soil surrounding plant roots; there, predatory fungi await their prey. These fungi release chemicals from lasso like loops to attract unsuspecting nematodes (tiny roundworms) moving through the soil in search of roots to eat. As the nematodes enter these loops, the fungi constrict the lassos, trapping the nematodes to digest them from the inside out. While the fungi have adapted this unique lifestyle as a way to find nutrients, this activity has the added benefit of protecting plant roots from the predation of nematodes.

> Not far from these fungi, other microorganisms are also hard at work making plant food. Nitrogen is the largest component of air and an essential building block of life — yet plants cannot use atmospheric nitrogen. They rely on a group of bacteria that can take this nitrogen gas and transform it into usable nitrogen food. This process is called nitrogen fixation and acts as a natural fertilizer promoting successful plant growth.

> • As water infiltrates and moves through soil to the water table below, diverse microorganisms serve as a natural

water filter of both chemical and living pollutants. Microorganisms consume the contaminants — thus removing them from the water supplies on which humans depend.

- In a constant competition for space and nutrients, microorganisms in the soil have become especially efficient at fighting and out-competing each other. The importance of these fighting mechanisms was realized when, in the 1920s, Dr. Alexander Fleming discovered that the common soil fungus *Penicillium notatum* contaminated and killed his cultures of disease-causing bacteria. Thanks to the follow-up experiments of Dr. Howard Florey, the antibiotic penicillin was isolated and became one of the first commercial antibiotics. Soils remain an important source of new medicines.

These examples exemplify the critical importance of soil microorganisms and our reliance upon them. However, with more microorganisms in a tablespoon of soil than there are people on Earth, there is much to be discovered about what is occurring right beneath our feet.[3]

SOME WORMS POSE A THREAT

Biologist Andrea Moore stated:

Most earthworms are not native to North America, since the last glacial period stripped the soil of most life: they've been

▲ *Soil is connected to many living things.*

▲ *Soil life.*

introduced here from Europe. In general, non-native species are a problem worldwide both on land and in the oceans, as some species can become invasive, rapidly changing an ecosystem, and cause negative impacts on other species and humans…. New worms pose a major threat to hardwood forests, where they would change the soil structure and growth dynamics of the ecosystem.[4]

BENEFITS OF BACKYARD VERMICULTURE

Vermiculture can benefit your backyard garden in the following ways:

- It enhances your existing composting operation.
- It introduces composting worms for a high-yield nutrient-rich fertilizer.
- It is similar to compost, but uses worms such as red wigglers and earthworms to help break down organic material.
- It has a higher amount of humus than compost, improving aeration and water retention tremendously.

Vermicompost is rich in nitrogen, phosphorus, and potassium and contains both macronutrients and micronutrients to benefit plant health and stimulate plant growth. It contains worm castings, partially decomposed organic materials, and organic waste with recognizable fragments of plants, food, and detritus materials. When you apply vermicompost, rich minerals are added into the soil. Most vermicompost contains plant growth hormones, increasing plant vitality and yields. In vermicompost, micronutrients that may ordinarily be washed away in heavy rains, such as magnesium and sulfur, are binded.

Research has shown that vermicompost can act as a natural pest deterrent because it promotes the synthesis of specific compounds.

In terms of affordability, vermicomposting is superior. The great product that it yields is by far worth the small investment. You can actually get started for free if you have a friend who keeps worms already. Just have your system in place first and ask them for about a dozen worms. Within a month or two, your population will start to increase.

In the retail market, natural fertilizers can be very expensive. Finished vermicompost sells for up to $35 for a 20-pound bag. A 20-pound bag of castings can be made in your basement or backyard for pennies, once your initial costs are paid.

If you are using reclaimed materials to build an outdoor bin, you just have to buy the worms and straw bales (to be used as occasional bedding and for insulation during winter months). The costs can really be kept down, as long as you are creative with your building resources.

You could even host a vermiculturist to demonstrate building a worm bin. Any we know would be happy to present a hands-on backyard workshop. They would probably even bring you starter worms, as long as there were at least five participants and each paid a workshop fee or gave a small donation for the presenter's time and travel. It would help to have separate piles of reclaimed lumber or pallets, baling wire, and organic materials already prepped, as well as bedding (shredded newspaper or office paper).

PURCHASING WORMS

Since there are roughly 1,000 worms per pound, they are sold by weight rather than by count. Worms can typically eat more than their weight per day. For an indoor worm bin, starting with 50 to 100 worms is fine. For an outdoor vermicompost bin, we started with 1,000 worms and they multiplied quickly.

Worms can be mail-ordered. The following are reputable companies that sell red wriggler worms:

- Uncle Jim's Worm Farm: 1-800-373-0555, unclejimswormfarm.com
- Planet Natural: 1-800-289-6656, planetnatural.com
- Red Worm Composting: redwormcomposting.com
- Gardener's Supply Company: 1-800-876-5520, gardeners.com
- Windy City Worms: wiggle-west@windycityworms.com; windycityworms.com
- Local Harvest: 1-831-515-5602, localharvest.org

Here are some approximate current prices ($US)

- $45 for 2,000 composting worms
- $35 for 1,000 red composting worm mix
- $30 for 500 red composting worm mix
- $30 for European nightcrawlers

▲ *Worms are often sold by the pound.*

HOME COMPOSTING

Have a composting system in place. There is an intimidating factor that comes into play with indoor home composting: Beginners often fear the dreadful smell associated with it. If done right, there is virtually no smell. The following methods have worked best for us after years of kitchen composting:

- Use a bin with a lid. Cut holes in the lid.
- Add equal parts wet and dry material. Be sure that there is enough oxygen and moisture in the worm bin. Anaerobic composting, the result of too much moisture, gives off a very foul smell. As long as you have bedding and food scraps, as well as enough moisture, you will create the optimal composting environment.
- Keep the bin in an area that is accessible, so that it is not easily forgotten. It should be far enough away from your main living space so

that the odor is not detected. We keep ours near the trash can.

- If you are really concerned about the odor and attracting fruit flies, keep the bin right outside your kitchen door or window.

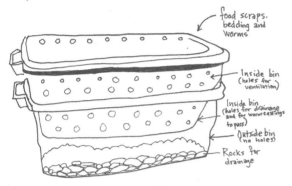

▲ *Indoor worm bin.*

▲ *The dos and don'ts of compost.*

Simple compost bins for kitchen scraps require the following:

- Small trash can with a pedal that lifts the lid
- Five-gallon bucket with a lid
- Small container with a lid (ice cream gallon bucket)

We empty ours every three days, and there is virtually no smell. If you are worried about an odor, keep a can of sawdust nearby and sprinkle on a scoop after each addition to the compost bin.

Several worm bin designs are specifically customized for indoor use. Be sure to have adequate amounts of food and bedding for the worms.

THE DOS & DON'TS OF COMPOST AND VERMICOMPOST

A compost bin and a vermicompost bin are different. Some items that can go into a compost bin should not go into a vermicompost bin.

Compost Materials

The following items can be composted:

- All food scraps (mainly fruit and vegetable scraps)
- Meat and bones (though it will attract wildlife, sometimes unwanted visitors such as raccoons)
- Dairy (also may attract unwanted visitors)
- Eggshells
- Coffee grounds
- Newspaper (black and white only, no color glossy)

- Cardboard, such as toilet paper and paper towel rolls
- Leaves
- Grass clippings
- Small twigs
- Plants removed from the garden after life cycle is complete. Do not add if they are infested with non-beneficial insects or are diseased.
- Weeds before they go to seed (not invasive weeds)

Vermicompost Materials

The following items can be composted:

- All food scraps
- Eggshells
- Coffee grounds
- Newspaper (black and white only, no color glossy)
- Cardboard, such as toilet paper and paper towel rolls
- Leaves
- Grass clippings
- Small twigs
- Plants removed from the garden after life cycle is complete. Do not add if they are infested with non-beneficial insects or are diseased.
- Weeds before they go to seed (not invasive weeds)
- Spent mushroom substrate such as grains or sawdust after mushrooms have ran their life cycle

What Not to Compost

It is important not to compost waste that should go to the landfill or be recycled such as plastic, Styrofoam, or any materials that won't decompose. Do not add invasive weeds and diseased or infested plants; instead, burn them away from the garden and compost bin.

PILE DIVISION

On a larger scale, compost can be placed into piles or long rows instead of bins. We like to divide ours into one-year, two-year, and five-year piles. The one-year pile has plenty of worms and microorganisms that are working hard to transform the organic matter into useable growing medium/fertilizer. It contains only materials that will decompose within 12 months, such as food scraps, leaf litter, newspaper, and grass clippings. It has an equal carbon and nitrogen ratio.

▲ *Cay and Iris help spread compost from a finished pile.*

The two-year pile contains everything in the one-year pile, but we add cardboard and manures from goats, rabbits, cows, and horses. We also include lots of fallen leaves, straw, and paper goods to this pile and turn it weekly.

The five-year pile contains everything the two-year pile has plus chicken manure. Since this is high in nitrogen, we try to neutralize it by adding more straw.

RESOURCES

Recycled paper and newspaper both make an excellent bedding for worms. Buy a simple paper shredder (after checking that friends and family don't have one that they are not using). Newspaper, thin cardboard, and black-and-white paper waste can all be shredded and kept in a bin with a tight-fitting lid in the garage or mud room. Ask friends and family to save newspapers for you. You might also check with your local newspaper office to see about getting their leftovers after distribution.

Fall leaves are a great addition to the compost pile and the vermicompost pile/bin. Leaf blowers usually come with an attachment that actually sucks and grinds up leaves and deposits them into a collection bag. This works well because the shredded leaves take less time for the worms to grind up, and they won't compact as much as whole leaves in the compost bin.

Grass clippings from untreated lawns are a wonderful addition to the compost pile and the vermicompost pile/bin. Lawn mowers may have a catchment container or bag for collecting clippings, which can then be added with leaf litter to the bins. This should only be done when a lawn is not treated with chemical pesticides.

Sawdust from untreated lumber can be added to a vermicompost bin. If you have a ton of sawdust from untreated lumber, you may be able to age it first by combining it in a separate pile with manure. Lumber mills could be a great resource for untreated sawdust.

Wood chips make an excellent filler material for long-term composting and are especially helpful for adding a carbon component to your large pile, for aging manure, and for a base layer in a long windrow system.

Spent grains are an excellent by-product from the brewing process. Readily available year-round from most large breweries, they can be a good source of food for microorganisms in the vermicompost bin during winter when vegetable scraps are not readily available. There are mixed reviews on using them for vermicomposting because of the amount of heat they let off when decomposing, as well as how they change the pH of the pile. Using spent brewing grains in the compost pile first would be a good idea. Let them start decomposing and cool down a bit. Do not put fresh spent grains directly into the compost pile; rather, age them for one to two weeks. One method for aging is to use a five-gallon bucket with several holes drilled in the bottom for drainage and airflow. Place about four handfuls of chip mulch at the bottom, add spent grains, and top with several more handfuls of chip mulch. This will allow the spent grains to cool off a bit, and decomposing will start after one to two weeks. Be sure to only add a few handfuls at a time in one corner of the bin. Do not cover the bin with spent grains, because you want the worms to be able to retreat if an area of the bin gets too warm for them.

Coffee grounds are readily available from most coffee shops. If they don't separate their grounds from the garbage, you could offer to provide a few clean buckets for them to dispense the grounds into. You can schedule a weekly pickup and drop off clean buckets each time. This is a great resource, especially if you are doing a large vermicompost system or windrow.

Animal manure is a great addition to the compost pile. Pre-composted or aged manure is better for the vermicompost bin. Some animal manures are better than others. Most offer good nutrition for worms, such as cattle, poultry, sheep, goat, hog, rabbit, and horse manure. Weed seeds in animal manure are often a disadvantage, but pre-composted manure can still be used. In most cases, the seeds need to reach a certain temperature in order to become nonviable. This factor varies for different types of manure and weeds.

Add the worm bedding — a mixture of shredded paper or torn newspaper, leaf litter, grass clippings, and small pieces of cardboard, such as toilet paper rolls — and spray with water until the mixture is wet.

The bedding should sit until it reaches the correct temperature. It should stay below 90°F for at least two days. Once the optimum

temperature has been reached, push aside the bedding, add the worms, and cover with the bedding. Food scraps can then be added slowly. A rule of thumb among well-known vermiculturists is that worms can eat their weight in one day.

After one to two months, harvest the bottom layer of vermicompost. Add a few handfuls of new worm bedding. Continue adding kitchen scraps, and the cycle will continue. (Adapted from goorganicgardening.com)

COMPOST AND VERMICOMPOST DESIGNS FOR YOUR BACKYARD

This section covers some basic designs for building compost or vermicompost bins in your own backyard and includes detailed instructions for using reclaimed/repurposed materials.

Simple Compost Boxes

Simple elevated worm boxes can be built using untreated wood and chicken wire or galvanized hardware cloth as a base. Place catchment bins underneath for easy worm harvesting.

Wire Fence Cylinder Compost Bin

Use a panel of scrap wire fencing, roughly ten feet long, with holes no smaller than 2" × 4". To form a cylinder, fasten the ends together with baling wire (overlapping them a few inches for extra support) or zip ties.

This design is great because over time you can use just one, or create multiples to place in predetermined areas you would like to have raised beds. With the wire cylinder, it is best to start the bins in the summer for a ready-to-go

WIRE FENCE CYLINDER COMPOST BIN

▶ *Wire fence cylinder compost bin.*

raised bed the following spring. Fill compost to the brim (leaf mulch, grass clippings, food scraps, and straw). There is no need to turn this bin; just keep adding organic material, and after six to eight months, simply lift the wire cylinder and you have a ready-to-plant garden bed in the spring.

Basic Cube Compost Bin

A simple compost bin can be made using reclaimed pallets, preferably heat-treated ones marked with the letters HT. Securely fasten

four pallets together upright with baling wire. Organic materials are added that are broken down by living organisms, microbes, fungi, and bacteria.

Vermicompost Bin

A vermicompost bin is essentially the same as a compost bin except that worms are added to help break down materials quicker. Worm castings can be harvested and used as organic fertilizer after about four months. A vermicompost bin can also be built using reclaimed heat-treated pallets. Construct it in the same way, except add a built-in trapdoor or removable slats to harvest worm castings.

For each design, place the fastened bin in a permanent area of your yard with one open end directly on the soil. It is not necessary to remove the grass in this location. To best activate the composting process, fill the bin with leaves, grass clippings, straw, and other organic matter. You may then begin adding kitchen scraps such as fruit and vegetable ends and peels, eggshells,

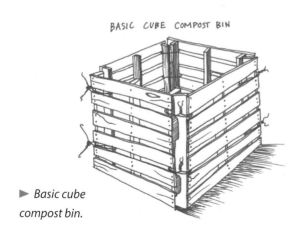

BASIC CUBE COMPOST BIN

▶ *Basic cube compost bin.*

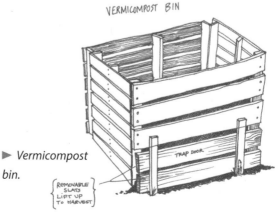

VERMICOMPOST BIN

TRAP DOOR.

{ REMOVABLE SLATS LIFT UP TO HARVEST }

▶ *Vermicompost bin.*

and coffee grounds. Avoid adding meat, dairy, oils, and citrus fruits.

Turn your compost regularly with a pitchfork to speed up the process, turning occasionally in a vermicompost bin to help aerate the compost. Do not cover the compost bin. It should be open to the elements. During dry spells, you may need to add water to your compost bin. Vermicompost bins can be built in boxes under a shelter for worm casting collection. If you want to build healthy soil and attract beneficial microbes, it is best to have the bin open to the elements and open to the soil below, rather than a closed container.

▲ *A worm bin can be incorporated into a grow box.*

Worm Bin Grow Box

Build a standard worm box with a hard plastic mesh front (with holes large enough for the worms to freely move back and forth). Build an additional box onto the front of the bin, where the mesh is, and plant your favorite garden varieties there.

Ann and Gord Baird's Veggie Washing Station/Worm Bin/Worm Tea Collector

Ann and Gord Baird, permaculturists with Eco-Sense, believe in stacking functions and keeping designs simple. They designed a simple way to conserve and utilize water by building a worm composter right next to a vegetable washing station. The washing station sink drains into a five-gallon bucket; this empties into a worm bin with holes at the bottom, resting in a water drum with a spout, which is raised off the ground. A separate bucket collects the worm

▲ *Worm bin washing station.*

leachate below. When washing veggies, they pour the wash water into the worm bin, and it flows through to the collection drum. This process saves water, gives nutrients from food waste to worms, and uses worm tea to water their fruit and vegetable plants.

Bathtub Worm Farm

Repurposing items that would ordinarily go into a landfill is necessary for those on a budget and a practical way to intercept landfill waste. For example, an old claw-foot tub with a few irreparable holes makes the perfect worm bin. Build a frame out of reclaimed materials or just rest the tub on stacks of cinder blocks. A

separate container resting underneath can be easily removed when worm tea is ready to be harvested.

Patio Bench Worm Bin

This design is adapted from *Worms Eat My Garbage* by Mary Appelhof from Seattle Tilth.[5]

Build a worm box using a 4-foot-by-8-foot sheet of ½-inch exterior plywood and five or six pieces of framing lumber (construction grade 2"× 4"). Cut the plywood into desirable sizes. Attach to a lumber frame. It can be weatherproofed with outdoor nontoxic stain or varnish.

▲ *Old claw-foot bathtubs can be transformed into a worm bin.*

▲ *Patio bench worm bin.*

Midwest Permacultures Worm Tower

This design is specific to individual garden beds. A large pipe with several dozen holes drilled through it is inserted into the ground. It provides a habitat for worms that have underground access to the soil in the bed. The concept behind this design is that the worms have plenty of access to nutrition and moisture and are able to explore their preferred habitat within the beds. They aerate the soil by adding air pockets that permit roots to go deeper and distribute castings at various levels, offering plenty of nutrition to the plants. This wonderful design removes a lot of the grunt work for the gardener.

One simple design uses two five-gallon buckets. Cut off the bottom and the top of one bucket and drill holes all over the other one (50 or more evenly spaced holes). Fit the first bucket inside the second. In a garden bed, dig a hole the size of one bucket. Insert the bucket and add a little soil around it. Next, add the ingredients for the worm farm. Fill the bucket ⅓ full with soil, add equal parts manure, veggie scraps, water, and a burlap sack, and cover with a lid. Evenly distribute one pound of worms around the outside of the bucket. Cover with the remaining soil. Add veggie scraps each week and be sure the worm farm is kept moist. (Based on design by Inga van Dyk.)

Bill and Becky Wilson have a very simple design for a worm tower, using three simple steps:

1. Drill ¼" holes into a PVC or plastic tube so that the worms can move freely in and out. The tube should be 2 to 2 ½ feet long and

▲ *Underground pipe worm farm or free-range worm farm.*

4 to 8 inches in diameter. Drill on a tarp or sheet to catch the bits of plastic.

2. Prepare a hole in the ground and bury the tube so that only 4 to 6 inches remain above the surface. Backfill around the tube but not in it, making sure that all the holes are below ground. A piece of window screen and a flowerpot as a cover will help keep out flies.

3. Fill the tube about half-way with a mixture of moist organic matter (straw, shredded newsprint, leaves, etc.) and kitchen scraps. Add a handful of red wriggler worms. Cover with a damp piece of burlap. To maintain the tower, simply add food scraps as available and water during dry weather to keep the worms and surrounding soil moist.[6]

Visit midwestpermaculture.com for more great garden ideas.

▲ *Rabbit cage over worm bin.*

▲ *Woven branches make a beautiful compost or vermicompost bin.*

Rabbit Cage over Worm Bins

Another example of stacking functions is keeping rabbits above open worm bins. The concept is that the rabbit droppings fall through holes in the cages into the bins, keeping the cages clean and providing an ongoing supply of manure for the worm bins. The rabbit cage is built with scrap lumber and chicken wire or hardware cloth. The holes should be large enough for the droppings to fall through but small enough so that the rabbits' paws do not get trapped.

Straw Bale Worm Bin

A simple worm bed can be made using 6 straw bales (2 on either side and 1 at each end) to form a rectangle in an area of your yard that gets partial shade, such as under a tree. Fill with leaves, newspaper, grass clippings, food scraps, and non-diseased plant remnants from the garden.

Woven Willow Worm Bins

If you are unable to buy lumber or have no access to scrap lumber or power tools, you can construct a worm bin using willow branches, young bamboo, or other long pliable branches (as well as some thicker branches), a hand saw, hammer, and nails. From this design, you can make permanent or moveable beds. Strip the leaves from 8 branches (at least 3 inches in diameter) that are flat at one end and pointed at the other. Using a hammer or sledge hammer, tap them into the ground in a square with 4 pieces at each corner and 4 in between. Holes may need to be slightly predug. Then weave the willow branches or bamboo between the branches and fasten with nails at the corner posts. For a moveable bed, make 4 separate windows using 2 long branches for the top and bottom, 2 smaller ones for the sides, and 3 smaller ones fastened evenly between the 2 end posts. Weave the willow or bamboo between the vertical branches.

Large Branch Bin

A large branch bin can be made from a fallen tree limb. Use long weatherproof nails or screws to fashion branches in a square or rectangle using the log stacking method. Fill with leaves, newspaper, grass clippings, food scraps, and non-diseased plant remnants.

LARGER VERMICOMPOST OPERATIONS

Growing Power, founded by Wil Allen, managed a large-scale vermicompost operation in Milwaukee, Wisconsin. It held about 5,000 pounds of compost in raised beds down the center of a high tunnel. They broke the compost down (it took about 6 to 8 months), presifted it, and then brought it into the worm bins. They layered about 5,000 pounds of worms in between the layers of soil. For approximately 4 months, the worms broke down the organic material into a usable form. This increased beneficial bacteria by 14 times, so the end result is nutrient-rich.

Once the worm castings were ready to harvest, they placed a 16-mesh screen over the worm bin. They added compost on top of it so that the worms go through the screen to where the compost is. After lifting the screens off and setting them aside, they harvested the castings using five-gallon buckets. New compost was added to the worm bins, and the worms and food scraps were returned to the bins as well.

WINDROWS

Windrows vary by size and scale. However, their basic concept is a long and often narrow berm of organic decaying material. For example, food waste, particularly fruits and vegetables, can be diverted from the landfill and placed in long narrow piles with chip-mulched pathways. Carbon materials such as leaves or old newspapers can be added to the berms. Place worms evenly over the windrows, and they will immediately get to work.

STOCK TANKS

Kathy and Joel Adams house their worms in elevated stock tanks with spigots. They have had a great deal of success keeping the moisture level of the worm bins between 70% and 85%. Kathy believes that the worms will die in a moisture level below 50%. They also keep a

▼ *An example of a windrow system.*

worm pile in wood chips. They add food scraps and peat moss and monitor the pH level regularly. They water their bins regularly but cover them if rain is forecast. They do not use tap water in their worm bins. According to them, "one worm can produce approximately 600 offspring in one year."

CARING FOR YOUR VERMICOMPOST BIN

The vermicompost bin should have a sweet earthy smell. It should not give off an offensive odor. If it does begin to smell bad, that may be a sign of an anaerobic environment. In this case, try turning it and add more carbon material, such as straw, wood chips, paper bedding, or cardboard, throughout the entire bin. If slime has developed, your bin may be too far gone. If

▲ *Show your worms some love.*

so, you can transfer that to an outdoor compost pile and combine it with wood chips, paper towel rolls, newspapers, etc.

FEEDING YOUR WORMS

As mentioned previously, worms eat more than their weight each day. As a general rule, one pound of worms needs at least one pound of food source daily. Proper nutrition is key to maintaining your worm bin.

Green Leaf Worm Farm recommends using a base of 18 inches of peat moss, corrugated cardboard, and shredded paper. Corrugated cardboard provides good habitat for raising worms.

VERMICOMPOST BIN CONDITIONS

Temperature Regulation

Optimal temperature for a worm bin varies by climate, elevation, time of year, and its location indoors or outdoors. A general rule is to keep the minimum temperature at 50°F to 80°F. The worms may survive extreme temperatures if they have the right moisture content and shade or insulation. Some vermiculturists have overwintered outdoor worms in below-freezing temperatures. Others don't like to stress their worms or risk losing them and will bring their worms inside their garage for the winter.

Moisture Content

Since worms breathe through their skin, their habitat should remain moist but not too moist. The proper balance of moisture and airflow is important. Standing water should never be present in a worm bin. It should also never dry out completely.

Proper Drainage

There should always be a drainage system in place for indoor worm bins. Holes drilled into the bin will usually suffice. More complicated worm bin designs have mesh screens to allow drainage but prevent flies and other insects from entering the bins.

Ventilation/Airflow

Since worms produce carbon dioxide, airflow is important. Having plenty of bedding in place ahead of time will help create air pockets. Other ideas are to add cardboard or toilet paper rolls throughout the bin facing in different directions.

Separating Worms

Under the right conditions, the worm population in a vermicompost bin can double every 90 days. Be sure you have a system in place to divide worms and place them into new bins or piles every few months to prevent overcrowding in the bin. Worms can be given away to fellow gardeners or sold at local farmers markets.

Insulation During the Winter Months

Several methods can be used to insulate the worms during the winter months. Our favorite is to simply cover the worms with tons of leaves. We go on secret twilight missions driving around neighborhoods that we know use sustainable landscaping methods. We collect the

▲ *Worms need to be separated as their population increases.*

brown leaf litter bags near the trash cans that people set out who don't want leaves in their yards. Also, before the temperatures get below freezing, we stack straw bales all around the bins to insulate them. Unless heavy snowfall is predicted, we rarely cover our bins. Then we just cover them with sheets of plywood.

The following list has ideas from friends and fellow worm farmers who have had luck overwintering their worms:

- Use a compost bin with a lid and just fill it with lots of organic material. Add a few layers at the top of the bin and close lid for the winter.
- Cover bin with burlap sacks.
- Cover bin with old tin scraps.
- Cover pile with an old blanket.
- Cover pile with an old door.
- Cover pile with a tarp and a few sandbags.

HARVESTING WORM CASTINGS

Because worm castings are essentially worm waste (manure), the harvesting process is different for each bin design, with the common goal being the removal of the bottom few inches that are fully decomposed.

There are several methods for harvesting worm castings, from a simple screen to a complicated casting tumbler. You can customize them based on your budget, the size of your operation, and your carpentry skills.

Small Worm Bins

For small indoor worm bins, place watermelon rinds or banana peels into the worm bin the night before you wish to harvest the castings. This gives the worms a reason to come to the surface, usually congregating on the peels and rinds. Simply put the peels, rinds, and worms in

▲ *Watermelon rinds can help attract worms to make worm castings easy to harvest.*

a separate container while you sift and harvest the rest of the worm castings.

Dump out the contents of your worm bin onto a large tarp. Hand sort all of the worms you see into the separate bin (with the majority of the worms, banana peels, and rinds). Pick out any large clumps of material that has not broken down yet and return them to the worm bin.

Here are two methods from Mary Appelehof's *Worms Eat My Garbage*:

Dump and hand sort by making cone-shaped piles, adding bright light to prompt worms to go to the bottom of the piles and then to remove the piles of worm castings and add them to a separate bucket. The worms can then be collected and weighed and added back to the worm bin with new bedding and food scraps.

Let the worms do the sorting by pulling all of the vermicompost to one side of the bin, add new bedding to the vacant side, and bury food scraps in new bedding. The worms will move into the new bedding in search of food. The vermicompost can be removed after 2 to 3 months and replaced with new food, and the process can continue.

A kitchen colander or mesh strainer could work for separating castings. The screen must have holes large enough for the castings to go through, leaving the worms and organic material that has not yet been broken down on the top of the screen.

Sifter Box

You can make a simple sifter box any size you wish, but 2' by 2' or 2½' by 2½' work well to fit over a standard wheelbarrow. Simply screw together untreated scrap lumber to make a frame. Cut galvanized mesh screen to fit the window and fasten using screws.

To sift, place a few handfuls of vermicompost in the sifter box. Shake them back and forth multiple times over the wheelbarrow. The worm castings should fall through the screen and into the wheelbarrow. The remnants on top of the screen, such as small pieces of mulch and twigs and larger food scraps, can be added back to the vermicompost bin.

Galvanized Hardware Cloth

Wil Allen has multiple worm boxes that are fairly shallow but wide. When the castings are ready to be harvested, he places galvanized hardware cloth or screen over them and adds food scraps such as banana peels and watermelon rinds on top. The worms come up to the surface, through the hardware cloth, to eat the decaying matter. He lifts off the screen, adds the worms and scraps on it to a new unfinished worm bin, and then harvests the finished bin.

Larger Operations

A large rotary sifter, or a trommel, can be made using scrap materials such as bicycle rims, lumber, zip ties, five-gallon buckets, metal pipes, and PVC pipes. Further, these contraptions can be made in a way that they can be bicycle-powered.

Storing Castings

Castings can be stored in five-gallon buckets in a clean, cool, and dark environment. The experts at Sierra Worm Composting recommend the following:

> The cardinal rule in castings is that you don't want them to dry out. Keeping them at 20% moisture ensures microbial

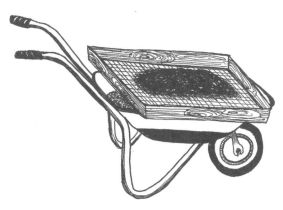

▲ *Sifter used over a wheelbarrow.*

▲ *Rotary sifter makes harvesting worm castings easy.*

life. Microbes die if the castings dry out completely. Depending on the quantity of worm castings you need to store, Ziploc bags (with a few air holes punched around the top) are good containers kept in a cool, dark place. Plastic garbage bags with air holes at the top could work for large quantities. The 20% moisture is attained when you take a handful, squeeze it, and the mass should just hold together. Any wetter and you'll need to dry it out a bit. If it's drier, simply spritz with a spray bottle or fine-mist from a hose and mix until the squeeze test succeeds. To take the guesswork out, I would suggest investing in a moisture meter. It's not a good idea to store longer than 6 months, certainly no longer than a year and always keeping tabs on the moisture content.[7]

WORM TEA

Joe Urbach summarized the differences between leachate, worm tea, and aerobic compost tea:

Leachate — is the correct word for the dark liquid that comes out of the bottom of your worm bin. If your bin is maintained correctly, you should have very little leachate and what you do have can be used safely (in 1:10 diluted form) on your ornamental plants. Sometimes leachate is incorrectly referred to as "worm tea." Some sites refer to it at as "worm wee," but even that is technically incorrect.

Simple Worm Tea — a mix of worm castings and water. Useful if you don't have an air pump but still want some liquid fertilizer from your worm bin.

Aerobic Compost Tea — an aerated mixture of worm castings, non-chlorinated water, and molasses or another microbial food source. It contains an active culture of microorganisms and should be used immediately, otherwise the benefit of aeration is all but lost.[8]

Leachate, Worm Tea, and Aerobic Compost Tea: A Clarification

Kathy and Joel Adams see great results in their garden using "worm juice" to fertilize their plants. Inside their elevated stock tanks, upside-down bread crates catch the debris and leave a space for the liquid to fall through, still maintaining a habitat for the worms and preventing them from drowning. They have added spigots to the bottom edges of the bins, with enough elevated space to fit five-gallon buckets. With this method, they have had a great deal of success keeping the moisture level of the worm bins between 70% and 85%. Kathy believes that the worms will die in a moisture level below 50%. They add food scraps and peat moss and monitor the pH level regularly. They keep their bins watered regularly but cover them if rain is forecast. They do not use tap water. The worm juice naturally collects in the base of the stock tank, filling the buckets beneath. To fertilize, they use two tablespoons per gallon of water to make a vermicompost tea.

For farm-scale vermicompost tea application, we have had luck steeping a large burlap sack of worm castings in the 200-gallon water tank attached to the waterwheel transplanter. We were able to fertilize with worm tea as we were planting, which really helped the crops.

GARDEN APPLICATIONS

Worm castings are the aggregate dark brown, rich soil medium found at the very bottom of the vermicompost bin. In garden applications, they make a nutrient-rich natural fertilizer that helps to boost soil immunity, increase soil fertility, increase plant health and disease resistance, strengthen roots, and improve yields and overall plant health. The following are specific applications for worm castings:

- For potted plants and small gardens, maximize the worm casting harvest by using sparingly.

- Worm castings help to improve germination time when added directly to a seed germination mix.
- Sprinkle over young seedlings to boost their growth.
- Side-dress larger plants to give them a head start against weeds.
- Sprinkle in the furrow before you transplant a row.
- Sprinkle on top of small garden beds before planting.

Results of using both compost and worm castings for plant vitality and growth, as well as building healthy soils, are rewarding. As diversified vegetable growers, we love our compost. It has made an enormous difference on crops, specifically heavy feeders such as tomatoes, eggplant, and peppers.

◀ *Children love to help tend to the garden. Applying vermicompost and watering are great ways for them to help.*

▲ *Our daughter Iris loves to help fertilize with worm castings and harvest the bounty.*

Chapter 4

Permaculture in Your Backyard/Bed Prep

I FIRST LEARNED THE TERM *permaculture* when I was 17 years old. Through my high-school environmental science major, I was in a group called Eco-Act, founded and facilitated by the Missouri Botanical Garden in 1981 to inspire Earth stewardship in youth. My mother helped me sell chocolate bars in order to pay for a trip to Costa Rica.

We visited the Punta Mona Center for Sustainable Living and Education, an 85-acre organic permaculture farm on the Caribbean coast, run by eco-entrepreneur Stephen Brooks. He and his sister Lisa started Costa Rican Adventures to educate international students about rainforest degradation, endangered species, and unsustainable agricultural practices, as well as solutions to these concerns. We visited the banana plantations where planes sprayed pesticides on the trees, causing nearby villages to suffer through the clouds of chemicals. We then visited the Bribri tribe at Kekoldi Indigenous Reserve in Puerto Viejo de Talamanca. They had been growing cacao trees for several generations in the understory of their food forests. They hand-ground the cacao and mixed it with tapa dulce, blocks of raw sugar. Walking through their food forest, witnessing such a diversity of tropical fruit trees

among the jungle backdrop is a memory etched in the catacombs of my mind.

The Bribri tribe had a deep unparalleled connection with their food. We witnessed the entire process of making chocolate: the pods were harvested from the trees; the pods were sliced open and the pulp removed; the beans were sorted, fermented, and dried in the sun. A respected grandmother in the tribe, whose hands were worn from years of hard physical labor, kissed each and every dried cacao bean before she ground the seeds by hand using a stone corn grinder. A rich drink was made using fresh goats' milk, hot water, raw sugar, and ground cacao. The experience of spending time with the Bribri tribe and exploring through the cloud forests and jungles and along coastlines of Costa Rica reaffirmed my love for the natural world and helped to strengthen the desire to do my part for the Earth.

Stephen, also the founder of Kopali Organics, an organic food company dedicated to supporting small farmers and providing a highly nutritious food source to the public, has been a major catalyst in the permaculture movement. He has taught thousands of individuals around the globe how to bring sustainability into fruition in their daily lives. Punta Mona is completely off the grid, using solar energy for

▲ Photo credit: Permission to use photo from Stephen Brooks, founder of Punta Mona Center for Regenerative Agriculture and Botanical Studies.

power, methane for gas, and growing 90% of the food for thousands of people per year at the retreat center. The property is rich in biodiversity with hundreds of fruit and nut trees towering over a food forest and dozens of raised beds in the kitchen garden. Various types of squash thrive on the hillsides. Chinampas, wetland gardens, are home to various fruits, vegetables, roots, leaves, and herbs. It is one of the most beautiful permaculture design models I have seen.

During my time at Punta Mona, I felt fiery ambition running through my veins. It all became clear: permaculture could be a solution! Well, at least it could if everyone in the world knew just how profound it was and if there were ways to simplify it and make it accessible to them.

On that life-changing trip, I learned the following ten central concepts of permaculture:

1. Permaculture incorporates the existing eco-system into the development plans without compromising the integrity of the land, water, or habitat of native flora and fauna.

2. Permaculture works with nature, not against it.

3. Permaculture gardens provide food for humans, animals, pollinators, and the soil.

4. Permaculture fosters symbiotic relationships.

5. Permaculture provides a global solution to widespread epidemics, including hunger and starvation, environmental degradation, deforestation, pollution, and reliance on fossil fuels.

6. Permaculture gardens help heal the land and its people by using plants to filter water, revitalizing contaminated soil, using grey water systems, implementing rain garden techniques, cultivating with the contours of the land, and growing more per square foot.

7. Permaculture promotes all aspects of sustainability and focuses on how all solutions for a greener future can work together. Integrating alternative energy systems into small-scale organic food production is just one way to implement these concepts.

8. Permaculture promotes healthy food, clean air, and clean water.

9. Permaculture focuses on the complex interrelationships within the food web and restores our balance with the natural world.

10. Permaculture is a catalyst for a sustainable future. Everyone is capable of practicing permaculture techniques.

Permaculture became the one steadfast way of life that I held dear to my heart throughout my twenties and thirties. Certified and specialized permaculturists all have different views on what it means to them and how to utilize it. That's the beauty of free will. Some permaculture experts may argue with my personal take on permaculture, but I do know this: it changed my life.

To me, permaculture is all-encompassing; it can be practiced every day in so many aspects of life, including thinking about human and planetary health, building and restoring, gardening and water conservation, sourcing food, cooking and eating, teaching, parenting, and so much more. Permaculture is an umbrella under which all the innovative resourceful Earth stewards may dream big while brainstorming real and practical solutions to the detrimental practices threatening the planet. Permaculture is inspiring. It stimulates the mind to think differently now for the future of the planet. Permaculture is alive with the possibilities of positive change. Beyond permaculture, there are many organizations and individuals across the globe that are rising to the occasion. The world is in desperate need of a paradigm shift.

As you read on, know that all suggestions are based on my experiences with the natural world, friends, family, mentors, and the Earth itself; suggestions that, if you resonate with them, can be adapted, altered, and formatted to fit into your own life. Permaculture has sculpted my life and has opened many doors to my desire to deepen my connection to the Earth while implementing daily solutions to the problems facing the world today, and my hope in writing this book is to share the exciting possibilities of implementing small, practical solutions with others.

Together, we can paint a beautiful oasis of food and abundance through backyard gardens, community gardens, sustainable farms, and permaculture villages that purify our air, improve our water quality, give nutrients to the soil, provide nourishment to families, and create habitats for pollinators. People from all walks of life are uniting to form a global transition into an abundant, healthy, regenerative world, and need a way to bring their dreams of this brighter future to fruition.

Permaculture concepts can be found at the heart of any eco-minded endeavor. Understanding their vast potential to guide us toward a regenerative future is vital to creating a paradigm shift. We have a last chance at clean air, clean water, and healthy soil, factors absolutely necessary for healthy survival. Permaculture can help us find ways that we, as individuals, can help heal the Earth and revitalize our air, water, and soil.

In 1978, Bill Mollison and David Holmgren coined the term *permaculture* to stand for "permanent agriculture," but the word has since developed a second meaning: "permanent culture." Bill was an instructor, and David was one of his undergraduate students. The book *Permaculture One* started out as David's undergraduate thesis. Bill developed a more hands-on approach to permaculture, while David focused on theories and broad perspective potential in permaculture. Both are equally revered as leading permaculture experts, but Bill is deemed the "Father of Permaculture." He founded the Permaculture Institute in Tasmania to teach permaculture principles through hands-on education. In *Introduction to Permaculture*, he outlines the major ones: relative location, multiple functions, multiple elements, energy efficient planning, using biological resources, energy cycling, small-scale intensive, accelerating succession, diversity, edge awareness, and attitudinal principles. Bill planted the way for thousands of permaculturists. He laid the foundation for Earth stewardship and is a hero among so many who wish to leave the world better than they found it.

While Bill and David coined the term "permaculture," a great deal of the insights are based on Indigenous wisdom. Cultures around the globe have held quintessential reverence for the natural world throughout history and have been practicing Earth stewardship for centuries.

The following explanation of permaculture is one that I wholeheartedly resonate with. It was a collective definition that was created by Lisa DePiano, Pandora Thomas, and Rafter Sass Ferguson: "Permaculture is an ecological design lens based on Indigenous wisdom by which we can observe and interact with everything in order to increase the health and well-being of everything to ultimately bring us into the next phase of planetary health."

Jason Gerhardt, defines permaculture as "a design paradigm that provides for human need by regenerating ecosystems, creating justice and peace, and thereby increasing permanence in human culture."

Toby Hemenway, one of my favorite permaculture authors and educators, offered a beautiful definition of permaculture. He passed away in December of 2016. May he rest in peace.

I think the definition of permaculture that must rise to the top is that it is a design approach to arrive at solutions, just as the scientific method is an experimental approach. In more concrete terms, permaculture tells how to choose from a dauntingly large toolkit — all the human technologies and strategies for living — to solve the new problem of sustainability. It is an instruction manual for solving the challenges laid out by the new paradigm of meeting human needs while enhancing ecosystem health. The relationship explicitly spelled out in that view, which connects humans to the larger, dynamic environment, forces us to think in relational terms, which is a key element of permaculture. The two sides of the relationship are explicitly named in two permaculture ethics: care for the Earth, and care for people. And knowing we need both sides of that relationship is immensely helpful in identifying the problems we need to solve.

First, what are human needs? The version of the permaculture flower that I work with names some important ones: food, shelter, water, waste recycling, energy, community, health, spiritual fulfillment, justice and livelihood. The task set out by permaculture, in the new paradigm, is to meet those needs while preserving ecosystem health, and we have metrics for assessing the latter. The way those needs are met will vary by place and culture, but the metrics of ecosystem health can be applied fairly universally. This clarifies the task set by permaculture, and I think it also distinguishes permaculture from the philosophy — the paradigm — required to use it effectively and helps us understand why permaculture is often called a movement. Permaculturists make common cause with all the other millions of people who are shifting to the new paradigm, and it is that shift — not the design approach of permaculture that supports it — that is worthy of being called a movement. Permaculture is one approach used by this movement to solve the problems identified by the new paradigm. To do this, it operates on the level of strategies rather than techniques, but that is a subject for another essay. Because we are, in a way, still in the phlogiston era of our ecological awareness, we don't know how to categorize permaculture, and we can confuse it with the paradigm that it helps us explore. Permaculture is not the movement of sustainability and it is not the philosophy behind it; it is the problem-solving approach the movement and the philosophy can use to meet their goals and design a world in which human needs are met while enhancing the health

of this miraculous planet that supports us.[1]

This image illustrates a comprehensive solution-based example of how a paradigm shift can create a world that works for everyone. It focuses on equality, environmental intelligence, spiritual awakening, food and resource localization, community building, and a unified desire for positive change. What if this could be implemented worldwide? Think of the possibilities!

The following was reproduced in my previous book, *Grow Create Inspire*,[2] with permission from Toby Hemenway.[3]

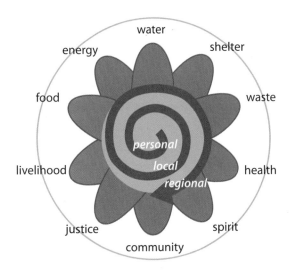

▲ Credit: Toby Hemenway

PERMACULTURE ETHICS

1. Care for the Earth
2. Care for people
3. Return the surplus

PRIMARY PRINCIPLES FOR FUNCTIONAL DESIGN

1. **Observe.** Use protracted and thoughtful observation rather than prolonged and thoughtless action. Observe the site and its elements in all seasons. Design for specific sites, clients, and cultures.

2. **Connect.** Use relative location: Place elements in ways that create useful relationships and time-saving connections among all parts. The number of connections among elements creates a healthy, diverse ecosystem, not the number of elements.

3. **Catch and store energy and materials.** Identify, collect, and hold useful flows. Every cycle is an opportunity for yield, every gradient (in slope, charge, heat, etc.) can produce energy. Reinvesting resources builds capacity to capture yet more resources.

4. **Each element performs multiple functions.** Choose and place each element in a system to perform as many functions as possible. Beneficial connections between diverse components create a stable whole. Stack elements in both space and time.

5. **Each function is supported by multiple elements.** Use multiple methods to achieve important functions and to create synergies. Redundancy protects when one or more elements fail.

6. **Make the least change for the greatest effect.** Find the "leverage points" in the system and intervene there, where the least work accomplishes the most change.

7. **Use small-scale, intensive systems.** Start at your doorstep with the smallest systems that will do the job, and build on your successes, with variations. Grow by chunking.

PRINCIPLES FOR LIVING AND ENERGY SYSTEMS

8. **Optimize edge.** The edge — the intersection of two environments — is the most diverse place in a system, and is where energy and materials accumulate or are transformed. Increase or decrease edge as appropriate.

9. **Collaborate with succession.** Systems will evolve over time, often toward greater diversity and productivity. Work with this tendency, and use design to jump-start succession when needed.

10. **Use biological and renewable resources.** Renewable resources (usually living beings and their products) reproduce and build up over time, store energy, assist yield, and interact with other elements.

ATTITUDES

11. **Turn problems into solutions.** Constraints can inspire creative design. "We are confronted by insurmountable opportunities." ("Pogo," Walt Kelly)

12. **Get a yield.** Design for both immediate and long-term returns from your efforts: "You can't work on an empty stomach." Set up positive feedback loops to build the system and repay your investment.

13. **The biggest limit to abundance is creativity.** The designer's imagination and skill limit

productivity and diversity more than any physical limit.

14. **Mistakes are tools for learning.** Evaluate your trials. Making mistakes is a sign you're trying to do things better.

RULES FOR RESOURCE USE

Ranked from regenerative to degenerative, different resources can:

1. increase with use;
2. be lost when not used;
3. be unaffected by use;
4. be lost by use;
5. pollute or degrade systems with use.

These principles are designed to be implemented into permaculture design projects and can apply to growing gardens, food forests, and farms in eco-villages. These plans and ideas can be scaled down or scaled up and are good guidelines to follow in any planting or community-building endeavor. Permaculture techniques work especially well in areas with low annual rainfall. When implemented correctly, these techniques are meant to be resilient and long-lasting. Some take more time to create but later require less labor for a high yield.

Permaculture begins with looking at the world through hopeful eyes, picturing a reality in which people attempt to work in harmony with the Earth, rather than against it. To look to nature for inspiration is a great way to truly absorb and observe the importance of biodiversity. For example, a native pollinator garden next to a vegetable garden promotes a symbiotic relationship between plants and pollinators.

Our plates would be empty without pollinators. Channeling and preserving water significantly reduces water waste, helps to retain moisture so the garden thrives. Building homes with natural materials found on building sites reduces reliance on synthetic and nonrenewable building materials, and is more energy efficient and very cost-effective. Building berms and swales allows for the channeling and preservation of water around a specific grouping of trees or crops. A berm is essentially a raised bed made from organic materials, and a swale is a specialized ditch that acts as a water preservation reservoir. Rainwater collected in the swale is channeled into the berm.

Personally, I have been following permaculture concepts and principles for nearly two decades and have been integrating them into methods of food production.

Growers around the globe help heal themselves, their communities, and their environment by bringing permaculture to life one seed at a time. The essence of permaculture is the ability to understand the symbiotic relationships between people and people, plants and people, plants and the Earth, and food production and the environment. Paying homage to each other as stewards of the Earth by offering support and encouragement is one way we can truly send out ripples of change to the world.

Real food grown from the Earth is the very point where all these relationships intersect. Throughout cultural history everywhere, the connection human beings have had to the land

and to their food has deepened by being in tune with nature and the changing seasons. For example, certain civilizations held grains, vegetables, fruits, nuts, and seeds as sacred. Rituals, ceremonies, and celebrations were held during planting and harvesting.

Understanding the complexity of nature's resilience and strength gives us a model to learn from. Sharing these observations with growers worldwide is very important for the future of the planet. We can inspire and teach each other based on our own observations. From witnessing a dandelion plant grow through the cracks of concrete to seeing a redwood tree sapling emerge from a clear-cut, we have so much to learn from nature. Cultivation methods have been passed down through scriptures, scrolls, and oral traditions. Innovative ways of growing food seem to be more prevalent today than ever because of social media. More people are experimenting with home gardening. Once you delve into the art of growing food, you discover

so many other possible endeavors, including herb-growing for medicine, food preservation, foraging for wild edibles, wild crafting, beer making, beekeeping, and animal husbandry. Growing food then becomes this momentous act with the potential to define the rest of one's life course. It was for me anyway. It brings about feelings of liberation and independence that are unmatched, empowering me to rely less and less on industrialized food systems.

PRACTICE PERMACULTURE IN YOUR OWN BACKYARD

- Grow an organic vegetable garden to feed your family, friends, and neighbors.
- Use straw to mulch or practice lasagna gardening and sheet mulching to suppress weeds. Integrate a food forest into your existing landscape.
- Plant perennial fruits and fruit trees.
- Get a rain barrel and use a rainwater catchment system to water your garden.
- Build simple bioswales to channel water.
- Start a compost pile to produce your own organic fertilizer and reduce waste.
- Build your soil by adding organic matter.
- Plant native perennial flowers to attract pollinators. Plant native trees to clean the air and provide a wildlife habitat.

PRACTICE PERMACULTURE IN YOUR COMMUNITY

- Volunteer at community gardens and farms.
- Offer your services to local growers.

- Become involved in food justice organizations in your community.
- Offer a free workshop series in your community.
- Gather funds to pay POC farmers and permaculturalists to lead workshops in your community.
- Start a free front-yard garden.

Natural ecosystems have painted our Earth with beauty in the form of forests, deserts, prairies, wetlands, mountains, valleys, rivers, oceans, glaciers. The "green hearts"of our time are creating new works of art on our Earth: prairie and wetland restorations, backyard gardens, fruit and nut orchards, community gardens, organic and biodynamic farms, and permaculture villages, all of which are purifying our air, improving water quality, returning nutrients to the soil, providing food to families, and creating habitats for pollinators. In gardens worldwide, we are planting seeds of change in fields of hope. People from all walks of life are waking up to the importance of sustainability by reading, listening, reflecting, brainstorming solutions, and enacting them.

It is vitally important for us to think seven generations ahead, to consider planetary and human health, and to respect the land as ancient cultures did long ago.

Being self-sufficient is no new endeavor, of course, but wading through the muck that the Industrial Revolution and mass consumption have left behind makes it seem new.

WELCOMING PERMACULTURE INTO YOUR LIFE

Pick a Manageable Permaculture Project to Implement

Perhaps your goal is to grow 70% of your own produce this year. Or maybe you would like to have a medicinal herb garden. Or, more generally, say you want to become more self-sufficient. Figuring out how a specific project designed with permaculture concepts can assist you with your personal goals is a wonderful place to start.

Permaculture Books

There are several very well-written books, each tailored to specific learning styles, that are available at your library or from the author. Permaculture creates paths of inspiration. Reader will follow the path that is right for them. Good books to start with include:

Bill Mollison, *The Introduction to Permaculture*, 2nd rev. ed., Tagari, 2002.

David Holmgren, *Permaculture: Principles and Pathways Beyond Sustainability*, Permanent Publications, 2011.

Toby Hemenway, *Gaia's Garden: A Guide to Home-Scale Permaculture*, 2nd ed., Chelsea Green, 2009. *The Permaculture City*, Chelsea Green, 2015.

Peter Bane and David Holmgren, *The Permaculture Handbook: Garden Farming for Town and Country*, New Society, 2012.

Mark Shephard, *Restoration Agriculture: Real World Permaculture for Farmers*, Acres USA, 2013.

Jessi Bloom and Dave Boehnlein, *Practical Permaculture: For Home Landscapes, Your Community, and the Whole Earth*, Timber Press, 2015.

There are also several great publications that give practical advice on Earth stewardship, self-sufficiency, alternative energy, regenerative gardening, and natural building. *Permaculture* magazine, *Mother Earth News, Orion Magazine,* and *Taproot* magazine are among my favorites.

Start Your Personal Revolution in the Kitchen

- Make a pledge to eat only fair trade, organic, non-GM foods.
- Support your local small-scale farmers and businesses that try to be more sustainable in your community.
- Reduce your consumption of processed foods packaged in single-use plastic.
- Grow your own fruits and vegetables and eat with the seasons to do your part to decrease food miles.

Permaculture Networks

Start a permaculture network in your community or check social media for local groups or meet-ups to join. Get together often. Organize and host workshops. Host a monthly Permablitz to work on projects together. Start a backyard revolution in your community.

Big City Permaculture

- Introduce permaculture projects and concepts into your local schools.

- Outdoor classrooms are more common than ever, and community service provides an excellent opportunity to get kids excited about growing food.
- Planting trees, installing vegetable gardens, building a rain garden, and landscaping with native plants are just a few ways to implement simple permaculture concepts into the school grounds.
- Visit urban farms and community gardens. Volunteer in neighborhood plantings.
- Host a tour of local permaculture projects or sustainable yards. In St. Louis, Terry Winkleman founded the Sustainable Backyard Network as a way of inspiring community members to grow their own food, collect rainwater, and share ideas for creating urban ecosystems. Winkleman organizes a Sustainable Backyard Tour each year that allows dozens of residents to showcase their eco-friendly backyards.

Permaculture Education

- Learn online through websites or free courses.
- Research what options suit you best.
- Research permaculture design courses in your area.

PERMACULTURE DESIGN PRINCIPLES

According to David Holmgren:

> The foundations of permaculture are the ethics which guide the use of the 12 design principles, ensuring that they are used in appropriate ways. These principles

are seen as universal, although the methods used to express them will vary greatly according to the place and situation. They are applicable to our personal, economic, social and political reorganisation as illustrated in the permaculture flower. Each principle can be thought of as a door that opens into whole systems thinking, providing a different perspective that can be understood at varying levels of depth and application.[4]

Here, we revisit the main permaculture principles and look at the potential of applying them to an edible landscape:

Observe and Interact

Observation is an important part of permaculture. It allows for careful planning based on information gathered from your site over a period of time. For example, studying the number of hours of sun each day that your specific edible landscape area will receive is an important

piece of information to know when deciding what to plant in that particular location. Other observations may include the annual rainfall, average rain during each rain event, slope of your land, water flow across the terrain, whether or not water pools in any areas, prevailing winds, shade coverage, and any other observations that could affect the edible landscape. Interacting with the land can occur once observations have been made over an extended period of time.

Catch and Store Energy

To catch and store energy means to create or adapt a system to capture a resource when it is in abundance and to store it for later use. Whether that be energy from the sun, water in the form of rainwater collection, or capturing and storing water from your roof to irrigate gardens, this approach helps to understand and hold reverence for renewable and

nonrenewable resources. One example is to cultivate a microclimate by planting Mediterranean drought- and heat-tolerant plants in a south-facing area near your home.

Obtain a Yield

Yields allow for a reward for all of the hard work you put into a system. For example, the goal for edible landscaping is to provide an abundance of edible food while creating an attractive and useful landscape. Yields are a main reason to

invest time and energy into a whole systems design.

Use and Value Renewable Resources and Services

Using and reusing the abundance that nature provides is an important component of reducing our reliance on nonrenewable resources. Reducing consumption is crucial if we want to see big change.

In an edible landscape, consider using resources found on site instead of buying new materials. For example, create an edge border to your edible landscape with fallen logs or branches found on your property or at a nearby location. Better yet, search for large fallen hardwood trees after a storm and inoculate them with mushrooms to border your garden. Instead of buying bags of organic fertilizer, make your own vermicompost by starting a vermicompost bin. Instead of buying trellises, make your own with long sturdy branches and twine. Instead of buying new labels, utilize old mini blinds cut into small sections.

Produce No Waste

Composting is an exceptional example of producing no waste. Food scraps, eggshells, coffee grounds, and recycled toilet paper rolls can be added to a compost bin. Upcycle plastic bottles as seed-starting containers; sheet mulch pathways with cardboard. Figure out ways to limit consumption. The zero-waste movement is a wonderful example that it is possible to produce very little waste. It takes sacrifice, perseverance, time, and energy, but it truly helps to reduce waste long-term while leaving a better future for our children and grandchildren.

Design from Patterns to Details

Designing from patterns to details is all about stepping back and looking at the big picture. By observing patterns in nature, we can integrate cultivated ecologies into existing natural or man-made systems. For example, my first experience with growing food occurred when I was a teenager. I spent an entire paycheck on seeds, soil, and plants to start a garden in my parents' backyard without looking at the natural patterns first. I spent hours on the details — selecting varieties, designing the garden on paper, researching companion planting and crop rotation. I spent weeks with my dad building a fence, adding new soil and compost, and planting the garden according to my design. I failed to make the initial observation that our backyard was mostly shade. It only got two hours of sun. Not much actually germinated or grew except for greens. It was a lesson I never forgot.

Integrate Rather than Segregate

An excellent example of this principle is integrating perennial guild plantings into an

orchard rather than separating it from a perennial planting. By increasing the biodiversity, plants are creating symbiotic relationships with each other, the air, the water, and the soil.

Use Small and Slow Solutions

Oftentimes, we want to see immediate results and receive instant gratification. Using small and slow solutions allows us to work smarter, not harder. An example in an edible landscape is to start with an initial plan after observation and then to slowly add design components over time. Perhaps you can start with a small pollinator garden. Simply planting milkweed could have a long-term impact for pollinators in your area.

Use and Value Diversity

Think about natural ecosystems. They are polycultures. Each ecosystem contains a plethora of diversity. Each plant and animal typically serves a purpose or has a function in that ecosystem. Each microorganism plays a role in that ecosystem as well. In an edible landscape, it is best

to plant a variety of plants that will take root, bloom, and set fruit during different times throughout a season. The goals for an edible landscape are to have a continuous abundance throughout each season; to create an attractive landscape with a variety of textures, colors, and blooms; and to inspire others to plant edibles in their front and backyards.

Use Edges and Value the Marginal

The point at which two ecosystems join or overlap is known as the edge. The edges are considered to be abundant, and biodiversity is rich. An example of an edge in edible landscaping is to perhaps create a hedgerow or a natural fence

line with fruiting shrubs such as elderberry, aronia berry, or a polyculture hedgerow.

Creatively Use and Respond to Change

Adapting to change is important. There are always factors that can cause a design to alter. Maintaining a flexible mentality toward design can help to ease the mind when change occurs.

In an edible landscape, some plants may not do well in your particular microclimate. While you may have strategically planned out a gorgeous design, the plants may have a different agenda. Perhaps a native currant came up in the spot you originally planted a different species that didn't do well. In that circumstance, allowing the currant to exist is an example of creatively responding to change. Working with nature rather than against it also helps this process. In our own yard, my husband noticed there were a dozen persimmon saplings that had sprouted when he went to mow the lawn. Instead of cutting them down, he mowed around each of the young trees. We sheet mulched around them and started interplanting perennials, fruit-bearing

shrubs, and red clover, a nitrogen-fixing cover crop. We now are stewards of a small but mighty persimmon grove polyculture.

Designing for Abundance

Before you begin:

Set goals for your edible landscape. They could be a combination of any of the following or your own personal goals:

- A continuous abundance from a front-yard garden, a perennial polyculture or a food forest

- Create a small ecosystem of beneficial insects and pollinators

- Aesthetics in the form of a beautiful array of heights, textures, and colors

- A social component is always a great idea. For example, our friend Matt Lebon of Custom Foodscaping and his partner, Deidre Kelly, said that when they introduced animals (first rabbits and then ducks) to their backyard

food forest in the city, they got to know their neighbors and developed friendships quickly. The social aspect of their edible landscape became a connection between the animals and the families walking by. They decided to plant perennials that the animals enjoyed near their enclosures so that passing neighbors could stop and feed the animals.

Think about strategies for the following:

- Water retention
- Weed management
- Crop planning, succession planting, local frost dates
- Planting zone-specific crops
- Planting pest- and disease-resistant varieties
- Planting requirements (height, sun/shade, spacing)

LANDSCAPE PLANNING

It is helpful to start with an aerial map of your site. You can then determine zones and sectors and create a rough drawing of your system's elements and components.

Below is a segment from the home system module that I am co-teaching as part of the Permaculture Women's Guild Online Permaculture Design Course facilitated by Heather Jo Flores and women from around the world.

Coming up with a permaculture design for your site allows you to see your home and site as a permaculture system that has ever-evolving and moving parts, to grasp a better understanding of the importance of identifying sectors that may influence or affect your site, to map out zones based on a sector analysis and how those zones intersect and how each home system component relates to the next.

Permaculture as a "placement science" depends on the designer to develop a systems-thinking approach for each individual site while relying on sector analysis to provide the information needed to place the zones. Natural sectors and human sectors are the outside forces coming on to your site, whether it be natural sectors such as sun, wind, rain, and water or human sectors such as pollution, pesticide drift, noise, etc.

The permaculture zones follow the principle of relative location. In zone mapping, the house is referred to as the centralized hub of human activity. The home is more efficient and functions better when everything has its place, when items are organized, and when clutter is minimal. Our homes are the places we retreat to. The home system is where we can reduce our carbon footprint while building a legacy of green handprints. It is important to start at home when designing the home system since it is our hub for activities. If our home functions well as a permaculture system, then our other permaculture endeavors will be more successful and we will have overall better organizational and design skills. We will delve into sector analysis and zone mapping in detail throughout the book.

In a permaculture design process, there are many factors to consider: global climate, topography, sectors, zones, principles, and the application of those principles in each zone. When looking at global climate, it is helpful to answer the following questions:

- Where are you on the map?
- What region are you in?
- What hardiness zone do you live in?
- What is the major landscape?
- What are the underlying characteristics of the ecosystem of your site?
- What are the major forces influencing your site?

Topography, or the reading of the land, is a helpful tool that describes the landscape and gives us insight into the shape, contour, curves, valleys, hills, and plateaus. The way the land is shaped tells us the story of how water moves through our site. How soils are created, formed, distributed, and often lost through erosion can give us the clues we need. Understanding the patterns of how water naturally flows on our site provides the foundation for design.

An important factor to consider is the actual ecosystem you are in. Was your land once a prairie, a savanna, a glade, an oak hickory forest, a temperate rainforest? Are you bordered by these defined ecosystems? These can dictate the types of species you will find growing wild on your site. In the realm of zones, they are descriptive of and defined by the amount of time spent in each of the zones, how often we visit an area, how long we stay, how we get to the various zones, and how the different zones relate to one another.

SECTOR ANALYSIS

Sectors represent directional forces that come from the outside world directly onto our site, such as a warm wind coming from the south, a cold wind coming from the north, a soft breeze that scatters seeds, the patterns of the sun, storms, frost, and fire. Other sectors could include soil composition, slope, the historical uses of the land, water flow, average rainfall, humidity, and wildlife.

Human sectors could include transit lines, roads, concrete, political regulations, nearby factories, street lights, crime, noise, pollution, pets, smells, pesticide drift, etc.

Utilizing specific sectors to our advantage is something we can consider when looking at the home system. For example, we want south-facing sunlight to warm our homes in the winter, and we want shade trees to help block the hot sun and cool our houses in the summertime.

Sectors, zones, and applied principles determine where to put what and why within each zone. The home system encompasses zone planning and refers to examining your own site with a permaculture lens, whether it be your home, garden, property, or farm. Observing your site is an important first step and an integral part of understanding its terrain, how water moves and flows on it, the patterns of sunlight and shade, the angle of the sun and its movements across the land, the wind, the rain, and the slope of the land. It's also important to pay attention to the bordering properties. Your neighbor could be clear-cutting, causing erosion and massive washouts that could affect your property line.

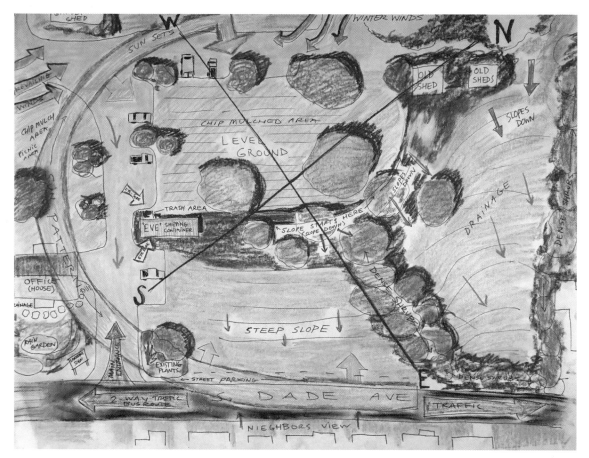

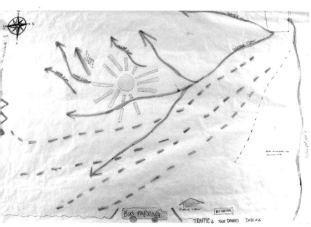

Here are two examples of sector maps. The first is a sector map that my husband, Farm Manager Eric Stevens did for EarthDance Organic Farm School.

Left is a sector map that I created for Earth-Dance Organic Farm School.

ZONES, SECTORS, AND THE HOME SYSTEM

In the realm of zones, they are descriptive of how frequently we visit an area, how long we stay, how much time we spend in each zone, the distance each zone is from the house, how we get to them, how the different zones relate to one another. For instance, the zones that require the most attention, maintenance, and daily care are the ones that are closest to your house. Convenience, efficiency, stacking functions, accessibility, organization, and proximity are all factors that come into play when creating or defining zones. We give more attention and thought to what we see more frequently with clear visibility. Zones should be identified not just in terms of location but also in terms of how often they are visited or managed: One, daily; Two, every other day; Three, once a week; Four, a few times a year; Five, almost never.

Here is an example of a zone map highlighting zones One to Five.

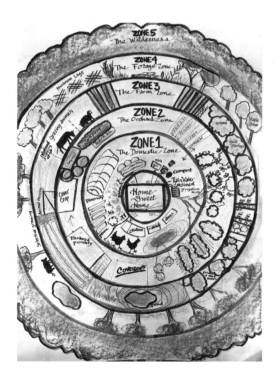

Zones are typically mapped out in concentric circles. However, the physical application of this map may not apply to everyone. For example, you may have a grove of trees that shades your home and surrounding area. This would mean that Zone One for you would contain vastly different components than someone who has full sun in Zone One.

Zone mapping is a framework or guide to navigate the art of planning an efficient design based on the layout of your land and all of the other factors discussed earlier. Not every site will have every zone.

Zones can change over time and adapt to your requirements. We then examine connections between elements and this ever-evolving web of connections and symbiotic relationships throughout the zones. It's good to first make an inventory of all the systems of your operation, a maintenance schedule, and a detailed description of the needs or requirements of each zone.

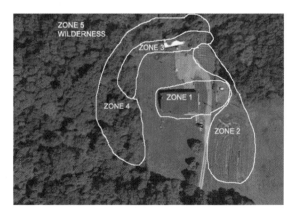

Once you have your site-specific factors and goals listed — such as slope in terms of rainfall, south-facing house, shade and sunlight analysis, energy-efficiency requirements, summer cooling, winter heating, etc. — then you can begin the process of zone mapping. Zones have to do with how we build, maintain, interact, and move through a permaculture system.

Zone One: Home Sweet Home, the Domestic Zone

Zone One includes home sweet home, the central hub of our activities: where we rest and recuperate, eat, sleep, gather, dream, and create.

Clear communication with all members of the household about where items go, how they need to be stored for easy access, and the importance of putting them back where they go are all crucial components to an efficient household. For example, tools should be clearly labeled and organized, gardening books could be kept near the seed library, and canning equipment could be stored in the kitchen.

Similar to the categorization of rooms in a home (kitchen, office, bedroom, living room, dining room), zone mapping allows us to be organized and efficient by grouping items into spaces that make sense. So often we lose time and energy looking for things we need. Placing what you use the most where you can access them easily saves valuable time that could be spent on other important endeavors.

For example, for the last several years, I have been going through the process of eliminating items that no longer serve me in my home. Each month, I dedicate a day to go through old bins of paperwork, fill a few bags of donation

items, reorganize spaces that are not functioning efficiently, etc. Through this activity, I have been able to organize my home zones by categories. Because my husband and I are multifaceted and have way too many hobbies, we have several functioning zones throughout our home.

We have an area that functions as a studio with shelves for clearly labeled art supplies. Another area designated to our gardening resources houses our seed library, gardening books, and supplies such as small tools and gloves. We also have a home apothecary, stocked with homegrown dried herbs, tinctures and oil infusions in process, herbal medicine supplies, and a related resource library. Our dining room, which also hosts workshops, has a huge farm table that serves multiple purposes: a place for family meals and a surface for arts and crafts and seed-starting.

Think of ways to maximize Zone One. Grow microgreens indoors to save time and increase nutritional intake during the cold months. Microgreens contain a plethora of phytonutrients. Grow a variety of houseplants that help filter the air and add life to your living space, plants that could be grown in a south-facing window that offer an edible yield such as kumquats and Meyer lemons. Houseplants such as aloe vera offer a medicinal yield. Other ways to maximize Zone One are sprouting, starting seedlings under grow lights, and growing kitchen herbs in a sunny window. A pantry for dry storage and canned goods and a root cellar can also maximize the home component. Zone One also includes the area directly surrounding your house that is easily accessible from it. Elements are placed in relation to this central hub based on how much attention they require.

Everything in Zone One typically requires daily care: visits, constant care and maintenance, and fruit and vegetable harvesting in peak season. Components may include greenhouses, cold frames, low tunnels, firewood storage, pet housing, workshop or woodshop, outbuildings used frequently, herb garden, salad garden, kitchen garden, perennial fruits, poultry and other small animals, compost/vermicompost bins, and irrigation hub. This area thrives on diversity, provided by fruits, vegetables, herbs, flowers, and nitrogen fixers.

Zone Two: The Home Orchard Zone

Characteristics of this zone include relatively close proximity to the house and regular maintenance, maybe every other day, not daily. Diverse species of fruit and nut trees, berries, vegetables, dwarf fruit trees, and flowers are also often included. Chickens and rabbits and other small animals that need regular care could also be housed in this zone as long as daily food and water systems are in place. Larger composting systems and windrows would be a great addition. This zone could have rotational grazing, small pastures, cover crops, permanent raised beds, permaculture guilds, nitrogen fixers, pollinator attractors, grazing between rows, interplanting of vegetables, and ponds.

Zone Three: The Farm Zone

Characteristics of this zone include less frequent visits, ongoing care, and maintenance, but less often. Typically, you would only need to visit Zone Three once per week, but if it includes a market garden, you would require more frequent visits during times of seeding, watering, weeding, and harvesting. A harvest and maintenance schedule can be set up for 3 days per week in this zone, or whatever amount of time meets its requirements.

Cultivation of these areas may be more extensive using mechanical cultivation but may be more manageable if using permanent raised bed systems.

Plant cover crops between rows and keep them mowed. Permanent raised beds with mulched pathways could limit the hours you spend weeding and watering.

Potential cash crops in this zone include grains, berries, vegetables, specialty crops, and medicinal herbs. It could also house a market garden, pastures, fruit crops, permaculture guild plantings and mixed orchards, beehives, large stands of pollinator-attracting plants and native flowers, large ponds, hedgerows, field crops, and large berry stands such as blackberries, blueberries, raspberries, juneberries, goji berries, gooseberries, and currants. This is a great zone for polycultures.

Zone Four: The Forage Zone

Characteristics of the forage zone include mostly wild, low-maintenance, partially managed, and minimal care. Zone Four still provides a functioning ecosystem and natural area such as a woodland, as an ecosystem and offers food and habitat for wildlife. It is a great zone to integrate a food forest and agroecological systems.

Zone Four is where you can practice ethical foraging, hunting, gathering, grazing. Forage for wild mushrooms and wildcraft medicinal herbs for your home apothecary, gather wild food from the forest floor, and do trials of interplanting shade-loving natives with local endangered plants such as ginseng and goldenseal. This area could contain a maple grove and a sugar shack, mixed trees and shrubs. Some of the trees could be selectively harvested and used to heat your home. Zone Four also has the potential to practice selective grazing to reduce fuel in the wild understory that could otherwise present a potential fire hazard.

Zone Five: The Wilderness Zone

The wilderness zone is a natural undisturbed ecosystem where we would practice little to no management. It is mainly an area set aside for observation, where we can gather information from studying nature's intrinsic intelligence: how plants relate to one another and how symbiotic relationships occur throughout the seasons. We can then distill this information and utilize the sacred wisdom to inspire how we create our own cultivated ecology within our site.

We are learning from the natural patterns and processes of nature. We are observing its resilience, rhythms, and life cycles: when plants, bud out, bloom, attract pollinators, bear fruit, and then go to seed. Utilizing this knowledge, we can try to recreate it within the various zones.

If you live in an urban environment, your zones will be very different from those listed above. You may only have a total of two zones

listed in your system. For example, if you have a small backyard that adjoins neighboring yards with only a fence line, you do not have a farm zone, a forage zone, or a wilderness zone. You may only have the domestic zone and the orchard zone.

Zone mapping is still useful. This mapping worksheet could be helpful to plan out the zones at your site.

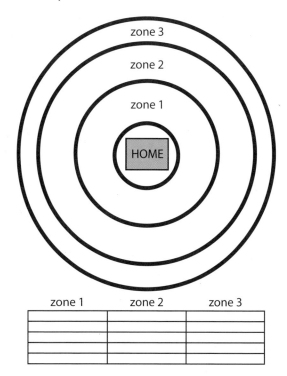

HOME SYSTEM AS A MODEL

When you begin to look at your own site with a permaculture lens, you begin to see your home as a system, to see how the zones intersect. Designing your home system simplifies your life and makes it more abundant and sustainable.

Systems thinking is a key component in permaculture.

One way to truly grasp this concept is by examining your existing home system as a model. How it is it functioning in real time at this present moment? Do you have a nice flow, or are obstacles constantly surfacing throughout the day in your system? How do you want to change it? Is it a simple change or a multifaceted series of complex changes that need to be done in phases?

When looking at the home system, it is important to think about the permaculture ethics and principles that are applied to each room, each zone in your home system.

How much of your comfort level are you willing to shift or sacrifice in the interest of ecological design, Earth stewardship, and Earth care. How do your daily choices affect those around you? How are your daily activities affecting the ecosystem you reside in? How can you make small and slow changes to be a part of the solution? Are there giant leaps you are willing to take?

Let's examine some other ways in which we can assess our system. Brainstorming and calculating ways to reduce water usage, energy consumption, transportation, and overall consumerism is an important process in integrating permaculture ethics into the home system.

Let's look at water usage. Are you using city water, well water, or rain water? How many gallons do you use per month. Can this change? Can you use less water? Find out how much clean water you could be collecting from your roof.

A friend places a few 5-gallon buckets in the shower while waiting for the water to warm up pre-shower. She then uses this water for her houseplants and garden. It is such a simple solution, yet it can save up to five gallons of water every time you shower.

Resources

https://green.harvard.edu/tools-resources/poster/top-5-steps-reduce-your-energy-consumption This poster illustrates five things you can do today to reduce your energy consumption.

"Accelerating the Global Transition To 100% Renewable Energy." https://cleantechnica.com/2017/09/28/accelerating-global-transition-100-renewable-energy/

West African Women and Water Training. This video provides a greater appreciation for water.

How to Switch to Solar Power in Your Home and Why Now Is the Time. This short video shows how to transition to solar energy. https://www.theguardian.com/us-news/video/2017/mar/01/solar-power-clean-energy-climate-change-video

Visit esf.edu/ere/endreny/GICalculator/Run offHome.html to calculate your total stormwater runoff.

Are all the components of your home and land functioning together seamlessly in a whole systems approach? If not, then it could be argued that they are a collection of separate permaculture-esque elements placed randomly.

For example, we have an indoor worm bin and an indoor compost bin in our kitchen, which limits the amount of daily time we spend taking compost out to the pile. We have a large outdoor compost system and several wire cylinders that we fill with compost and food scraps, leaf litter, and grass clippings. After decomposition occurs in the cylinders, we will simply lift them up and we have a raised bed ready to go.

We are a drop-off site for friends and neighbors. The worm bin stays inside until the castings are harvested and used to fertilize our seedlings and transplants while the worms enjoy our food scraps. When the worm population gets too large

for our home worm bin, we bring part of the worm population to the outdoor worm bin.

Soil health is crucial. We have the duty and responsibility as permaculturalists, gardeners, farmers, and Earth stewards to treat the soil with reverence, to build healthy soils on our sites, and to educate about the importance of soil on this planet. It takes roughly 500 years for 2.5 cm of topsoil to form.

I highly recommend watching the video of Vandana Shiva: *Vandana Shiva: Save Our Soils, Save Our Seeds, So That We Can Save Humanity.*[5]

Another important example of integrating permaculture principles and ethics through hands-on action is integrating guild plantings into your home system. Here is a wonderful example of a fruit tree guild planting from the Resiliency Institute.

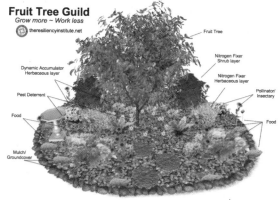

In a basic guild planting, a fruit tree is placed in the center and will provide long-term yields. Plants that are placed around it serve purposes for the soil, the tree, each other, wildlife, and humans. Nitrogen-fixing plants help fix atmospheric nitrogen, making it readily accessible for plant roots; dynamic accumulators, such as comfrey, draw nutrients from different levels of the soil into its roots and transfers the nutrients up through the leaves, which can then be "chopped and dropped" around the tree as a fertilizer.

Mediterranean and other aromatic herbs such as sage and lavender are grown to attract beneficial insects but deter pests, as do alliums such as Egyptian walking onions and garlic chives. Perennial native flowering plants are placed to attract native and beneficial pollinators. Perennial fruits are placed in the understory of trees, far enough from the tree to meet their light requirements. Finally, the area can be composted and heavily mulched to add nutrients and suppress weeds. These individual systems are working together for the greater good. The end product is a thriving micro-ecosystem that provides long-term benefits to humans, small wildlife, and pollinators. We will dig deeper into guild plantings in Chapter 6.

BED PREP

In this section, I will discuss a myriad of tried and true methods (that have worked for us) of soil building and sheet mulching, as well as innovative methods of weed suppression to maximize crop yields and vitality, therefore increasing profits if you plan to sell your bounty.

Weed pressure can be daunting. Successful weed management in organic agriculture is a challenge which requires patience, preventive measures, dedication, and a commitment to following through with the systems put into place. Weed seeds germinate quickly, causing an influx of growth during spring and summer. Preventative weed management strategies are crucial to maintain crop integrity, to help decrease pests and diseases, and to decrease the potential for pathogens.

Luckily, several techniques can prevent the potential for weeds to overtake crops. For beginning gardeners, the approach I recommend is to build raised beds and then add new

Resources

"Plant a Fruit Tree Guild." An article on guild planting from the Resiliency Institute, http://www.theresiliencyinstitute.net/grow/plant-fruit-tree-guild/

"How We Made a Garden of Edible Delights: Monoculture to Permaculture." An article about how founder of *Permaculture* magazine, Maddy Harland, transformed her site from grass to garden! https://www.theguardian.com/lifeandstyle/2014/jul/09/how-we-made-a-garden-of-edible-delights-monoculture-to-permaculture soil. A mixture of half topsoil and half compost that is free of weed seeds will save hours of weeding. We go through a local company, St. Louis Composting, that sells bulk certified weed seed-free blends at a reasonable rate. We can get a truck bed full of these blends for around $30. They also offer the option of delivering large quantities. Check with your local Extension office to see what your options are for this type of soil/compost blend. We often add mushroom compost, vermicompost, and other soil amendments. If you plan to build raised beds, I would recommend using a broadfork to break up the soil and then add an initial layer of cardboard, burlap, and chip mulch to help suppress the weeds.

From Grass to Garden

If you want to transform your lawn into an edible oasis, there are variety of ways to go from lawn to bounty. If you are starting from scratch on an area that has long been lawn, or in our case prairie, the initial thought is to mow and till. While this would be effective, it may not be the most environmentally sound way to go about it. Tilling the soil kills beneficial bacteria and microbes, worms, fungi, and other soil life. It may be necessary to till once and then form no-till permanent raised beds. It really depends on the size of your garden plot and the type of soil that you have.

If you are installing a small front-yard garden, a digging fork or broadfork would work just fine to break up the soil enough for the roots of the garden plants to grow.

If you are ambitious and serious about no-till, you could use a broadfork to loosen the soil

and scatter a multispecies cover crop to help create a network of biopores to aerate and provide water to the soil. The cover crops should grow at least a few months. A scythe can be used to chop down the growth, which would then rest on the soil for a few weeks. This adds biomass and creates an environment for microbes and soil life, resulting in a rich tilth over time. Transplants can be directly planted into the cover crop patch. If you choose this method, select an annual cover crop. This works best in the fall so that the cover crop can winter kill. It is best to select the correct seasonal cover crop. Cover crops will be discussed in more detail later in this chapter.

Vinegar Method

Using commercial-grade vinegar or horticultural vinegar (20% acetic acid) on an area of grass you wish to have a future garden has proven to be effective. The grass will die and will most likely not return, depending on what type it is. Caution should be used when handling acetic acid. Be sure to wear goggles, gloves, and a mask. The area sprayed should be left to rest for at least 3 weeks before turning over the soil. There is some potential for the acetic acid to lower the pH of your soil. Compost and organic matter should be added to the patch before planting.

Sod Cutters

If your lawn is mostly zoysia grass, you may consider renting a sod cutter for garden prep. This machine, with its oscillating knife that cuts grass below the roots, slices long blanket-like strips of the grass, which can then be rolled up and moved. These can be repurposed or composted. Sod cutters can be rented from your local hardware store for around $50–$80 for 4 hours.

No-till Method

The no-till method creates living healthy soil in which microbes, beneficial bacteria, and fungi are provided an environment to carry out their intrinsic functions, allowing them to complete the process of nutrient absorption and decomposition, and in turn build healthy soils.

Adding clean, weed-free soil to garden beds can maximize long-term health of soil, reducing the reliance on tillage. Maintaining the permanent raised beds is important. They should be weeded regularly during the first few months.

Berm and Swale System

The concept behind a berm and swale system is essentially digging out trenches to collect, absorb, and hold water while simultaneously building permanent raised beds (berms) with the excavated soil. The swales increase moisture retention while decreasing the need for irrigation. The elevated beds allow plants to have a better chance at survival.

The berms can be covered with landscape fabric, heavy mulch, or burlap sacks and planted with guild plantings. Fruit trees and shrubs are integrated with Mediterranean aromatic herbs; allium family species such as Egyptian walking onions, garlic chives, and Welsh onions; dynamic accumulators such as comfrey; and nitrogen-fixing plants including leadplant, New Jersey tea, and false indigo.

Occultation

Occultation is a weed suppression method that is done by smothering the weeds using a thick black silage tarp. This can be done throughout the growing season and is most successful when left for 3 to 4 weeks.

Solarization

Solarization involves covering the soil with clear plastic for 6 to 8 weeks in order to kill soil pests. According to Beth Hanson, in an article published in Rodale's *Organic Life* magazine:

> Solarization involves concentrating the sun's energy in the top 12 to 18 inches.

The heat trapped below the plastic can reach highs of 140°F in the top 6 inches, killing weed seeds, insects, nematodes, and many fungal and bacterial pathogens, including those that cause verticillium wilt, fusarium wilt, potato scab, damping off, crown gall disease, and phytophthora root rot. The beneficial effects from solarization are greatest near the soil surface and decrease with depth.[6]

Bed Prep 101

The following methods have worked well for us for the last several years. These suggestions can be scaled up or down as you see fit.

It is best to not till or disturb the soil once the beds are prepped, as this may bring up weed seeds from lower levels in the soil.

1. Form beds using a shaper implement or by hand with a rake, shovel, broadfork, or pitchfork. Most beds are formed in the 30-inch bed system that market gardeners use for a number of reasons. The space is utilized better when crops are closer and more condensed, which also means fewer weeds; it allows for the farmer to step over the bed with a wide stance; it limits erosion; and for season extension, fewer materials are used.

2. Water the beds or allow them to get rained on.

3. Occultation tarps can be placed on immediately or within 24 hours once beds have been watered. The wet soil and warmth of the tarps create an optimal environment for weed seeds to germinate. They continue to grow under the tarp and are starved of light. They exhaust themselves to the point of termination, creating a weed-free bed once tarps are taken off 2 to 3 weeks later.

4. Once tarps are removed, landscape fabric can be placed on beds prior to planting.

Sheet Mulching

Sheet mulching involves adding many layers to the soil. It typically starts with a layer of cardboard and newspaper to suppress weeds,

followed by layers of leaf litter, straw, grass clippings, and compost. The primary functions of sheet mulching involve suppressing weeds, preventing weed growth, and building soil. It also increases soil moisture retention, adds nutrients to the soil, and increases soil organic matter and diversity. Sheet mulching is typically done in the fall so that the beds can be planted in the spring.

Gathering Resources

Become a drop-off site for compost, leaves, grass clippings, and wood chips. This allows an abundance of materials to be in close proximity. Often, tree trimmers will drop off chip mulch at your site. Coffee roasters will give away stacks of burlap sacks. Check local you-pick farms and garden centers for leftover straw bales after fall events.

FREE TO LOW-BUDGET GARDENING

The following materials and supplies are very useful to the backyard gardener. Some of these can be found in your household, while others can be sourced free or at low cost in your own community.

- Free compost: Most city parks have a free composting system. Usually, you need to haul it yourself in a pickup truck.
- Burlap sacks: Most coffee roasters will give burlap sacks for free, especially to community gardens.
- Wood chips: Tree-trimming companies will often deliver wood chips to community gardens for free. If you see a tree trimmer in your

neighborhood, ask them to deliver to your yard. Put down a few tarps to prevent a large mess and for easy hauling once the pile gets low.

- Crates: Some bakeries and restaurants will give away old crates.
- Pallets: Some large businesses such as grocery stores, nurseries, and hardware stores will give away pallets to community gardens or backyard gardeners. It is best to get pallets that are labeled HT (heat treated).
- Straw bales: Straw bales make excellent additions to the backyard garden. Several bales can be formed into a rectangle and used as garden beds, compost piles, worm habitats, etc.

For seed starting, these items can be diverted from the landfill and reused:

- Toilet paper rolls
- Paper towel rolls cut into sections
- Newspapers, folded into cubes
- Cardboard boxes
- Coffee bags
- Recycled soda or water bottles with the tops cut off

GARDENING TIPS: WATER CONSERVATION

Rainwater catchment is a simple and effective way to conserve water that is essentially free. In St. Louis, about 45 minutes from where we live, the Metropolitan Sewer District offers grants for stormwater mitigation, rain gardens, and rainwater catchment systems such as barrels and cisterns. Check your local municipality to find out if they offer rebate programs for stormwater mitigation.

Rainwater can be harvested from rooftops or other impermeable surfaces. Catchment systems can be as simple as a rain barrel connected to the end of a downspout, an easy way to catch and store water that can then be used to irrigate gardens with soaker hoses.

To help catch and store water that can help during a drought, dig small narrow trenches or swales around raised garden berms to retain water. As you are planting, add water into a trench first if you are planting into a row, or add to each hole before you transplant. This gives the plants enough water for a few days or even a week.

When watering a small garden, water the base of each plant instead of the whole bed. This helps to conserve water.

Cover Crops

Cover crops are a cost-effective way to add soil amendments and living mulch. They offer a protective layer and help to loosen soil without tillage, thus allowing aeration and water absorption. Cover crops help to prevent soil erosion and increase soil health and diversity, water retention, soil organic matter, and nutrient uptake.

Some common cover crops include red and white clover, oats, mustards, tillage radishes, sorghum-sudangrass, wheat, winter rye, buckwheat, cowpeas, barley, hairy vetch, and Austrian winter peas. These are typically used on small-scale no-till farms, as well as in large-scale no-till agriculture. They are highly effective in the garden setting, especially in restoring soil health in urban settings and in overly farmed rural areas.

▲ *Hairy vetch and peas.*

▲ *Daikon radish.*

According to the NRCS (Natural Resources Conservation Service), the following seasonal cover crops are recommended for restoring soils.[7]

Cool-season Grains (Winter Rye, Wheat, Triticale, Spelt, Barley, and Oats)

Winter rye is a hardy cool-season cover crop that suppresses weeds and provides a great deal of biomass. Rye should be grown with a legume such as red clover or hairy vetch. Wheat, triticale, and spelt are great hardy cover crops that can also help to suppress weeds and add biomass. These varieties can be sown in the early spring and are often mixed with clover, vetch, and peas. Barley has deep roots and can be grown easily and helps to control erosion and suppress weeds.

Warm-season Annual Grains (Buckwheat and Sorghum-sudangrass)

Buckwheat is a quick-growing summer crop and is typically used to smother weeds.

▲ *Oats.*

Sorghum-sudangrass produces a great deal of biomass and helps to increase soil organic matter. It grows quickly and gets tall. It can be mowed a few times. It can be interplanted with buckwheat or cowpeas.

Legumes (Clover Varieties, Hairy Vetch, Soybeans, Cowpeas, and Alfalfa)

White and red clover are cool-season, low-growing perennial cover crops that are deep-rooted and produce moderate levels of nitrogen. They also provide nectar for bees in early spring. Clover can handle foot traffic.

Hairy vetch is a hardy, cool-season, nitrogen-producing cover crop that helps to increase nutrient availability. It attracts beneficial insects by offering habitat and food. It can help suppress early spring weeds. Soybeans and cowpeas are summer legumes that help to suppress weeds and produce nitrogen. They can be interplanted with sorghum-sudangrass. Alfalfa is a cool-season perennial legume that helps to reduce compaction, fixes nitrogen, and also is wonderful for attracting beneficial insects. It can be grown with small grains.

Brassicas (Forage Radish, Forage Turnips, and Mustards)

Brassicas are helpful when planted after spring veggie crops, except for brassica vegetable crops. They can be planted in early fall as well as a winter-kill cover crop. Forage radish and forage turnips provide deep roots which help to reduce soil compaction and suppress weeds. Mustards grow quickly and provide a great deal of biomass and can help prevent erosion. These all should not go to seed.

Grasses

Grasses include cool-season annual and perennial ryegrasses. They can provide a great deal of biomass and help to prevent erosion.

GARDENING FOR BEGINNERS: PLANTING YOUR FIRST GARDEN

Growing food is a simple and rewarding experience. It can be intimidating for the beginning gardener, but with a little effort, a continuous bounty soon outweighs the challenges and steps necessary to achieve a well-maintained garden.

I recommend you start planting the things that you love to eat or that you find beautiful. Chances are your passion for gardening will grow with each changing season. You can start a balcony container garden or a small backyard garden for less than $20. Embrace organic!

Gardening Step One: Determining Your Zone and Soil Type

The first steps are to determine which planting zone you reside in and the type of soil you have in the location you wish to grow a garden. The plant hardiness zone map helps to determine which plants will thrive in your area. What may be blooming in spring in your backyard at a specific time may still be dormant in other parts of the country or vice versa. If you reside in the United States, visit www.planthardiness.ars.usda.gov to determine your zone, or do a web search of your specific region, or contact your local university Extension offices. Zones are determined by day length, soil temperatures, climate, air temperatures, and first and last frost dates.

For example, tomatoes thrive in hot temperatures while greens thrive in cooler temperatures. However, there are plenty of loopholes in gardening. For instance, you can find the time on the calendar year that mimics the place of origin of a specific plant. There specific times are indicated by soil temperature when certain plants thrive and will vary from zone to zone. For instance, Mediterranean herbs thrive in Midwest summers. Plants that wouldn't typically grow in a cooler climate, such as ginger, can grow inside of a temperature-regulated high tunnel or greenhouse.

It will also be beneficial to determine locations for your edible landscape and garden areas and to make notes about their microclimates, for example, where it is sunny, shady, and windy. Note also whether a plant will be grown on a slope. Making and keeping diagrams and drawings of your garden areas is very helpful!

Some plants grow well by directly sowing them into the ground, such as root vegetables and greens. Others do best when seeds are planted in a small container or a multi-cell seed tray indoors under grow lights or in a greenhouse so that roots are well-established before being transplanted outdoors. For example, carrot seeds thrive when planted directly into the ground, whereas tomatoes do best when transplanted.

To determine your soil type, you can go the precision route and get a soil test through your local Extension office that helps to determine its biochemistry. The amount of different minerals and nutrients indicates which plants will thrive in that specific soil structure. The analysis also allows you to compare the ideal nutrient levels to those present in your specific soil. Typically, the test will come with suggestions about how

to best improve soil composition. For urban and suburban soils, test them for heavy metals and lead contamination. If your soil is contaminated, it may be best to find another plot of land. If it is mildly contaminated, I would suggest bioremediation through a combination of mycoremediation and biochar. I would also suggest not planting in the contaminated soil but rather building tall raised beds with new soil. Fruit trees can be planted in mildly contaminated soil if bioremediation is simultaneously occurring. The fruit will take several years to produce, and it is my understanding that the fruiting bodies do not contain the contaminants.

For a less complicated route, use a pitchfork or a shovel to turn over the soil in a section where you want your garden. Is your soil hard clay or mud? Is it loose and loamy? Is it sandy or rocky? Look around your yard and make notes of which plants are already thriving. Clay soil and sandy soil benefit from the addition of compost. Good growing soil has a nice variety of organic materials and aggregates, it is loose and loamy, and the humus (organic material formed from decomposition of plant and animal matter) is dark in color.

Gardening Step Two: Choosing Seeds Based on Your Zone and Soil Types

Seed selection is an important part of planning your garden, yet many beginning gardeners feel intimidated by this process. It is more than just thumbing through seed catalogs and choosing the most eye-catching varieties. The factors to consider include heat resistance, drought tolerance, disease and pest resistance, and the climate in which the specific variety thrives. Check with your local farmers, gardeners, or the local Extension office for help choosing varieties that do well in your region. Follow these simple steps to ensure a stress-free seed selection process!

1. Make a list of your favorite fruits and vegetables. It is important to grow what you love to eat, so that the harvest will not go to waste. You can also plan to donate and share your harvest with friends, family members, neighbors, and community food banks.

2. Determine whether or not your favorites will grow in your specific growing zone. From here, cull a modified list of seeds that you will want to obtain for your garden.

3. Determine the specific growing requirements for your chosen plants, including light requirements, spacing, and water needs. Make sure to record this information in an easily accessible location, such as a gardening journal or a paper taped to your refrigerator. Not only will writing it down help you remember and learn about these plants, it will also be a useful resource for all future gardening adventures.

4. Every plant has many different varieties. Choose seed varieties that are specific to your needs. It is best to choose varieties that are acclimated to your zone but also drought resistant, pest and disease resistant, etc. If you are in a wet climate, you would not choose a drought-resistant variety but rather a variety that tolerates wet climates

and the pests or diseases associated with wet climates.

5. Once you narrow down your varieties, order the seeds through a reputable company that signs a non-GMO pledge, such as Seeds of Change, Johnny's Selected Seeds, Baker Creek Heirloom Seeds, the Rare Vegetable Seed Consortium, Southern Exposure Seeds, Botanical Interest Seeds, Seed Savers Exchange, Strictly Medicinal Seeds, or Morgan County Seeds. You may also consult staff at local nurseries; they are often eager and excited to help.

6. Select new varieties as well as heirloom seeds. Try something new each time you buy seeds. You will be amazed at the incredible and beautiful variety within a single species of plant! We love to grow beautiful and unique specialty produce and don't believe anyone should feel limited by conventional varieties of plants.

BEGINNER'S SEASONAL GUIDE TO ORGANIC VEGETABLE GARDENING

(This guide, with its Midwestern perspective, may not be suited for your region. Check your local Extension office for a regional planting guide.)

Winter

The winter is a great time to start planning your garden and ordering seeds. Seedsofchange.com has an excellent variety of organic seeds. Rareseeds.com (Baker Creek Heirloom Seeds) is a great resource for heirloom seeds.

Organize your seeds according to planting dates. For small-scale gardening, accordion organizers work well.

Start the following seeds indoors under grow lights or in a greenhouse mid-February through mid-April: broccoli, bok choy, kohlrabi, cabbage, onions, scallions, eggplant, early tomatoes, and peppers.

Sketch the layout of your garden or edible landscape showing where you want each crop to go. Keep in mind companion planting, light and water requirements, height, spacing, and aesthetics. Many vegetable gardening books are available at your local library that offer plans ranging from raised beds to acre plantings. See also edible landscape garden designs in Chapter 7.

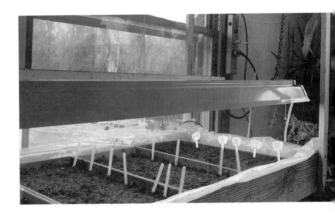

and compost. Next, add half compost and half topsoil. Finally, your top layer should be well-decomposed compost mixed with topsoil. You want your top layer to have a fine tilth so that it is easy to sow seeds.

Early Spring

Prepare your space as soon as the ground is thawed and slightly dry, typically early March in the Midwest. Use a broadfork or a potato fork to turn over and gently break up the top layer of soil. A hard rake or hoe can also be used to break the soil up into smaller pieces. Your goal should be a fine tilth. Be sure to add plenty of compost, bags of leaves, grass clippings, and cow manure, horse manure, or green manure before you prep. These soil additions will feed your plants throughout the year.

You can easily create raised beds with straw bales, untreated scrap wood, or heat-treated pallets. In a raised bed, additions of any of the following layers help create good living soil and provide organic pathways for roots: leaves, followed by straw, grass clippings, more leaves,

Spring

After the last frost, when the ground can be worked, plant seeds directly into the ground for spinach, carrots, peas, chard, kale, salad mix, lettuce, radishes, beets, and turnips.

You may purchase established vegetable plants (that you were not able to plant from seed in late winter or early spring) and transplant them into your garden. Nurseries carry a variety of plants for vegetable gardening.

Plant comfrey as a chop-and-drop plant near your beds as it is a natural fertilizer. Cut leaves added to garden beds as mulch will add extra nutrition.

Weed regularly. For young seedlings, be sure to keep the soil weed-free with hand tools. It's a good idea to lightly weed your garden by hand on a regular basis to save time in the long run and improve the quality of your garden and edible landscape.

For transplants, the use of barriers such as weed cloths, sheet mulching, straw, and compost are important for suppressing weeds and retaining moisture.

Use soaker hoses on your beds. Keep your seed beds well-watered until they sprout. Water on a regular basis once plants are established, though their needs vary from plant to plant.

Late Spring

Tomatoes, winter squash, summer squash, cucumbers, melons, peppers, beans, okra, raspberries, blackberries, and herbs such as basil and dill can be planted to enjoy in the summer. You may plant them from seed in your prepared garden beds or from transplants. Plant potatoes from seed and sweet potato slips.

Summer

In the summer, plant the same crops you planted in early spring. You can repeat the process with warm-season crops and then again for fall crops. Be sure to follow a planting guide for your zone or region. Save seeds from your favorite varieties.

Fall

Plant carrots and greens to overwinter and enjoy the next spring, saving seeds from your favorite varieties. Harvest everything from your garden before the first frost. Clear out your garden beds and cover them with cardboard, tarps, or landscape fabric.

Late Fall

Late fall is a good time to cut back dying plants, remove unwanted debris, and put garden areas to rest for the winter. This only applies to regions that experience winter freezing.

START A BASIC GARDEN FOR $50 (10' × 3' EDIBLE LANDSCAPE BED)

The wonderful thing about gardening is that it can be done simply by collectively gathering resources and sharing the end harvest.

This guide factors in the kindness of neighbors, the generosity of friends and relatives, and the resourcefulness of the gardener's mindset. With $50 and some creativity, you can create a basic garden in your front or backyard using the minimum amount of new tools and resources. You are not only saving money but also promoting the use of recycled materials. Starting a garden bed can be done during any season. Beds for spring planting are typically prepared in the previous fall or winter. Throughout the world, gung-ho gardeners always find a way to grow food, despite the season. Check with your friends and neighbors. See what seeds they are sowing when you get started. The barter system is tremendously helpful for gardening. Sharing resources is one of the best ways to approach life in general, I've found!

First, gather your resources. In our estimation, these are the only things you'll need to buy.

Seeds and plants: $30. Seed packets average about $3 per packet, or you can save your own. Neighbors and friends can buy bulk seed orders together to save money. Plants average $3 each. Smaller nurseries tend to have better prices.

Garden forks: $5. You can find a used garden fork in decent condition from friends, flea markets, Craigslist, or Freecycle networks. A garden fork is heavy duty and has four long tines typically forged from a solid piece of carbon steel, making it great for turning over compacted soil. If you can't find one to buy in your budget, borrow one.

Compost: $6 per bag or free from a friend or farmer. Most cities have a free compost program.

Straw bales: $3. Check Craigslist under "farm and garden" or ask a local farmer. Straw bales can often be purchased at farm or seed stores.

Garden hoses: Most folks already own a garden hose. Neighbors might have an extra you can borrow, in exchange for a few homegrown vegetables.

Tools: If you have a higher budget, consider investing in a broadfork, a tool that loosens and aerates the soil without disturbing the living network of microorganisms, bacteria, and fungi. The tilther, a pricy drill-powered mini-tiller, helps tremendously in that it allows just the top inch of soil to be loosened in order to prepare a fine seedbed for direct seeding of crops.

Now, stock up on the following free and repurposed useful supplies.

Chip mulch: Shredded limbs and trunks of trees are good for pathways, mulching around trees and perennial natives, shrubs, and flower and herb beds. It helps to protect roots, maintain moisture levels, and is also a good smothering base for a future garden bed. If you dump and spread chip mulch in your future garden bed and let it rest for one year, it not only smothers the weeds but also breaks down into more of a loam humus layer, making it an excellent foundation for permaculture garden beds or edible landscapes.

Free chip mulch can be dropped off to your location by contacting your local tree-trimming company or by visiting getchipdrop.com.

Perennial (native) plants and divisions to attract pollinators: Free from friends or neighbors.

Vessels for starting seeds (save these throughout the winter to start seeds in the spring):

- Coffee bags
- Cardboard toilet paper rolls
- Water bottles
- Recycled plastic quart containers
- Reused milk cartons
- Egg cartons

Plant labels made from recycled materials (use permanent marker, crayons, or waxed pencils):

- Old venetian blinds, cut individually to the desired size.
- Recycled yogurt containers cut into strips
- Reused popsicle sticks

Soil: Some city parks may offer the following free soil options:

- Fill dirt: Good for a base layer or filler, but the nutrient level is unpredictable.

• Topsoil: Generally the top 2 inches of soil, this is more nutrient-rich and is good for bringing your garden soil nutrients up to a more balanced and preferred level to benefit the plants.

• Compost: A combination of various detritus materials with a soil base which includes mostly yard waste such as leaves, grass clippings, small branches, and twigs.

• Sand: Very useful especially when mixed with compost for growing herbs. Sand is also a good additive for fast drainage. It also works well mixed with compost for starting seeds to promote better drainage, as a top dressing, or as mulch for heating up the soil around the base of herb plants.

Free mulch for garden beds:

• Black-and-white newspaper (no color or glossy ink)

• Leaves or leaf litter from your yard or neighbors

• Grass clippings

• Weeds before they go to seed (as you weed your garden, lay the pulled weeds down flat around each plant to act both as green manure and a weed suppressor)

• Burlap coffee bags

Chapter 5

_____

Your Edible Yard — Natural Alternatives to Herbicides and Pesticides

NATURAL WEED MANAGEMENT

I N MY EXPERIENCE, the best course of action for natural weed management is to take preventative measures to suppress weeds. As mentioned in the previous chapter, starting with fresh soil free of weed seeds reduces labor-intensive weeding in the long run. Sheet mulching, occultation, and solarization are very effective methods of weed suppression. When facing large weeds initially, it is best to mow those first. It is crucial to not let weeds go to seed.

Transplants are often more successful in an organic farm setting. First, they are off to a great start as their roots are established before they go in the ground. They achieve canopy quickly meaning that they will cover the soil, shading out the weed seeds.

Intensive planting and maximizing the square footage of the garden with a variety of plants will help to create an herbaceous layer over the soil which will help to starve the weeds of light.

Some weeds, such as violets, may provide a lovely ground cover in your vegetable garden. Violets are a wild food and could offer delicious and nutritious greens and flowers that can be added to salads when other greens are not in season. Other weeds, such as spiny pigweed, will out-compete cultivated crops. Pigweed stems are

covered with thorns and are very hard to remove once they become large established plants. Wild hops vine is a weed that will take over very quickly and is hard to remove. It is important to note that weeds are maintaining soil structure, in most cases helping to prevent erosion, and creating biomass for the soil. Most weeds are attracting pollinators during their flowering stages. A number of highly nutritious edible weeds can be utilized for food and medicine. Dandelion, purslane, lamb's-quarters, plantain, yellow wood sorrel, red clover, yarrow, and wild onion are some of the most common edible or medicinal weeds that grow in our garden. I will discuss these amazing weeds as well as my favorite ways of preparing them later in this chapter.

Sheet Mulching

Sheet mulching, also referred to as lasagna gardening, is essentially layering compost, leaf mulch, grass clippings, newspaper, more compost, and straw or mulch around each plants to help suppress weeds, add nutrients, and retain moisture. Sheet mulching can be done around your established transplants as well.

Landscape Fabric

Landscape fabric is a tried-and-true method of weed suppression. Though it can be expensive, it is heavy-duty, durable, and offers a long-term strategy specifically for perennial plantings,

such as permaculture berm and guild plantings. Landscape fabric is woven from a permeable material that allows rainwater and irrigation water to seep into the soil while retaining heat and suppressing weeds.

Plastic Covers

Biodegradable Plastic is highly effective at suppressing weeds. The downsides to biodegradable plastic are that it is very expensive, and specialized equipment may be needed to lay it in the rows effectively. Additionally, it is not environmentally friendly in the sense that it may take several years to decompose or the plastic may go

to the landfill at the end of the growing season. The process by which it is produced may not be completely environmentally friendly.

Compost

The application of heavy compost is a great way to utilize stacking functions, including feeding the plants, adding nutrients to the soil, retaining moisture, and suppressing weeds. Adding several inches of weed-free compost on your existing bed not only is wonderful for the soil but can smother the buried weed seeds.

Heavy Mulching

Heavy mulching involves using 4 to 12 inches of straw, leaves, wood chips, or other organic material on hand. Ideal for perennials planted in permanent beds, it is used to suppress weeds, minimize soil compaction, provide a protective layer, and increase mycorrhizal activity. It breaks down after a season, creating a humus layer and becomes a foundation for a future garden bed. Heavy mulching with straw is applied to crops such as strawberries and garlic to prevent weeds. Check out the book *One Straw Revolution* by Masanobu Fukuoka.

Mulched pathways can be created using cardboard, burlap, or wood chips. Living pathways can be created by planting resilient cover crops such as hairy vetch, red clover, white clover, or miner's lettuce.

Weeding Tools

Weeding requires regular observation and attention. The optimal time to weed is when a seedling is less than an inch tall, even better is when they first sprout. A tine weeder rake and a wire weeder are best used when weeds are at their white thread stage: the root looks like a white thread when pulled up.

A **hula hoe** is a long-handled hoe that is shaped like a stirrup with sharpened edges on the front and back side, allowing you to use it in a shuffle-like motion while only weeding the surface of the soil. This hoe is used on beds or in fields with exposed soil or areas with small aggregates.

A **wheel hoe** has the same weeding effect as the hula hoe, but instead of it being fastened to a long handle, it is more like a high wheel cultivator, where there is one wheel in front of the hoe, and has two handles that guide it down the row. A wheel hoe can be used on beds between rows of direct seeded, transplanted, and established crops and to keep pathways weeded.

The **tine weeder** rake looks like a landscaper's rake, but the tines are thin heavy-duty wires spaced close together. This rake scratches the surface of the soil to prepare seedbeds or can be gently guided over well-rooted crops, combing over the soil, killing tiny weed seedlings.

The **wire weeder** is a small handheld tool with an ergonomic handle made of plastic. This tool is typically double-sided with a thin but heavy-duty wire shaped slightly like a trapezoid on either side, except one side has a narrow-shaped opening for getting into tight spaces. This tool is best used for hand weeding very close to established plants without harming them. There are no sharp edges anywhere on the tool. It is effective in lightly cultivating the soil

while killing small weed seedlings. This is a great tool for school groups or untrained volunteers.

Large weeds can be pulled by hand, but caution is advised. The roots of large weeds often disturb the soil as they are being pulled, causing new weed seeds to surface and germinate quickly. If you plan to pull weeds by hand, it would be a good preventative measure to sheet mulch around your plants directly after.

Organic or OMRI Certified Sprays and Other Natural Herbicides

There are many effective natural herbicide sprays on the market, but they can be expensive and may not work on all weeds. Some of these, even if the active ingredients are all natural or plant based, may still pose health concerns. It is important to read the labels to find out health risks. Even natural sprays may advise wearing gloves, long sleeves, masks, and safety goggles when applying them. Caution is advised. I tend to not use these sprays because we are on a tight budget.

Agricultural vinegar has been proven effective, but as mentioned in the previous chapter, caution is advised. Oftentimes, these sprays could affect the fruits, vegetables, flowers, and herbs growing in your garden.

NATURAL PEST MANAGEMENT
Companion Planting

Companion planting is an excellent way to keep garden pests at bay, for example, interplanting onions or hot peppers next to susceptible crops. Find out which pests are most prevalent in your region and plant crops that will deter them.

Companion planting is also a great way to add healthy diversity to your garden. Plants such as borage and marigolds help attract pollinators while deterring unwanted pests from the garden. Marigolds and nasturtiums can help repel beetles and aphids. Carrots growing next to tomato plants offer shade and relief from the summer heat.

Though companion planting is widely practiced and can sometimes be a useful technique, current evidence does not prove the effectiveness of companion planting.

Beneficial Insects

Introducing beneficial insects can help with pest issues. Ladybugs prey on aphids. Ground beetles prey on Colorado potato beetles, cutworms, and caterpillars. Green lacewings prey on whiteflies, aphids, and caterpillars. Damsel bugs prey on cabbage worms and mites. Braconid wasps prey on caterpillars and aphids. If you choose to release beneficial insects, it is best to first plant flowers, herbs, and perennials they are attracted to. For example, ladybugs are attracted to dill, ground beetles are attracted to clover, green lacewings are attracted to coriander, damsel bugs are attracted to mint and fennel. Typically, beneficial insects are attracted to aromatic herbs.

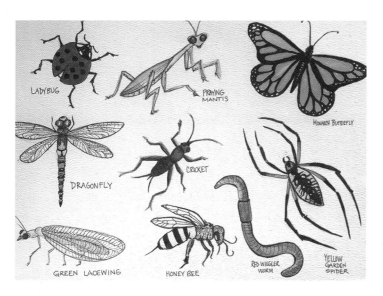

◀ *This image illustrates some common beneficial insects in the garden.*

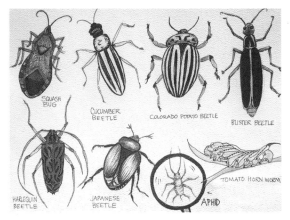

▲ *This image shows some common garden insects that can cause significant damage to crops.*

Row Covers

Row covers are usually a white airy material used to create a physical barrier from swarms of insects and migrating birds. They also help to protect crops from frost. Row covers can be used to slightly extend the growing season.

Netting and Cages

Insect netting is a fine mesh net that prevents insects from making themselves at home on your crops. Bird netting can be placed over fruit trees and berry bushes before the berries ripen

to prevent birds from eating all the berries. I don't use netting because I encourage wildlife. Additionally, we live on ten acres, and the birds have plenty of access to native flora. In an urban environment, netting may be necessary to prevent birds, squirrels, and other wildlife from enjoying the fruits of your labor.

Adding a chicken-wire cage over your prized crops can prevent rabbits and squirrels from nibbling on your crops.

Trap Cropping

Trap cropping helps to soften the blow of pest and insect damage to your prized crops. For example, try planting a summer squash away from your main garden a week or two before you plant your main crop. Ideally, this will attract the insects to the trap crop while your other plants should remain unaffected for a while. Squash bugs are very hard to get rid of though. I would recommend choosing varieties that are disease and pest resistant.

Hand Picking

Removing insects by hand, such as cabbage loopers and horn worms, might be necessary. If the problem is too intense, it may just be best to remove that plant from your garden altogether. Place it in a bucket of vinegar water to prevent the insect from going to your neighbors' crops or feed them to your chickens.

Sprays

Natural sprays such as Py-Ganic and Dipel can be effective, but they are expensive.

Homemade sprays can be made in the blender (use an extension cord to make this outside!). Caution is necessary when making these highly irritating sprays at home. Goggles, gloves, and masks must be used when making potent natural pest sprays.

½ cup water
4 raw onions (chopped)
10 whole cloves of garlic
12 cayenne peppers

Combine all ingredients in the blender and process until smooth. Line a colander with cheesecloth and strain mixture into a large pot.

Dilute with 1 gallon of water. Pour strained mixture into a backpack sprayer or small spray bottles. Be sure to label clearly, keep out of the reach of children, and use precautionary methods when applying. Always wear gloves, a mask, and goggles when handling or applying this spray.

Apply to crops to prevent pests or to treat plants which have harmful insects on them.

There are hundreds of recipes and remedies for natural pesticides. Contact your local Extension office or Master Gardener chapter to source recipes from them, based on the specific pests which plague your region.

Linda Gilkeson, author of *Backyard Bounty* says,

While DIY pest treatments aren't regulated in the US, note that in Canada, any substance used to control insects, weeds, or microbes must be a registered product with a Pest Control Product number from the Pest Management Regulatory Agency and the use of an unregistered substances including substances such as acetic acid or any home recipe preparation is illegal. Further, it is also important to remember that if homemade preparation works to kill pests it may well also kill beneficial insects and many also damage the leaves of plants so great care and consideration should be taken.

Crop Rotation

Crop rotation should be done after the crop's life cycle ends. Avoid planting vegetables from the same plant family in the same location year after year; do so only once every few years. The soil needs a break from heavy feeders, as well as a variance in root depth. For example, some vegetables are light to medium feeders, while others are heavy feeders. Crop rotation limits insect and pest problems and helps to return vital minerals and nutrients back to the soil.

According to the Rodale Institute: Different plants have different nutritional needs and are susceptible to different pathogens and pests. If a farmer plants the exact same crop in the same place every year, as is common in conventional farming, they continually draw the same nutrients out of the soil. Pests and diseases happily make themselves a permanent home as their preferred food source is guaranteed. With monocultures like these,

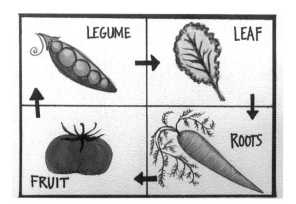

increasing levels of chemical fertilizers and pesticides become necessary to keep yields high while keeping bugs and disease at bay.

Crop rotation helps return nutrients to the soil without synthetic inputs. It also works to interrupt pest and disease cycles, improve soil health by increasing biomass from different crops' root structures, and increase biodiversity on the farm. Life in the soil thrives on variety, and beneficial insects and pollinators are attracted to the variety above ground, too.[1]

An article titled "A Quick Guide to Crop Rotation & Vegetable Families," published by *GrowOrganic.com*, makes the following recommendations:

The basic rule: Wait 3 years until you replant families in the same place.

Why? Soil borne diseases build up when similar plants grow in the same space for more than a year. You don't want to deal with club root, fusarium wilt, or verticillium wilt, do you? If you keep moving the plants, you'll help thwart the diseases.

Just like any family, not all members of plant families look alike. See which relatives surprise you the most![2]

Steve Albert, in an article for the *Harvest to Table Gardening* blog, suggests the following crop rotations:

Crop Rotation by Harvest Groups

Crop rotation by harvest groups is a simple rotation strategy: rotate leafy crops, root crops, and fruiting crops. Harvest group rotation is not a precise crop rotation method (for example, peppers are light feeders and tomatoes are heavy feeders, but both are fruiting crops — but it is an easy way to group plants and to remember the rotation from one year to the next. A simple three-year crop rotation divides crops into their harvest groups:

1. Leafy crops — including members of the cabbage family such as broccoli, Brussels sprouts, cauliflower
2. Root crops
3. Fruiting crops (flowering crops)

Into this mix you can add cover crops to follow fruiting crops. Because fruiting crops are almost all summer crops — tomatoes, peppers, squash, melons, eggplants — they finish harvest in early autumn and their planting area can be replanted with a winter cover crop such as winter rye or fava beans. In spring, the cover crop is turned under and leafy crops can be planted to continue the rotation. This rotation would look like this:

1. Fruiting crop   3. Leafy crop
2. Cover crop   4. Root crop[3]

Plant Families

GrowOrganic.com has compiled a list of plant families and the varieties that belong to each family:

Nightshades
(Solanaceae, heavy feeders)
Tomatoes
Tomatillos
Eggplants
Peppers
Okra (some say it's a mallow)
Potatoes
Morning Glory (heavy feeders)
Sweet potatoes

Melons, Squash, and Cucumbers
(Cucurbits)
Cucumbers
Zucchini and summer squash
Watermelons
Musk melons
Pumpkins
Gourds

Goosefoot
(Amaranthaceae)
Beet
Spinach
Chard
Quinoa
Orach

Sunflower
(Asteraceae)
Sunflowers
Jerusalem artichokes
Lettuces (surprised?)
Endives
Artichokes

Cole (Brassica, heavy feeders)
Broccoli
Brussels sprouts
Cauliflower
Cabbage
Kale
Collards
Radishes
Kohlrabi
Rutabagas
Turnip
Mustard

Onions (Allium, light feeders)
Onions
Leeks
Chives
Garlic

Peas (Legumes, soil enriching crops)
Peas
Runner beans
Bush beans
Fava beans
Garbanzo beans
Peanuts

Grasses
Corn
Millet
Rice
Barley
Wheat
Rye

Parsley
Carrots
Parsnips
Celery
Fennel
Cilantro/Coriander

Pollinator Gardens

Pollinator gardens are essential to every healthy garden system. Without pollinators, our plates would be empty. Every vegetable garden should

integrate plants and flowers that attract pollinators such as honeybees and butterflies, as well as other beneficial insects such as ladybugs. Native flowers from your region are the best to attract pollinators. However, companion plants such as borage, calendula, and marigolds serve a dual purpose: they attract pollinators as well as keep harmful pests away from your crops. Bright, showy, colorful flowers such as zinnias also attract pollinators.

By following these steps, you will acquire a green thumb in no time and will be enjoying a lovely garden and a bountiful harvest of fresh, homegrown, seasonal, organic produce this summer and fall. Avid vegetable gardeners are able to enjoy the fruits of their labor year-round with careful planning and maintenance, and over time, you will too!

Wondrous Weeds

Many households go to great lengths to achieve perfectly manicured lawns. I do not. My motto is that if it's growing, invasive or not, every plant has a purpose, whether it be for pollination; erosion prevention; food for animals, insects and people; or just for the sake of photosynthesis. Ralph Waldo Emerson said, "A weed is just a plant whose virtues have not yet been discovered." In today's fast-paced world, it is hard not to lose our connection with nature and the understanding that we have an innate symbiotic relationship with plants and animals. We are inevitably responsible for the future of our planet. We are so busy with the reality and rituals of everyday life that we hardly notice the

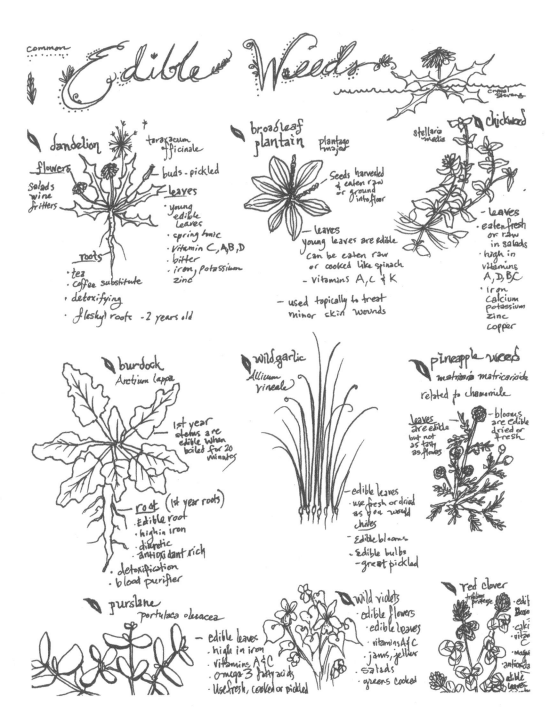

beauty beneath our feet, and even worse, we see what could ultimately heal us as something that is a nuisance. Serrated dandelions, soft and delicate red clovers, dainty wild onions and garlic, succulent chickweed, and burly plantain are among the first to emerge, even before the grasses begin to green. They have all been dormant throughout the bitter cold winter and are ready to reach for the sun. The wild greens in spring are vibrant, and herbalists around the world consider them to be spring tonic plants.

Foraging for wild edible greens and mushrooms is one of our family's favorite pastimes, as well as a survival skill and lesson in character building that we enjoy teaching our children. They learn that weeds thrive in a myriad of growing conditions and under severe environmental stress, making them incredibly resilient and highly adaptable — like a dandelion growing through the cracks of concrete.

For centuries, weeds have been used worldwide for food and to treat ailments such as headaches, nausea, menstrual cramps, cold and flu symptoms, as well as labor and birth. Your local library should have a selection of books on native plants and wild edibles specific to your region.

Identifying plants can be a complex endeavor because many look alike, making them difficult to distinguish. Dandelion and plantain are easy to identify because they are everywhere. Plants look slightly different when growing in diverse conditions or throughout various stages of their growing cycle. It is best to do your own research and always keep a native plant identification book with you. Taking someone's word on plant identification may not be the best idea, especially if they are not trained. When foraging, it is a good rule of thumb to only harvest a small amount; never take the entire stand of plants. Typically, it is a good idea to only harvest one-quarter of what you find, if the plant population is abundant and thriving. Also, foragers should practice ethical harvesting by using appropriate techniques to remove plants.

Here are a few of my favorite edible weeds that grow in abundance in the Midwest and some throughout the United States.

Burdock

Burdock root is edible and medicinal. Rich in calcium, potassium, copper, iron, chromium, flavonoid, and vitamins, it is mucilaginous, meaning it coats the mucus membranes. Roots from first-year burdocks can be harvested from early spring through late fall and cooked just like other root

make sure the area is not sprayed with chemicals. It is high in vitamins C, A, and B and packed with phytonutrients, magnesium, potassium, selenium, manganese, and zinc.

I enjoy taking nature walks with my children. They love to help me harvest chickweed because it is easy to pull! We bring it home, wash it, and make a salad. I combine beeswax and an oil infused with chickweed, plantain, comfrey, and dandelion for a salve that works well for cuts and scrapes.

vegetables. It can be dehydrated and made into a detox tea or added to a coffee substitute blend of dried roots that include dandelion and chicory. Burdock root is excellent for detoxifying the liver, stimulating the appetite, and aiding digestion. It has antifungal and antibacterial properties.

Dandelion

Dandelion, a powerful detox herb, has a plethora of medicinal uses. The roots are a powerful antioxidant and a friend to the digestive system. They can be roasted and used as a coffee substitute.

The greens make an excellent pesto or salad and are high in vitamins and minerals. The flowers are high in iron, beta-carotene, and

Chickweed

Chickweed is found in sunny and shady areas of most backyards. If you wild harvest chickweed,

growing throughout the United States, maybe even in your own backyard. Just remember, as with any wild edible, be sure you identify it correctly before harvesting it. Lamb's quarters are highly nutritious, packed with iron, vitamin C, calcium, riboflavin, and niacin. We have been enjoying them at La Vista since we began farming here. They actually contain trace elements of gold and silver, which is a natural antibiotic.

To clean lamb's quarters, immerse the whole plant and gently shake a few times. Use the leaves like spinach, cooked or raw. Add them to salads, smoothies, soups, stews, pastas, dough, cannelloni, or lasagna.

vitamin C. Aesthetically, they make a nice garnish for any dish and are absolutely gorgeous in a refreshing herbal lemonade. Dandelion fritters are one of my favorite wild food dishes.

Plantain

Plantain has been used throughout history as a panacea, meaning a medicine that is used to treat everything. It has antibacterial, astringent, and anti-inflammatory properties. Young leaves can be eaten raw and are loaded with vitamin

Lamb's Quarters

Lamb's quarters, also referred to as poor man's spinach, wild spinach, or goosefoot, is found

C and calcium. Plantain is one of the main ingredients in first-aid salve. To treat insect stings quickly, simply pluck a leaf of plantain, tear it apart, and use a little saliva to make an instant paste. Hold it on the sting for at least a minute.

Red Clover

Red clover is a wonderful weed that grows wild in pastures and fields worldwide. Native to Western Asia, Europe, and Africa, it is a source of phytoestrogens, plant-based estrogens. It can aid in menstrual cramps, PMS, hot flashes, and other symptoms of menopause. Red clover can also be helpful in treating the common cold and flu, as it helps loosen phlegm, and is good for the heart, keeping arteries flexible. It is rich in vitamins and minerals including calcium, potassium, magnesium, and vitamin C.

Stinging Nettles

Stinging nettles, native to North America, Asia, Europe, and Africa, grow wild in woodlands, prairies, and savannahs. It can be hard to distinguish between wood nettles and false nettles. In fact, for years I had been confusing stinging nettles with wood nettles (which are also highly medicinal) until a herbalist friend described their differences. Stinging nettle leaves have a very distinct pattern of three major veins running lengthwise down the center. The leaf pattern is opposite and the leaves are lanceolate. Wood nettles have more ovular leaves with a pinnate venation. Also, their bottom leaves are alternate, and their top leaves are opposite. The stinging hairs that run the entire length of the stem cause an immediate burning and itching reaction in the skin. Some herbalists intentionally run their hands and arms into a stinging nettle patch as a successful method of treating arthritis.

Nettles are one of the most amazing medicinal herbs. Used to treat cold and flu, digestive upsets and skin disorders, they are also a good tonic for the urinary tract, kidneys, heart, and lungs. Stinging nettles are also revered as a wild edible, eaten by Native Americans for their high nutrient content, rich in iron, potassium, calcium, and vitamin C. The leaves can be made into a nutrient rich infusion. Simply boil a pot of water and add stinging nettle leaves. Simmer on low for 30 minutes. Allow nettles to steep overnight. Strain through cheesecloth.

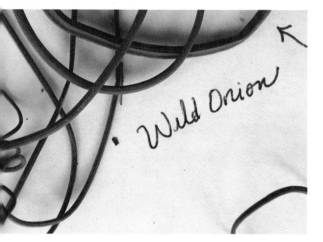

Wild Onions

Wild onions can be found in the spring and summer throughout the US. They look like grass but are hollow and tubular, found in clusters, and have a very potent onion flavor. Use them just as you would chives, scallions, or onions. Cut with scissors and serve raw in salad, cooked with meals, or added to flavor sauces and soups. Wild onion soup is delicious served with wild onion biscuits.

Onions have been used historically to treat respiratory infections. They contain high anticancer sulfur compounds and help regulate healthy cholesterol levels.

Chapter 6

Choosing the Right Plants

CHOOSING THE RIGHT PLANTS for your region is an important step to a successful garden or edible landscape.

There are several moving parts in the equation of plant health. In order for plants to thrive, they need proper nutrition, the right soil type, adequate sunlight or shade, sufficient moisture, and enough space to spread out and for their roots to grow.

LIGHT REQUIREMENTS

Plants have varying light requirements. Most vegetable, fruit, and herb varieties require full sun for up to 8 hours per day in order to reach their full potential. Morning sun is typically less intense and a bit cooler than afternoon sun, which can be very intense and often scorching. If dry and unwatered plants are exposed to several days of afternoon sun, they may suffer tremendously.

SPACING

Each plant variety has specific spacing require-ments for optimal health. Some need a foot between them; others can thrive when closer together. Check the seed packet or tag of the plant variety for recommendations.

HEIGHT CAPACITY

Some plants grow low to the ground while other plants tower over the garden reaching up to 12 feet at full maturity. When planning and plant-ing a garden, it is best to research the height capacity of each plant. For example, when cre-ating an attractive herb garden, the low-growing herbs (6" or less) should be at the front of the bed. The 6" to 12" plants should be behind the 6" grouping. Taller varieties should be at the back, spaced according to height capacity.

It is a good practice to read each of the seed packets, do your research, and make yourself a handy chart of all the things you are growing. Include seeding recommendations, spac-ing, light requirements, and other important information.

TYPES OF PLANTS

Annual plants generally die back after one growing season. Sow tender annual seeds in trays for transplanting and sow hardy trans-plants directly into the ground.

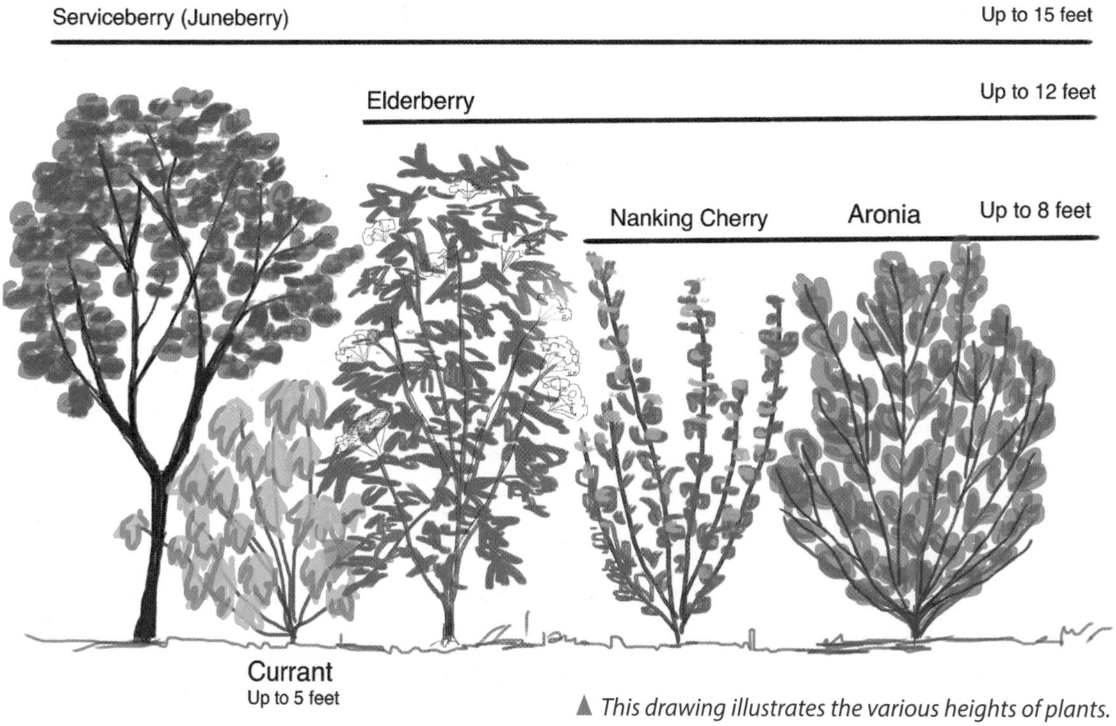

Serviceberry (Juneberry) — Up to 15 feet

Elderberry — Up to 12 feet

Nanking Cherry   Aronia — Up to 8 feet

Currant — Up to 5 feet

▲ *This drawing illustrates the various heights of plants.*

Benefits of Companion Planting

Companion planting is an excellent way to reduce pest damage and add healthy diversity. For example, onions or hot peppers can help deter pests from nearby susceptible crops. Include specific crops to discourage pests that are most prevalent in your region. Carrots growing near the base of tomatoes help aerate the soil, providing space for water and nutrients to reach their roots. In turn, tomatoes provide shade for them in the heat.

Such companion plants — including borage, marigolds, aromatic herbs, and native perennials — also help attract pollinators and beneficial insects. This simple way of promoting biodiversity creates a flourishing ecosystem in your yard that also helps with crop success.

▲ *Attract pollinators with flowers native to your region.*

Perennial plants return year after year and are resilient. Some spread quickly. Be sure to research growth patterns before planting.

Biennial plants return one year and go dormant for the next, alternating this growing cycle.

Hardy plants, perennials and annuals, tend to be resilient, survive harsh or extreme conditions, and are drought, heat, and cold tolerant.

Tender plants, perennials or annuals, often do not withstand cold temperatures. They usually require more maintenance and are often more delicate, with vulnerabilities to disease, pests, extreme temperatures, drought or periods of heavy rain, and even prolonged exposure to sun or shade.

ZONE HARDINESS

According to the United States Department of Agriculture, "the USDA Plant Hardiness Zone Map is the standard by which gardeners and growers can determine which plants are most likely to thrive at a location. The map is based on the average annual minimum winter temperature, divided into 10-degree F zones."[1]

When choosing plants, it is important to find varieties that are hardy to your specific zone. For example, we are on the edge of 6a and 6b. For our garden and farm, I make sure to research the hardiness of each plant and only consider varieties that are hardy to our zone before purchasing and planting. Because some will be hardy in multiple zones, I often choose those that are hardy in zones 5 to 8.

Breakdown of zones by the USDA Plant Zone Hardiness Map:

Zone	Temperature in degrees (F)	Zone	Temperature in degrees (F)	Zone	Temperature in degrees (F)
Zone 1a	-60 to -55	Zone 5b	-15 to -10	Zone 10a	30 to 35
Zone 1b	-55 to -50	Zone 6a	-10 to -5	Zone 10b	35 to 40
Zone 2a	-50 to -45	Zone 6b	-5 to 0	Zone 11a	40 to 45
Zone 2b	-45 to -40	Zone 7a	0 to 5	Zone 11b	45 to 50
Zone 3a	-40 to -35	Zone 7b	5 to 10	Zone 12a	50 to 55
Zone 3b	-35 to -30	Zone 8a	10 to 15	Zone 12b	55 to 60
Zone 4a	-30 to -25	Zone 8b	15 to 20	Zone 13a	60 to 65
Zone 4b	-25 to -20	Zone 9a	20 to 25	Zone 13b	65 to 70
Zone 5a	-20 to -15	Zone 9b	25 to 30		

DISEASE RESISTANCE

According to Paula Flynn with Department of Plant Pathology at the Iowa State University Extension:

> The use of resistant or tolerant varieties is an inexpensive and easy means of controlling plant diseases in crops where such varieties are available. Their use can also help cut down on the use of pesticides for disease control.

> The term resistance or tolerance does not mean that the plant is completely immune to disease. It refers to a plant's ability to overcome to some degree the effect of the pathogen. Also, no variety is resistant or tolerant to all diseases. For instance, the initials VF by a tomato variety indicates resistance to the fungal diseases Verticillium wilt and Fusarium wilt, but does not mean that the variety is also resistant to the common leaf diseases.[2]

INSECT RESISTANCE

Insect pests are one of the most difficult problems in the realm of gardening. One effective strategy to this pressure is to choose varieties that are naturally resistant to insects. Check with your local Master Gardeners association or your local university Extension office to inquire about these varieties.

CHOOSING THE RIGHT PLANTS FOR YOUR REGION

When choosing plants, you want to first gather information about your specific region. For example, does it have a wet or dry climate? Are there prolonged periods of drought or rainfall? What are the average low and high temperatures throughout each season? You want to tailor your plant selections to these relative conditions.

Drought tolerant varieties can withstand extended periods without water. If you live in a desert climate or an area with little rainfall, choose these varieties.

If your region has extremely harsh winters, choose cold hardy annuals and perennials that can withstand prolonged frigid temperatures.

PLANTING TIMES

Planting time varies by region. Multiple successions can be planted during the appropriate window. Check your local garden club or university Extension office to obtain a zone-specific planting chart. I have created this handy chart for our region.

If you live in a zone with harsh winters, be sure that you know the last frost date of the spring and the first frost date of the fall, as guidelines. For example, in zone 6a, where I live, the last frost date is typically between March 15 and 30, but we did have several light frosts in April and unseasonably cold temperatures in May this past spring. Our first frost date is typically between November 1 and 15. However, last fall, we had our first frost in mid-October. If you want to be sure your planting and harvesting during optimal times, check your seven-day forecast well before the anticipated last and first frost dates.

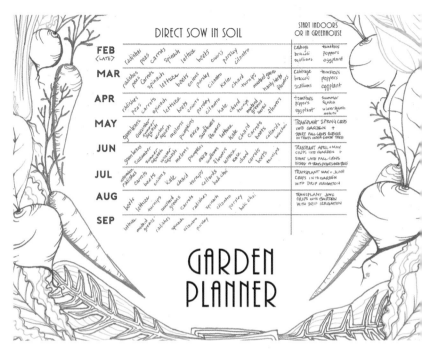

GUILD PLANTINGS AND FOOD FORESTS

Guild plantings resemble small food forests, providing layers mimicking the canopy layers of a forest. They comprise a diverse array of plants

◀ *Guilds can be planted to create a micro-ecosystem, maximize space, and increase yields.*

that are useful in creating a micro ecosystem, helping to enrich the soil and provide abundant yields, food and shelter for wildlife, and nutrition and medicine.

Small guild plantings are excellent for compact spaces but can be also be scaled up and set in various patterns and designs, offering symbiotic relationships between their multiple varieties. These low-maintenance gardens provide abundant harvests throughout most seasons and beauty in any front or backyard.

Our friend Matt Lebon, of Custom Foodscaping, has transformed his small city plot into an edible oasis. He has dozens of guild plantings in his backyard food forest. (See photos in Chapter 8.)

I have been inspired by his work installing permaculture guilds and food forests throughout our region. Some of the information below is from our many plant-centered conversations over the years.

There are many layers to a food forest. I am using the terms food forest and permaculture

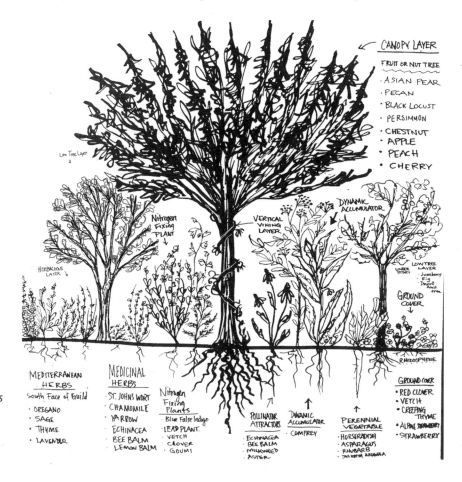

▶ This image illustrates the many layers of a food forest or guild planting.

guild planting interchangeably throughout this chapter. Based on our experience, we plant permaculture guilds in groupings to eventually create a food forest. A food forest can be scaled down or up depending on the size of your plot.

Geoff Lawton, in an article, states:

Forests are ecosystems with a diversity of plants, animals, and fungi. They were designed by nature to have perfect balance. A food forest is a version of this in which the different, balanced components produce food. When we understand how nature creates its ecosystem, we can model that with productive species to produce food sustainably, with minimum inputs for maximum outputs.

Forests have layers. At the top is the: (1) canopy layer followed by (2) understory trees, (3) bushes and shrubs, and down to (4) herbaceous layers. Under the ground, there are (5) root yields, and at the surface, there are (6) groundcovers. There are also vertical layers of (7) climbers.[3]

Food forests can be adapted using various region-specific crops. For example, a food forest planted in a tropical rainforest climate may contain bananas, mango, guava, tamarillo, and cassava, while one in the US Midwest may contain persimmon, elderberries, juneberries, aronia berries, red clover, and horseradish.

The following detailed description of each of the food forest layers or guild planting components is adapted from Temperate Climate Permaculture.[4]

Canopy Layer

The canopy layer comprises tall fruit and/or nut bearing trees. In a small guild planting, a large fruit tree such as an apple, Asian pear, pawpaw, persimmon, cherry, peach, or plum could be the central canopy tree.

Take caution when planting trees. Call your local utility companies to make sure there are no buried lines in your chosen area. Be sure there are no power lines above the area.

Understory Tree Layer

The lower tree layer comprises dwarf fruit trees and smaller nut trees.

Bush and Shrub Layer

This layer comprises understory fruit-producing shrubs and bushes, such as juneberry, elderberry, gooseberry, currant, berries, and aronia. Also in this layer are nitrogen-fixing shrubs such as Siberian pea shrub.

Herbaceous Layer

The herbaceous layer comprises dynamic accumulators, nitrogen-fixing plants, alliums, perennial vegetables, pollinator attractors, and herbs (Mediterranean and medicinal), as well as annual companion plants such as marigolds and nasturtiums.

Dynamic accumulators such as comfrey can be planted throughout the guild. They gather specific minerals and nutrients and store them in a more bioavailable form throughout their tissues in high concentrations

Nitrogen-fixing plants such as Siberian pea shrub, blue false indigo, and leadplant could be planted throughout the guild in order to fix atmospheric nitrogen.

I like to integrate a variety of plants from the **allium family** such as Egyptian walking onions, Welch onions, scallions, garlic, common chives, or garlic chives. These alliums help deter unwanted pests from the garden.

Perennial vegetables such as rhubarb, Turkish rocket broccoli, sea kale, and asparagus can also be added to the herbaceous layer to provide biodiversity and a continuous supply of food throughout the seasons.

Perennial flowering **pollinator attractors** could be planted to help attract native and beneficial pollinators that will in turn help to increase the yield of the fruit-bearing crops.

On the south- or southwest-facing side of the guild, I plant aromatic **Mediterranean herbs** such as lavender, rosemary, sage, oregano, and thyme, which are heat and drought tolerant and can help absorb heat. These provide continuous abundance as **culinary and medicinal herbs**. They are aromatic and attract beneficial insects and pollinators during their flowering stages.

Ground Cover Layer

The ground cover layer, which can comprise plants such as red clover, are planted to help suppress weeds, retain moisture, fix nitrogen, add soil organic matter and biomass, help prevent erosion, and act as a living mulch. It also helps build soil fertility.

Interplant the ground cover with low-growing perennial fruiting crops such as everbearing or alpine strawberries. Strawberries work well for edges of guilds, bordering beds, and lining pathways as well. Sylvetta arugula, a perennial vegetable, can also be planted in this layer.

Rhizosphere Layer

The rhizosphere layer comprises plants with deep roots, specifically root vegetables. A perennial vegetable option for this layer is horseradish, a nutrient-rich medicinal food. I like to stack functions and integrate burdock in this layer, which can be eaten as a root vegetable and also has many medicinal properties.

Vertical Layer

The vertical layer comprises vining or climbing plants such as passionflower, grapes, or American groundnut but should not be planted until the central tree is well-established.

Note: For any of the above-mentioned layers, find out which varieties of perennials grow and yield well in your climate.

The following two layers are sourced from Food Forests Grow:

Aquatic/Wetland Layer: These are a whole host of plants that thrive in wetlands or at the water's edge, at the edge of a forest. There are many plants that grow only in water.

Mycelial/Fungal Layer: This layer describes the mushrooms that live mostly underground in the soil of the forest. Fungal networks live in healthy soils. They will live on, and even within, the roots of plants in the Forest Garden. These underground fungal network transport nutrients and moisture from one area of the forest to another depending on the needs of the plants.[5]

CANOPY LAYER FRUIT AND NUT TREES

Apple Trees

When choosing an apple variety, it is best to purchase a reliable variety from a local nursery, one that is drought-tolerant and resistant to insect damage and disease. Apple trees grow best in full sun and well-drained loamy soil. Some varieties need to be near another apple tree in order for cross-pollination to occur. Golden

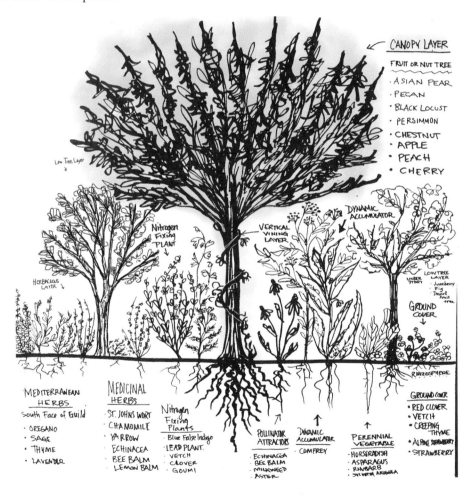

CANOPY LAYER

FRUIT OR NUT TREE
- ASIAN PEAR
- PECAN
- BLACK LOCUST
- PERSIMMON
- CHESTNUT
- APPLE
- PEACH
- CHERRY

Low Tree Layer

Herbaceous Layer

Nitrogen Fixing PLANT

VERTICAL VINING LAYER

DYNAMIC ACCUMULATOR

LOW TREE LAYER
UNDER STORY
- Juneberry
- Fig
- Dwarf fruit tree

GROUND COVER

RHIZOSPHERE

MEDITERRANEAN HERBS
South Face of Guild
- OREGANO
- SAGE
- THYME
- LAVENDER

MEDICINAL HERBS
- ST. JOHNS WORT
- CHAMOMILE
- YARROW
- ECHINACEA
- BEE BALM
- LEMON BALM

Nitrogen Fixing Plants
- Blue False Indigo
- LEAD PLANT
- VETCH
- CLOVER
- GOUMI

POLLINATOR ATTRACTORS
- ECHINACEA
- BEE BALM
- MILKWEED
- ASTER

DYNAMIC ACCUMULATOR
- COMFREY

PERENNIAL VEGETABLE
- HORSERADISH
- ASPARAGUS
- RHUBARB
- SYLVETTA ARUGULA

GROUND COVER
- RED CLOVER
- VETCH
- CREEPING THYME
- ALPINE STRAWBERRY
- STRAWBERRY

▲ *Apple tree.*

▲ *Asian pear tree.*

delicious is typically a good general tree to plant for cross-pollination purposes. The Liberty apple tree, a great disease-resistant variety that is hardy to zones 4 to 8, bears fruit within 2 to 4 years and ripens in early fall. It can grow up to 15 feet tall and 15 feet wide. Stark Bro's Nurseries recommends Cortland or Freedom varieties for cross-pollination.

Asian Pear Trees

A wonderful addition to guild planting, Asian pears are prolific producers, drought-tolerant, and disease-resistant. For the most part, they are also insect-resistant, meaning not incurring a lot of damage. Most Asian pear varieties are hardy in zones 4 to 8. Depending on the variety, they can grow up to 20 feet tall and 15 feet wide. They grow best in full sun and well-drained, nutrient-rich soil.

Asian pears start producing fruit in the 3rd or 4th year, typically ripening in early fall. These crisp and delicious pears store very well and

typically have very little insect damage. Asian pears need to be planted near another pear tree in order for cross-pollination to occur. Stark Bro's Nurseries recommends Bartlett, New Century Asian pear, or Housi Asian pear for cross-pollinating.

▲ *Peach tree.*

Peach Trees

We have seen great results in Zone 6a with the Redhaven variety. Hardy in zones 5 to 8, this self-pollinating and disease-resistant variety is easy to grow and has very little maintenance needs other than pruning. It grows best in full sun and well-drained loamy soil. This tree can reach up to 15 feet tall and 15 feet wide. The Redhaven variety, a prolific producer, bears fruit within the first few years, typically ripening in mid-July. The fruits have very little insect damage.

▲ *Cherry tree.*

Cherry Trees

We have seen great results with a variety called Stella sweet cherry, which is hardy in zones 5 to 8, that grows best in full sun and well-drained loamy soil. This prolific producer typically bears fruit in the first 5 years, usually ripening in June. It has moderate disease resistance and is self-pollinating.

Apricot Trees

Apricot trees are often finicky. One of the heaviest-bearing varieties is the Wilson Delicious, a prolific producer that is hardy to zones 5 to 8. It grows best in full sun and well-drained soil, typically bearing fruit within the first few years, which ripens in late June or July. This self-pollinating variety can grow up to 20 feet tall and 20 feet wide.

▲ *Fig tree.*

Fig Trees

We have seen great results with the Chicago hardy fig, hardy to zones 5 to 10, though it will need to be pruned and mulched to survive harsh winters. In some warmer zones, figs can grow to 30 feet tall and 35 feet wide. They don't get that big in our zone (zone 6a) because we have very cold winters, and we have to prune them back and apply heavy mulch each fall. Figs grow best in well-drained loamy soils and full sun, but they will tolerate partial shade. This prolific producer bears fruit within the first

2 years, typically ripening in July, and keeps producing through early fall. Chicago hardy figs are drought- and heat-tolerant. In my experience with this variety, I have not noticed much disease and insect pressure.

▲ *American persimmon tree.*

▲ *Pawpaw tree.*

American Persimmon Trees

The American persimmon is a timeless fruit tree native to North America and hardy to zones 4 to 9. The genus name, *Diospyros*, means "fruit of the Gods." Persimmons grow well in full to partial sun in a variety of soil types, but prefer well-drained sandy soils. It takes about 3 to 5 years for a young tree to bear fruit, which are delicious when ripe. They do contain soluble tannins that make them impossible to eat until they are fully ripe.

Pawpaw Trees (*Asimina triloba*)

Pawpaws, the largest fruit indigenous to North America, grow in woodlands and forests. Hardy to zones 5 to 8, they grow well in partial-full sun in most well-drained soils with a pH of 5.0 to 7.0. They take about 3 years to bear fruit; cultivated varieties need cross-pollination. Hand-pollinate pawpaws using pollen from other varieties (genetically different varieties). The fruit resembles a mango, with the consistency of an overripe one, but tastes like banana custard. They make a great addition to a guild planting or food forest.

▲ *Mulberry tree.*

▲ *Wild plum tree.*

Mulberry Trees (*Morus rubra*)

The Illinois everbearing mulberry hardy to zones 4 to 8, is native to eastern and central North America. It grows well in full sun and prefers well-drained sandy or loamy soil with a pH of 5.5 to 6.5. It takes only 1 to 2 years to produce fruit, which are dark purple, long, and delicious. This tree is drought-tolerant and is self-pollinating.

Wild Plum Trees (*Prunus americana*)

Native to the US Midwest, this plum tree grows in woodlands, alongside streams, and in pastures. It grows well in full sun to partial shade and in well-drained soils. In the wild, this tree grows in sandy or rocky soils and is susceptible to pests and diseases when left unobserved. When cultivated, it works well as a hedgerow. Its small plums aren't that pleasant when eaten raw but make excellent jams and jellies.

Mexican Plum Trees (*Prunus mexicana*)

Native to northern Mexico and the central US, this plum grows in woodlands and thickets. It grows well in full sun to part shade, is hardy in zones 6 to 8, and produces small oval fruits. Unlike the American (wild) plum, the Mexican plum has very many disease or pest concerns.

Japanese Plums

The Starking Delicious, a Japanese plum, is easy to grow, disease resistant, and a prolific producer with delicious fruit. This variety is hardy in zones 5 to 9 and reaches heights up to 20 feet. It needs pollinators such as Shiro or Ozark Premier. Stark Bro's Nurseries exclusively sells this variety.

▲ *Hawthorn tree.*

Hawthorn Trees (*Crataegus monogyna*)

The hawthorn can be found in Europe, the Mediterranean, Afghanistan, and North America. It is drought-tolerant, hardy to zones 4 to 8, and grows well in full sun-partial shade in a variety of moist soil types. The leaves can be used for tea. Western herbalists consider the edible berries to be food for the heart, used historically to restore a normal heartbeat and improve circulation.

Dwarf Fruit Trees

Dwarf fruit trees, which typically grow 7 to 11 feet, are best suited to compact spaces, education gardens, potted on rooftop gardens, school gardens, and small community gardens. Although not as prolific as semi-dwarf or standard fruit trees, they do produce an abundance of full-sized fruits in compact spaces. Check your local plant or tree nurseries for varieties that do best in your climate. Bonfire dwarf

peach, dwarf Giraldi mulberry, dwarf northstar cherry, and North Pole columnar apple are varieties that are popular for edible landscapes.

Dwarf Weeping Mulberry Trees (*Morus alba*)

The dwarf weeping mulberry makes a lovely addition to an edible landscape. It grows to about 12 feet in height and width, producing long weeping branches like a willow. Hardy to zones 3 to 9, this makes a great playhouse for kids. The berries are smaller than standard mulberry varieties but just as delicious. This variety is disease- and pest-resistant as well as drought-tolerant. It grows well in full sun or partial shade in a variety of well-drained soils.

American Chestnut Trees (*Castanea dentata*)

The American chestnut is native to North America, specifically the eastern US. Hardy to zones 4 to 8, it grows quickly and prefers full to partial sun and moist well-drained acidic soil but will tolerate dry and clay soil. This variety is susceptible to chestnut blight, but the American Chestnut Foundation has been working on rigorous breeding programs to work on blight-resistant hybrids. Its nuts are edible, though they are covered with sharp, spiny husks. The American chestnut is listed on the Slow Food Ark of Taste catalog for its characteristics of being prolific: up to 6,000 nuts can be harvested from one tree.

Chinese Chestnut Trees

The Chinese chestnut, native to Korea and China, can reach between 40 and 60 feet. Hardy to zones 4 to 9, preferring full sun and

▲ *Chinese Chestnut Tree.*

▲ *Hickory tree.*

moist, well-drained acidic soil, it is heat- and drought-tolerant and resistant to chestnut blight. The nuts are edible, though they are covered with sharp, spiny husks.

Hickory Trees

Worldwide, there are 17 species of hickories, 15 of which can be found in Canada and the southern and eastern US. Shellbark hickory trees, native to the rich floodplains and bottomlands of the US, are a low-maintenance tree with very few pests. They reach heights of 80 feet, produce the largest nuts of all hickories, and grow well in full sun and most soil types. Drought-tolerant, Shellbark hickories used to be very prolific, but this species has dwindled significantly.

Shagbark hickories grow well in full to partial sun and well-drained soil. Cultivars such as Abundance and Grainger yield delicious oval nuts in as little as 3 years. Syrup can be made by boiling down the bark and adding sugar.

▲ *Hazelnut tree.*

Hazelnut Trees

Hazelnut trees, hardy to zones 5 to 8, grow well in full sun and well-drained loamy soils. In hot climates, they are best planted as an understory tree, with some shade. They can grow up to 18 feet in height and width. For cross-pollination to occur, place them within 40 feet of another variety of hazelnut. They are prolific producers but can take up to 10 years before bearing nuts.

SHRUB LAYER/LOW TREE LAYER
Fruit Producing Shrubs:
The Understory Layer

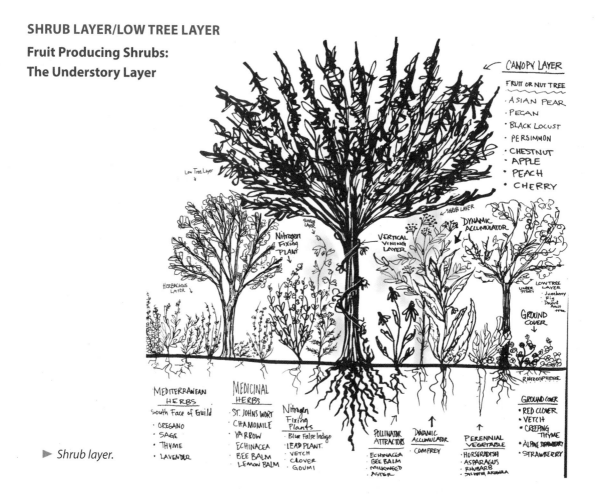

▶ *Shrub layer.*

▲ *Goumi.*

Goumi (*Elaeagnus multiflora*)

Goumi is a fruiting shrub native to Russia, Japan, and China. This nitrogen-fixing plant is hardy to zones 4 to 9, reaches heights of 6 to 10 feet, and grows well in full sun to partial shade in well-drained soils. A very prolific plant, it produces delicious small edible fruits. It is resistant to most pests and diseases and provides flowers for pollinators and abundant fruit for birds and other wildlife.

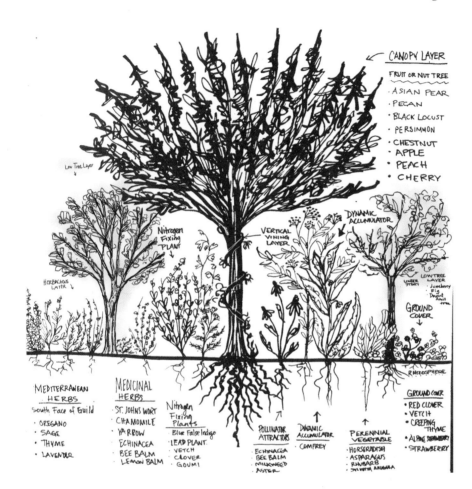

CANOPY LAYER

FRUIT OR NUT TREE

· ASIAN PEAR
· PECAN
· BLACK LOCUST
· PERSIMMON
· CHESTNUT
· APPLE
· PEACH
· CHERRY

Low Tree Layer

Nitrogen Fixing Plant

VERTICAL VINING LAYER

DYNAMIC ACCUMULATOR

LOW TREE LAYER
UNDER STORY
· Juneberry
· Fig
· Dwarf fruit tree

GROUND COVER

HERBACEOUS LAYER

RHIZOSPHERE

MEDITERRANEAN HERBS
South Face of Guild
· OREGANO
· SAGE
· THYME
· LAVENDER

MEDICINAL HERBS
· ST. JOHNS WORT
· CHAMOMILE
· YARROW
· ECHINACEA
· BEE BALM
· LEMON BALM

Nitrogen Fixing Plants
Blue False Indigo
· LEAD PLANT.
· VETCH
· CLOVER
· GOUMI

POLLINATOR ATTRACTORS
· ECHINACEA
· BEE BALM
· MILKWEED
· ASTER

DYNAMIC ACCUMULATOR
· COMFREY

PERENNIAL VEGETABLE
· HORSERADISH
· ASPARAGUS
· RHUBARB
· SYLVETTA ARUGULA

GROUND COVER
· RED CLOVER
· VETCH
· CREEPING THYME
· ALPINE STRAWBERRY
· STRAWBERRY

◀ Low tree layer.

Aronia Berries (*Aronia melanocarpa*)

The aronia is native to North America, primarily near the Great Lakes Region, and is hardy to zones 3 to 7. This multi-stemmed shrub can reach up to 8 feet and grows well in full sun and partial shade in a variety of well-drained soils. It produces small dark purple-black berries within 2 to 3 years. The bitter berries, which can be juiced or made into syrups, jellies, and fruit leather, are highly nutritious and rich in antioxidants. This wonderful pollinator attractor has

▲ Aronia Berries.

minimal disease and pest pressure and is a great addition to guild plantings.

▲ *Juneberries.*

Juneberries (*Amelanchier spp.*)

Also called service berries and saskatoon berries, these large multi-stemmed shrubs are native to the US and Canada and are hardy in zones 4 to 9. They grow well in full sun to partial shade and in average well-drained soil types. There are many cultivars. Autumn Brilliance (*Amelanchier × grandiflora*), a common shrub that grows up to 20 feet tall, produces abundant small fruit, similar to blueberries, that can be eaten fresh or made into jams, jellies, syrups, and pies. The Juneberry, which is resistant to most pests and diseases, provides food and shelter for wildlife and attracts pollinators.

▲ *Gooseberries.*

Gooseberries (*Ribes uva-crispa; Ribes grossularia*)

Gooseberries are in the Ribes family, native to northern Africa and Europe, and hardy in zones 3 to 8. Several varieties make lovely additions to edible landscapes and guild plantings. Gooseberries grow well in full sun to partial shade and prefer well-drained soils with a pH of 6.0 to 6.8. They grow up to 5 feet tall, and most are covered with large sharp thorns. Gooseberries need to be pruned regularly to encourage growth and the production of fruit. They are susceptible to pests and diseases, so be on the lookout for signs of damage. Stark Bro's Nurseries has great resources to naturally treat these issues.

Jostaberries (*Ribes missouriense; Ribes × nidigrolaria*)

Jostaberries, a cross between gooseberries and currants, are hardy in zones 4 to 7 and grow well in full sun to partial shade in well-drained sandy soils with a pH between 6.0 and 6.5. These thornless bushes produce sweet/tart dark purple (nearly black) berries that are delicious raw or made into jams and jellies. Jostaberries grow to be between 3 and 6 feet tall.

▲ *A mix of black currants and red currants.*

Currants

Currants, in the Ribes family, are hardy in zones 4 to 6 and grow well in full sun to partial shade in moist well-drained loamy or sandy soils with a pH of 6.2 to 6.5. Bushes grow to about 5 feet high and 6 feet wide. After about 2 years, they produce clusters of edible berries that can be enjoyed fresh or made into jams and jellies. Currants are typically resistant to most pests and diseases.

There are many different colors and varieties of currants. The Red Lake currant yields abundant delicious fruit and ripens in mid-summer. The Black Consort currant produces large clusters of black berries and is hardy in zones 4 to 8.

▲ *Golden currants.*

Golden currants or Buffalo currants produce vibrant clusters of small berries.

Goji Berries (*Lycium barbarum; Lycium chinense*)

Goji berries, native to China, are hardy in zones 3 to 10. The bushes are easy to grow, disease- and pest-resistant, as well as drought-tolerant.

▲ *Goji berries.*

They grow well in full sun and well-drained soil, reaching up to 6 feet in height. Most goji berries are self-pollinating and abundant producers, yielding delicious sweet small berries that are rich in antioxidants.

Jujubes

Jujubes, large deciduous shrubs native to Asia, India, and Europe, are hardy to zones 6 to 9. They grow well in full sun and well-drained sandy soils, reaching heights of 30 to 40 feet, depending on the climate. Jujubes are drought tolerant and disease and pest resistant. They produce delicious edible fruits that have been used medicinally by many cultures.

Quince (*Cydonia oblonga*)

Quince shrubs, native to Western Asia and the Middle East, are hardy in warm-temperate climates in zones 5 to 9. They grow in full sun and partial shade in well-drained soils with a low to medium pH, reaching up to 30 feet tall. Their large fruits resemble pears and have a tart and astringent flavor, so they are often made into jellies or preserves. Quinces are susceptible to some pests and diseases.

Nanking Cherries (*Prunus tomentosa*)

Nanking cherries, native to Asia, are drought-tolerant, medium-dense shrubs hardy in zones 3 to 7. They grow well in full sun and in a variety of well-drained soil types, reaching heights of 6 to 10 feet. In early to mid-summer, medium-tart cherries ripen that can be eaten fresh or made into jams, jellies, and pies.

▲ *Nanking cherry.*

Elderberries (*Sambucus canadensis*)

Elderberry shrubs, native to eastern North America and Europe, are hardy in zones 3 to 9 and grow well in full sun to partial shade, in moist well-drained soils. Mostly pest- and disease-resistant, they reach heights of 12 feet,

▲ *Elderberry.*

span out wide, and make excellent hedgerows. They can flower and bear small clusters of fruit in the first year but start producing huge umbels of edible fruit in later years. The berries are rich in vitamins and minerals and high in antioxidants but should not be consumed raw. They can be cooked down into highly nutritious and immune-boosting elderberry syrup.

We buy our stem cuttings from River Hills Harvest: riverhillsharvest.com

▲ *Witch hazel.*

Witch Hazel (*Hamamelis virginiana*)

Witch hazel is one of my favorite shrubs to grow. One of the only winter bloomers, it is known as a harbinger of spring in many regions. It is hardy in zones 4 to 8 and grows best in full sun or filtered shade and well-drained soil, reaching up to 20 feet tall. Witch hazel attracts a variety of pollinators. The bark extract and flowers made into a hydrosol have long been revered for their skin tonic properties.

RUBUS FAMILY PLANTS

Blackberries

Blackberries are a wonderful addition to perennial food systems. However, they do spread, so be sure you have an area dedicated to them. Additionally, they need to be trellised and pruned regularly. We only grow a self-pollinating variety called Triple Crown thornless blackberries, which is heat-tolerant and hardy in zones 5 to 9. In full sun and well-drained loamy soil with a pH of 6.0 to 6.8, they can reach up to 5 feet high and over 4 feet wide. This variety will start producing delicious large berries within 2 years.

▲ *Blackberries.*

▲ *Red Raspberries.*

▲ *Honeyberry.*

Red Raspberries (*Rubus idaeus*)

Several varieties of raspberries are native to portions of Asia and North America and hardy in zones 4 to 8. Some heat-tolerant varieties grow in zone 9. Red raspberry canes grow well in full sun and well-drained loamy soils with a pH of 6.0 to 6.8, reaching about 5 feet tall and up to 4 feet wide. Stark Bro's Nurseries offer a tried and true prolific variety called Heritage red raspberry that produces delicious small-medium fruit from June to October, depending on the zone. It takes up to 2 years to bear fruit.

Honeyberry (*Lonicera caerulea*)

Also known as haskap, honeyberries, a deciduous shrub native to Canada, Poland, Russia, and Japan, is hardy in zones 3 to 7. They grow up to 4 feet tall in full sun to partial shade, in rich, moist, well-drained soils, and are resistant to most pests and diseases. Their delicious small oval fruits can be eaten raw or made into jams and jellies. In order to bear fruit, two compatible varieties are needed for cross-pollination.

Thimbleberry (*Rubus parviflorus*)

Thimbleberries, which are similar to raspberries, are a spineless bush native to the western US, hardy in zones 3 to 9. They grow up to about 4 feet tall in partial sun and rich, well-drained soils.

Salmonberry (*Rubus spectabilis*)

Salmonberries, a species of brambles hardy in zones 5 to 9, grow well in full sun or partial shade in rich, well-drained soils, up to 6 feet in height and width. They are often found in open forest environments. The yellowish-pink ripe berries were a very important food source for Indigenous peoples in the Pacific Northwest.

HERBACEOUS LAYER

Dynamic Accumulators

Dynamic accumulators are plants whose roots gather various minerals and nutrients from the different layers of the soil and store them in bioavailable forms in the leaves. Their leaves can be chopped and dropped at the base of fruit trees and shrubs to act as a natural fertilizer and to improve soil fertility

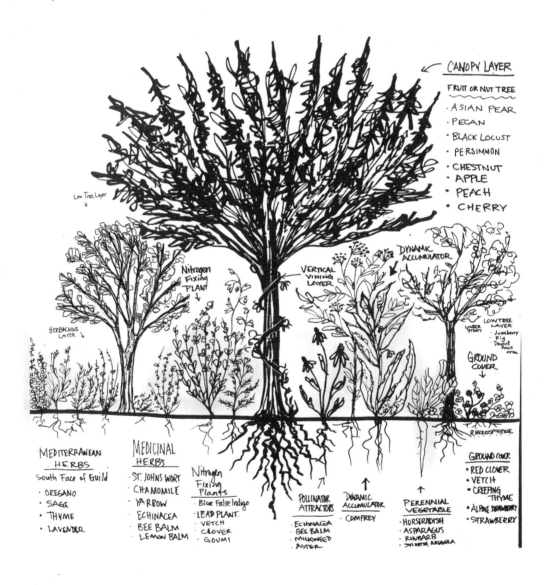

CANOPY LAYER

FRUIT OR NUT TREE

- ASIAN PEAR
- PECAN
- BLACK LOCUST
- PERSIMMON
- CHESTNUT
- APPLE
- PEACH
- CHERRY

Low Tree Layer

DYNAMIC ACCUMULATOR

VERTICAL VINING LAYER

Nitrogen Fixing PLANT

HERBACEOUS LAYER

LOW TREE LAYER
UNDER STORY
- Juneberry
  Fig
  Dwarf
  fruit
  tree

GROUND COVER

RHIZOSPHERE

MEDITERRANEAN HERBS
South Face of Guild
- OREGANO
- SAGE
- THYME
- LAVENDER

MEDICINAL HERBS
- ST. JOHNS WORT
- CHAMOMILE
- YARROW
- ECHINACEA
- BEE BALM
- LEMON BALM

Nitrogen Fixing Plants
- Blue False Indigo
- LEAD PLANT
- VETCH
- CLOVER
- GOUMI

POLLINATOR ATTRACTORS
- ECHINACEA
- BEE BALM
- MILKWEED
- ASTER

DYNAMIC ACCUMULATOR
- COMFREY

PERENNIAL VEGETABLE
- HORSERADISH
- ASPARAGUS
- RHUBARB
- SYLVETTA ARUGULA

GROUND COVER
- RED CLOVER
- VETCH
- CREEPING THYME
- ALPINE STRAWBERRY
- STRAWBERRY

▲ *Comfrey.*

▲ *Siberian pea shrub.*

Comfrey, *Symphytum officinale,* is a dynamic accumulator and can be chopped and dropped — meaning the leaves can be chopped with a knife or scythe and then dropped on the garden beds in the guild and around the fruit tree to help fertilize the plants naturally. Comfrey also has medicinal properties, and its flowers attract pollinators.

Nitrogen-fixing Plants

Siberian pea shrub, *Caragana arborescens (fruticosa),* a perennial legume hardy to zones 2 to 9, makes an excellent hedge, reaching 20 feet high if left to mature or pruned to stay a medium size. It is great for guild plantings that are spaced out a bit more.

It adds nitrogen to the soil as its roots grow and leaves fall. The flowers attract pollinators and birds. The small lime-green peapods are edible, as are the protein-rich dried seeds that must be cooked first.

▲ *Blue false indigo.*

Blue false indigo, *Baptisia australis,* fixes atmospheric nitrogen and has the ability to convert it into a readily available form for plants. It is drought-resistant, attracts various pollinators, and has long been revered by Indigenous cultures for its medicinal properties.

Leadplant, *Amorpha canescens*, has nodulated roots that contain nitrogen-fixing bacteria. It helps prevent soil erosion and attracts pollinators, such as butterflies, bees, moths, beetles, and an array of beneficial insects. Indigenous cultures have long revered leadplant for its medicinal properties.

Allium Varieties

▲ *Egyptian walking onions.*

Egyptian walking onions, *Allium proliferum,* a beautiful perennial (in zones 3 to 9), are striking in an edible landscape, growing to about 3 feet tall. They are called walking onions because they grow, bloom, go to seed, and then fall over, setting roots near the base of the parent plant. The small bulbs are delicious, as are the green onion-like leaves. The topsets can be harvested and planted.

Welsh onions, *Allium fistulosum*, are a hardy perennial herbaceous onion that can be cut time and time again and enjoyed as green onions (scallions). They attract beneficial pollinators and help to deter pests. They look beautiful in an edible landscape, especially when flowering.

There are so many varieties of **onions**. They make a beautiful landscape plant and add texture to any garden design. I have had great success with Candy, Red Long of Tropea, Cipollini, and Ailsa Craig.

▲ *Garlic.*

Garlic, *Allium sativum*, an amazing addition to edible landscapes, takes a long time to grow, but it is worth it. We have been growing and saving bulbs for seed from a German red hardneck variety for nearly a decade. In zone 6a, we plant garlic in full sun and well-drained soil in late October or early November, apply about 6 inches of straw to the beds, and harvest in early to late July. Garlic is highly nutritious and has immune-boosting properties. It is best to find garlic for planting that is hardy to your zone and acclimated to your specific region.

Perennial Vegetables

Perennial vegetables such as rhubarb, Turkish rocket broccoli, sea kale, asparagus, and others can also be added to the herbaceous layer to provide biodiversity and a continuous supply of food throughout the seasons.

▲ *Elephant garlic.*

▲ *Rhubarb.*

Elephant garlic, *Allium ampeloprasum var. ampeloprasum*, a biennial plant in the onion family, is really easy to grow and very attractive in an edible landscape. Hardy in zones 3 to 9, its large bulbs are nearly the size of a medium onion but can be separated into cloves like garlic. It has great flavor and is a bit milder than garlic. The green tops can be used as scallions, the flowering scapes are edible, and the flowering tops are delicious in salads.

Rhubarb, *Rheum rhabarbarum L.*, is a perennial vegetable that grows long thick stalks from a central plant, the size of a small bush, in zones 4 to 7. Avoid planting this in a children's garden because the young toxic leaves could resemble rainbow chard to children and beginning gardeners.

Rhubarb crowns can be planted in early spring. It is tolerant of cold and heat and resistant to disease and pests. The stalks are often cooked and made into strawberry rhubarb pie.

Turkish rocket broccoli, *Bunias orientalis,* grows up to 4 feet tall in zones 4 to 7, providing a continuous abundance of nutritious and delicious small broccoli florets. It grows best in full sun but can tolerate partial shade. It has been found to not be bothered by deer and rabbits.

▲ *Butterflies on milkweed.*

▲ *Asparagus.*

Asparagus, *Asparagus officinalis,* grows well in zones 3 to 8. Crowns planted in spring and heavily mulched with straw will take a couple of years to establish. The young stem shoots start to emerge when the weather is warmer, usually around 50° F. Most varieties of this nutrient-rich vegetable are disease- and pest-resistant and tolerant of drought, heat, and cold.

Pollinator-attracting Plants

Check with your local garden center to find out what the best native pollinator-attracting plants are in your region. In our area, my favorite native pollinator-attracting plants are butterfly milkweed, swamp milkweed, common milkweed, beebalm, New England aster, St. John's wort, leadplant, New Jersey tea, Tradescantia, black-eyed Susan, gray-headed coneflower, blue false indigo, and selfheal.

▲ *Butterfly milkweed.*

▲ *Swamp milkweed.*

▲ *New England aster.*

▲ *Common milkweed.*

▲ *St. John's wort.*

▶ *Beebalm.*

Low-growing Fruit

▲ *Alpine strawberries.*

▲ *Everbearing strawberries.*

Alpine strawberries, *Fragaria vesca,* a low-growing perennial groundcover that is hardy in zones 5 to 9, are an everbearing variety that yields multiple flushes of delicious small berries. They help to suppress weeds and prevent erosion, growing well as an understory plant in partial sun to partial shade, and prefer rich, moist, organic soils that are slightly acidic. These compact plants typically grow between 5" and 8" tall and spread by way of the runners.

Everbearing strawberries, *Fragaria × ananassa,* low-growing perennials that provide intermittent harvests from spring through fall, are very easy to grow but must be mulched thoroughly with straw to suppress weeds. We had great luck with a day-neutral variety from Nourse Farms called Evie 2 that is hardy in zones 4 to 8 in well-drained soils with a pH of 6.5 to 6.8. From our experience, this variety was mostly pest- and disease-resistant.

▲ *Garden Huckleberries.*

Garden Huckleberries (*Solanum melanocerasum*) are not frost hardy but will grow well in most zones in full sun and well-drained soil. They can be started by seed and may fruit within 2 months, reaching about 2 feet high. They make a wonderful annual in the garden, producing small dark purple/black berries that must be cooked or boiled before eaten. The unripe green berries are poisonous. Caution should be taken because a close relative in the nightshade family is very poisonous. Be sure you plant and label the right variety. Some nightshade varieties grow like weeds.

Wintergreen berries, *Gaultheria procumbens,* an evergreen groundcover native to eastern North America, is hardy in zones 3 to 8. It grows well in full and partial shade in moist, rich, well-drained soils that are slightly acidic. Fruit appears in the fall and lasts through the winter. The bright red edible berries can be eaten raw or made into jellies.

Culinary Herbs

Perennial and Mediterranean herbs are best suited for guild plantings. However, annual herbs can be interplanted into guilds to maximize your garden space area.

Herbs can be grown in your kitchen window, in containers on your balcony or deck, or directly in your yard. I have even experimented with bringing containers inside mid-fall to keep the herbs as houseplants for the winter. Parsley, sage, rosemary, and lemon verbena have done the best with this method.

I like to stock up on culinary herbs throughout the season because most offer an array of healing properties. After they hang-dry or dehydrate, I make a blend that includes thyme, oregano, sage, basil, savory, mint, lemon balm, echinacea root, chamomile, and dandelion leaves and store it in a Mason jar. Throughout the winter, I prepare tea from this for my family and myself to boost our immune systems and to aid in the relief of cold and flu symptoms. Herbs also improve respiratory function, purify the blood, cleanse the liver and kidneys, and relieve stomach upsets. Most of the culinary herbs also contain antibacterial and antiviral properties.

Below is a list of some of my favorite culinary herbs, followed by medicinal herbs that are regular fixtures in my garden.

▲ *A variety of basil.*

▲ *Anise hyssop.*

Anise hyssop, *Agastache foeniculum* (perennial/ full sun/ prefers warm to hot weather/ prefers well drained soil)

Culinary uses: Anise hyssop flowers have a delightful flavor and are a great addition to salads.

Medicinal properties: The leaves can be made into a soothing tea that tastes like black licorice. Anise hyssop has been used historically to treat cold and flu symptoms and relieve congestion.

Basil, *Ocimum basilicum* (annual/full sun/likes warm weather/prefers well drained and moist soil)

Culinary uses: Basil is known for its unique flavor and for being crushed into pesto. It makes a wonderful addition to pasta sauces,

sandwiches, salads, and many Italian dishes. Purple basil can be crushed into delicious pink lemonade. Lemon basil can be used to flavor fish or poultry. Cinnamon basil makes a delicious tea. Holy basil (tulsi) also makes a wonderful tea and is considered a sacred herb in many religions.

Medicinal properties: Basil has strong antibacterial and antioxidant properties. It helps alleviate indigestion, cold and flu symptoms, asthma, and bronchitis. It is high in magnesium and helps to improve blood flow.

The plethora of basil varieties include purple basil, African blue basil, and Siam Queen Thai basil, which can be grown from seed or transplanted starts. Other well-known varieties, including lemon basil and cinnamon basil, each have their own unique flavor characterized by their names.

▲ *Common chives.*

▲ *Garlic chives.*

Chives, *Allium schoenoprasum* (perennial/full sun/tolerates warm and cool weather/prefers fertile soil that is moist and well-drained)

Culinary uses: Chive leaves have a mild onion/garlic flavor and are an excellent addition to any savory meal. They are easily cut with kitchen scissors. The flowers are also edible.

Medicinal properties: Chives have antioxidant properties and help to lower cholesterol and blood pressure. They are high in vitamins A, C, and K and rich in calcium and iron.

Garlic chives, *Allium tuberosum* (perennial/full sun/tolerates warm and cool weather/ prefers fertile soil that is moist and well drained)

Garlic chives are a wonderful perennial herb that can be used just like common chives. Garlic chives have long, slender, flat leaves. They do spread quickly, so be mindful where you place them in your garden.

Culinary uses: Garlic chives have a robust garlic flavor and are a wonderful addition to any savory dish. They resemble leeks in that their leaves are flat, as opposed to standard chives, which are hollow and tubular.

Medicinal properties: Garlic chives have antibacterial properties and can be applied to minor skin ailments such as bites or scrapes to aid in healing. The leaves can aid in digestion and improve kidney function.

Cilantro, *Coriandrum sativum* (annual/full sun/likes cool or mild weather/prefers well drained soil)

Culinary uses: Cilantro is notorious for its love-it-or-hate-it reputation around the world. It is known for its unique flavor in salsa but has also been used in several ethnic cuisines.

Medicinal properties: It aids in digestion, eases pain in menstrual cramps, and helps to

▲ *Cilantro.*

relieve colic in infants after breastfeeding mother drinks cilantro tea.

Coriander: I love adding coriander, the flavorful seeds of the cilantro plant, to curry, soups, stews, salsa, and rice dishes.

Dill, *Anethum graveolens* (annual/full sun/ likes cooler weather/prefers well-drained soil)

▲ *Dill.*

Culinary uses: Dill is known for its unique slightly salty addition to pickled cucumbers. I use dill as a natural salt substitute.

Medicinal properties: It aids in digestion, is soothing for anxiety, and is rich in mineral salts.

Epazote herb, *Dysphania ambrosioides* (annual/ full sun/prefers warm weather/well-drained soil)

Culinary uses: Epazote, native to Central and South America, was highly revered by Aztec cultures for its culinary and medicinal uses. It has a very distinct flavor. Do not consume epazote seeds and flowering tops, as the seeds are poisonous. Its use is contraindicated for pregnant women.

Medicinal properties: Epazote has a number of minerals and vitamins including B vitamins, folate, as well as antioxidants. It has been historically used to treat digestive upsets, boost immunity, and enhance metabolic activity.

▲ *Fennel.*

Fennel, *Foeniculum vulgare* (annual/full sun/likes warm weather/prefers well drained moist soil)

Culinary uses: Fennel bulb is an aromatic herb with a flavor like anise or licorice. The bulb can be chopped, tossed in olive oil and, roasted with root vegetables or added to soups and salads. There are specific seed varieties for fennel herb and fennel bulb plants.

Bronze fennel is an amazing herb that produces an abundance of fennel herb. Varieties such as Orion fennel produce a large bulb that can be harvested and chopped to add to roasted vegetables.

Medicinal properties: Fennel has been used to treat anxiety and depression, as well as digestive upsets and colic in babies.

sugar or honey infused with concentrated herb tea, is delicate and tasty.

Medicinal properties: For centuries, lemon balm has been called the "vitality herb" and used to treat ailments including anxiety, cold and flu symptoms, fever, digestive complaints, headaches, and insomnia. Lemon balm can also act as a natural insect repellent; crush a handful of leaves and rub them on your skin.

▲ *Lemon verbena.*

Lemon verbena, *Aloysia citrodora* (tender perennial/full sun to partial sun/prefers warm-hot temperatures and rich well-drained soil)

Culinary uses: Lemon verbena, with its extraordinary lemony aroma and flavor, offers a lovely addition to salads and tea.

Medicinal properties: Lemon verbena has been used historically for relieving digestive issues. It can help reduce heartburn and, as a mild sedative, offer soothing support for anxiety and insomnia.

▲ *Lemon Balm.*

Lemon Balm, *Melissa officinalis* (perennial/full sun/ likes warm weather/prefers moist and fertile soil)

Culinary uses: Use lemon balm, cut into thin strips with scissors, fresh in salads, as a garnish for fish, or to make a delicious tea or elixir. Lemon balm cordial, a syrupy liquor made from

▲ *Lovage.*

▲ *Mint.*

Lovage, *Levisticum officinale* (perennial/full sun/ tolerates warm and cool weather/prefers moist soil)

Culinary uses: Lovage, also known as cutting celery, has a strong and crisp celery-like flavor but with more floral notes. It can grow up to 6 feet tall. Fresh or dried lovage makes a good addition to vegetable stock and savory dishes such as soups, stews, and casseroles.

Medicinal properties: Lovage has been used to treat headaches, digestive upsets, and fatigue.

Mint, *Mentha L.* (perennial/full sun or partial shade/likes warm weather/thrives in various soil conditions)

Mint will spread profusely so it is best to plant in containers unless you want an area completely overtaken with it.

Culinary uses: Mint makes a wonderful fresh addition to Thai and Vietnamese dishes, as well as fruit salads and ice cream. Mint and yogurt are a surprisingly delicious combination, as in Mediterranean cucumber salad. It can also

be used in many beverages like lemonade and various cocktails.

Medicinal properties: Mint has a cooling effect on the body, is great for the digestive system, and is helpful in easing fevers. Mint tea makes a great soothing gargle for sore throats. My favorite mint varieties include ginger mint, apple mint, chocolate mint, and pineapple mint.

▲ *Oregano.*

Oregano, *Origanum vulgare* (perennial/full sun/ likes warmer weather/prefers well drained soil)

Culinary uses: Oregano, known for its potent flavor in Italian and Greek foods, has actually been used worldwide for centuries. Its zesty flavor complements many savory dishes, such as soups, stews, sauces, beans, and rice.

Medicinal properties: Oregano has antibiotic, antibacterial, and antifungal properties. Tea made from fresh or dried oregano is good for aiding in digestion, relieving menstrual cramps, and easing coughs and colds.

▲ *Papalo.*

Papalo, *Porophyllum ruderale* (annual/full sun to partial sun/ tolerates warm temperatures)

Papalo, used commonly in Mexico and South America, has a unique flavor, a combination of cilantro and hot peppers. Unlike cilantro, papalo plants tolerate hot temperatures.

Culinary uses: Papalo can be used as a cilantro substitute in salsa, soups, or stews. A little goes a long way.

Medicinal properties: Papalo has been used historically by cultures in Mexico and South America to reduce high blood pressure and to aid in stomach disorders.

▲ *Flat leaf parsley.*

Parsley, *Petroselinum crispum* (biennial/full sun/ tolerates warm and cool weather/prefers moist well-drained soil)

Culinary uses: Parsley, a wonderfully flavorful herb, can be used fresh in salads or added to smoothies. Notorious for its reputation as a garnish, it makes a fresh and delicious addition to any savory dish. There are primarily two different types, curled and flat leaf. Parsley is the key ingredient in tabouli.

Medicinal properties: Parsley, one of the most medicinal culinary herbs, is high in iron, calcium, vitamins K, A, C, and B vitamins. It is rich in antioxidants, has anticancer properties, helps to strengthen the immune system, can aid in digestion, and offers relief for colds and flu.

▲ *Sage.*

▲ *Rosemary.*

Rosemary, *Rosmarinus officinalis* (tender perennial in northern climates/full sun/likes warm weather/needs well-drained soil)

Culinary uses: Rosemary is a lovely culinary herb that pairs well with root vegetables, such as potatoes and turnips, and in bread.

Medicinal properties: This nutrient-rich herb contains phytonutrients as well as iron, potassium, and calcium. It is high in vitamins A and C and has antioxidant, antibacterial, and anti-inflammatory properties. It has been used to treat depression, headaches, as well as cold and flu symptoms.

Sage, *Salvia officinalis* (hardy perennial/full sun/likes warmer weather/prefers light well-drained soil)

Culinary uses: Sage, most commonly used in homemade stuffing, is also a delicious addition to many savory dishes including soups and hearty stews. Pan-fried sage turns crispy and silvery and makes a great addition to pastas or butternut squash bisque.

Medicinal properties: Sage has a very long history as being a highly revered medicinal herb. This tonic herb can be used to treat colds, flu viruses, fevers, and sore throats. It has been used in First Nations cultures for centuries as a smudging and clearing herb.

Thyme, *Thymus vulgaris* (perennial/full sun/likes warm weather/prefers well-drained soil)

Thyme, one of the most cold-hardy herbs, will be found alive and well under a layer of ice in the herb garden.

▲ *Thyme.*

Culinary uses: Thyme, one of my favorite herbs to use in every savory dish, has a rich spicy flavor that is excellent in soups, hearty stews, pasta dishes, and breads.

Medicinal properties: An antiseptic herb, thyme aids in digestion, alleviates cold symptoms, clears congestion in the lungs, helps to eliminate toxins in the body, and reduces fever, chills, aches, and pains. Drink a honey-sweetened tea steeped with fresh or dried thyme.

Medicinal Herbs

Medicinal herbs can be grown from seed or transplants. It is best to source perennial divisions or cuttings locally to be sure the varieties are acclimated to your environment. Check with a herb-loving friend or your local herbalist, who can be found through a nearby herb store, apothecary shop, or health food store.

Perennial divisions are simply a small portion of an established plant that is typically cut with a shovel (roots and all); the mother plant will still

▲ *This image illustrates a variety of medicinal herbs.*

thrive. Transplant this into a pot or directly into the ground. It will most likely take it a while to recover from transplant shock while it gets used to the new growing conditions. As long as it is buried deep enough and gets adequate sun and water, it should grow well. Some plant nurseries sell medicinal plant starts that can be directly transplanted into your medicinal herb garden.

The following are some of my favorite medicinal herbs to grow.

▲ *Calendula.*

Calendula, *Calendula officinalis* (annual that reseeds itself/full sun/likes warmer weather)

Calendula, one of my favorite herbs, has edible flowers that make nice decorations to cakes and cupcakes.

Medicinal properties: Calendula flowers accelerate healing and have been used to aid the lymphatic system. A first-aid salve help heal minor cuts and scrapes. Calendula is antifungal, anti-inflammatory, antimicrobial, and antispasmodic and is a known astringent, with diaphoretic properties.

▲ *Borage.*

Borage, *Borago officinalis* (annual that reseeds itself/full sun/likes warmer weather)

Borage is a beautiful plant with edible young leaves and bluish-purple flowers, which attract beneficial pollinators. Used medicinally since medieval times, it is known for its antidepressant and anti-inflammatory properties. Borage flowers are mostly used in salads and to decorate cupcakes.

Chamomile, *Matricaria chamomilla* (annual that reseeds itself/full sun & partial shade/does well in moderate warm weather)

Chamomile flowers have one of the most magical aromas. Chamomile soothes the mind, body, and spirit and, as a mild sedative, aids in sleep. It can help alleviate headaches, skin

▲ *Chamomile.*

rashes, digestive upsets, and menstrual cramps. Chamomile is safe for children in small doses. It is anti-allergenic, antibacterial, anti-inflammatory, antifungal, antiseptic, and antispasmodic.

▲ *Purple coneflower.*

Purple coneflower, *Echinacea purpurea* (perennial/full sun/likes warmer weather)

Echinacea is an amazing medicinal herb. The whole plant can be used. As a herbalist, I have been making tinctures for years, my favorite being an immune-strengthening tincture that includes echinacea. When made into a salve, echinacea can treat minor cuts, wounds, scrapes, or burns. In root form, it helps to alleviate and reduce cold and flu symptoms and boosts the immune system. Echinacea is anti-inflammatory, antiviral, antifungal, and antibacterial and acts as a blood purifier.

▲ *Hibiscus roselle.*

Hibiscus roselle, *Hibiscus sabdariffa* (full sun/moist well-drained soils)

Roselle is a lovely species of hibiscus native to West Africa but grown worldwide. Hardy in zones 8 to 11, it can also grow as an annual in lower zones. We grow it as an annual in zone 6a, and it produces beautifully. Roselle can grow up to 8 feet tall and 5 or more feet wide in warmer zones. The vibrant red calyces, left behind after blooming, can be eaten fresh or dried and made into lovely teas, jellies, or syrups.

Medicinal properties: Roselle calyces are used medicinally around the world. One of the applications is helping to lower blood pressure. Roselle has been used historically in folk medicine as a diuretic herb. Some cultures use the young leaves in soups and stews.

▲ *Lavender.*

Lavender, *Lavandula augustifolia* or *L. officinalis* (perennial/annual/full sun/likes warm weather/ prefers sandy well-drained soil)

Some varieties are perennials in parts of the world. Check to see which variety grows best for your region.

Lavender also has many culinary uses. It is the spotlight herb in Herbes de Provence, a popular blend containing savory, oregano, rosemary, and thyme. With its sweet flowery flavor, lavender makes a delightful addition to lemonade and granola and sweets such as cookies and scones. Lavender lemon shortbread cookies are one of my favorites. Lavender honey lemonade is a refreshing summertime drink.

Medicinal properties: Lavender has a soothing effect on the body. It can be used to treat digestive upsets. It has antibacterial and antiviral properties and is rich in antioxidants.

▲ *Mullein.*

Mullein, *Verbascum thaspus* (perennial/ full sun or partial shade/likes warmer weather)

Mullein, which is found in the wild in glades and along streams and rivers throughout North America, can also be planted from seed. It grows in a rosette pattern, forming a large central stalk in its second year. Mullein grows in zones 3 to 9, is drought and heat tolerant, and attracts pollinators.

Medicinal properties: Mullein is a lung tonic herb and can help alleviate symptoms of respiratory ailments such as asthma and lung deficiency.

Stinging nettles, *Urtica dioica* (full sun and partial shade/well-drained, nutrient-rich soils)

Native to North America, Asia, Europe, and Africa, stinging nettles grow wild in woodlands, prairies, and savannas They can also be propagated from seed, or divisions can be taken

▲ *Stinging nettles.*

▲ *St. John's wort.*

from established plants. The stingers are very unpleasant on the skin, so use precaution when working with nettles.

One of the most amazing medicinal herbs, they are used to treat cold and flu, digestive upsets, and skin disorders and are a good tonic for the urinary tract, kidneys, heart, and lungs. Stinging nettles are also revered as a wild edible, eaten by Native Americans for their high-nutrient content, rich in iron, potassium, calcium, and vitamin C. The leaves can be made into a nutrient rich infusion. Simply boil a pot of water and add stinging nettle leaves. Simmer on low for 30 minutes. Allow nettles to steep overnight. Strain through cheesecloth. Soak the leaves in water or lightly steam or boil to remove the stingers. Plants grow up to 4 feet tall.

St. John's wort, *Hypericum perforatum* (perennial/full sun/likes warmer weather)

St. John's wort is a mood-enhancing and uplifting herb used to treat anxiety, sleep disorders,

and mild depression. Its tiny yellow flowers "bleed" red when crushed.

Medicinal properties: St. John's wort is alterative, antifungal, and antispasmodic and acts as an astringent, blood purifier, diuretic, nervine, and sedative.

▲ *Tulsi.*

Tulsi (Holy Basil), *Ocimum tenuiflorum* (tender perennial/ full sun/likes warmer weather)

Holy basil, an aromatic herb that has both culinary and medicinal value, likely originated in India, where it is revered as an incarnation of the Hindu goddess, Tulsi. It plays an important role in Ayurvedic medicine. Tea made from the leaves can ease cold and flu symptoms, inflammation, and digestive upsets. Tulsi is antibacterial, antifungal, anti-inflammatory, and antioxidant.

▲ Yarrow.

is alterative, antifungal, antiseptic, astringent, diaphoretic, homeostatic, and a stimulant.

Edible Flowers

Edible flowers can be grown as a lovely addition to an edible landscape. Research each variety to check for height and sun requirements.

▲ Wormwood.

Wormwood, *Artemisia absinthium* (perennial/full sun/likes warmer weather)

Wormwood is a spectacular silvery plant that grows extremely tall and spreads quickly. An anthelmintic herb, it helps to expel parasites from the body and is also used to treat digestive upsets including nausea and heartburn. Wormwood is anti-inflammatory, anthelmintic, antipyretic, antiseptic, and tonic.

Yarrow, *Achillea millefolium* (perennial/full sun/likes warmer weather)

Yarrow, a delicate-looking aromatic herb, can be used to stop bleeding, treat cold and flu symptoms, and purify the blood. Yarrow

▲ A mix of edible flowers (yarrow, borage, calendula, cilantro).

My favorite edible flowers include: anise hyssop, apple blossoms, basil, black locust, borage, calendula, chamomile, chervil, chicory, chives, chrysanthemum, coriander, crabapple blossoms, dandelion, dianthus, dill, day lilies, English daisy, fennel, garden peas, garden sage, grape hyacinth, hibiscus (rose of China and rose of Sharon), hyssop, lavender, lemon balm, lemon blossoms, marigolds (pot marigold, African marigold, and signet marigold), marjoram, mustard, okra, orange blossoms, oregano, nasturtiums, pansies, pineapple sage, plum blossoms, radish, redbud, red clover, rose petals, rosemary, scarlet runner beans, scented geraniums, squash blossoms, summer savory, thyme, violets, winter savory, and yucca.

Groundcover Layer

Red clover, *Trifolium pratense*, a wonderful perennial groundcover, is a nitrogen-fixing plant

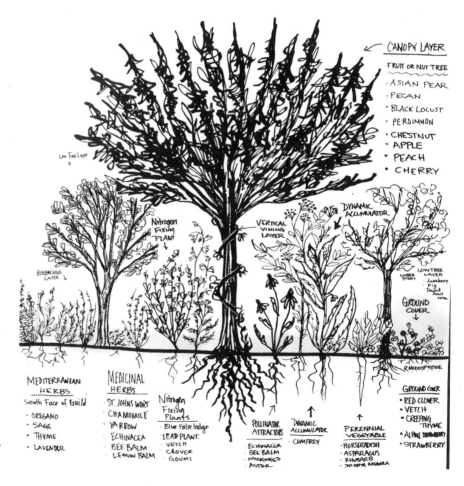

▶ This image illustrates the low-growing plants of the groundcover layer.

▲ *Red clover.*

that provides food for pollinators and has medicinal properties. It is heat-tolerant, cold-hardy, drought-resistant, and has low pest pressure.

Creeping thyme, *Thymus serpyllum*, an exceptional lawn substitute, is easy to grow and hardy to zones 4 to 9. It forms dense mats and spreads sporadically but can blanket a small area in a few years. Creeping thyme is edible and can be used just like regular thyme. It attracts pollinators and provides a protective layer over the soil.

Violets, *Viola odorata*, a lovely low-growing groundcover, have beautiful edible and medicinal dark green leaves and vibrant purple flowers. Hardy in zones 3 to 9, they are one of the first flowers to bloom in the spring.

▲ *Violets.*

Corsican mint, *Mentha requienii*, a low-growing groundcover that is hardy to zones 6 to 10, grows best in shade but can handle some sun. It is not a drought-tolerant plant, so it needs to be watered regularly for optimal growth. It is self-seeding and does spread quickly. It has a lovely aroma and a strong mint flavor.

Vertical Layer

The **American groundnut,** (*Apios americana*) is a deciduous nitrogen-fixing perennial vine, hardy in zones 3 to 10, that produces edible beans and tubers. Boil the tubers for 20 minutes

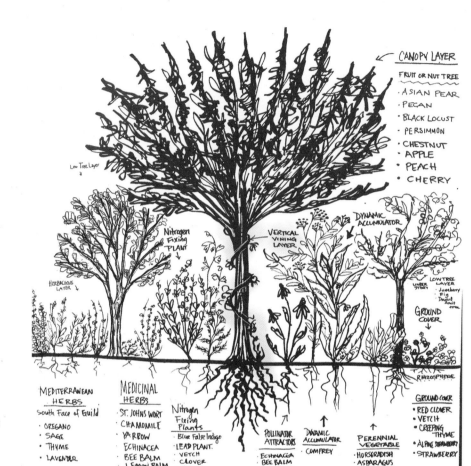

CANOPY LAYER

FRUIT OR NUT TREE
· ASIAN PEAR
· PECAN
· BLACK LOCUST
· PERSIMMON
· CHESTNUT
· APPLE
· PEACH
· CHERRY

Low Tree Layer

Nitrogen Fixing PLANT

DYNAMIC ACCUMULATOR

VERTICAL VINING LAYER

HERBACEOUS LAYER

UNDER STORY

LOW TREE LAYER
· Juneberry
· Fig
· Dwarf fruit tree

GROUND COVER

RHIZOSPHERE

MEDITERRANEAN HERBS
South Face of Guild
· OREGANO
· SAGE
· THYME
· LAVENDER

MEDICINAL HERBS
· ST. JOHNS WORT
· CHAMOMILE
· YARROW
· ECHINACEA
· BEE BALM
· LEMON BALM

Nitrogen Fixing Plants
· Blue False Indigo
· LEAD PLANT
· VETCH
· CLOVER
· GOUMI

POLLINATOR ATTRACTORS
· ECHINACEA
· BEE BALM
· MILKWEED
· ASTER

DYNAMIC ACCUMULATOR
· COMFREY

PERENNIAL VEGETABLE
· HORSERADISH
· ASPARAGUS
· RHUBARB
· SYLVETTA ARUGULA

GROUND COVER
· RED CLOVER
· VETCH
· CREEPING THYME
· ALPINE STRAWBERRY
· STRAWBERRY

► *This image illustrates the vertical layer.*

▲ *Passionflower.*

before eating. It can grow over 6 feet high, taller in some climates. The flowers attract pollinators.

Passionflower, *Passiflora incarnata,* a vining perennial that is hardy in zones 5 to 10, grows well in full sun and partial shade. It produces gorgeous otherworldly flowers that attract many pollinators and have medicinal properties, primarily as a sedative and sleep aid. The passionflower vine produces dozens of edible passion fruits.

CREATE CULTIVATED ECOLOGIES

Find out which plants are rare, dwindling, or are on the endangered plant list in your area and grow them in your own yard. In our region, ginseng, goldenseal, echinacea, Solomons seal, bloodroot, and trillium are dwindling in population. Whenever possible, I plant these seeds in our garden.

▶ *A variety of native plants we have cultivated in our own garden.*

Fun Facts

Some shade loving landscape plants have edible parts! The fiddlehead portion of the ostrich fern is edible when cooked.

Hostas, when they first emerge as shoots, are edible.

▲ *Rosa Rugosa Rosa rugosa is the variety of rose that provides medicinal rose hips.*

▲ *In Ann and Barry Stevens' yard, ostrich fern and hostas look beautiful in a shade-loving edible landscape.*

TREES TO CONSIDER FOR A LARGER PROPERTY

▲ *Birch tree.*

Birch (*Betula L.*)

Birch trees have been used historically to make canoes. There are several varieties of birch trees. The river birch, native to the southeastern US, is especially beautiful in a landscape. This fast-growing tree reaches 90 feet, grows well in full sun or full shade, is heat tolerant, and is hardy to zones 4 to 9. This semi-aquatic tree grows along rivers, floodplains, and lakes and provides a natural source of erosion control. Its sap can be tapped to make into a lovely syrup.

Black Locust (*Robinia pseudoacacia*)

The black locust tree, thought to be native to the Appalachian Mountain Range in the eastern US, has become naturalized throughout other regions and portions of southern Canada. A rapid spreader, plant it only in areas where long-term land management will take place. The black locust has a myriad benefits: It fixes nitrogen, grows very quickly, makes a wonderful windbreak, and can provide shade for grazing animals. When interplanted with other crops, this tree has been found to enhance the growth of other species, including barley and black walnuts. The flowers, an excellent food source for honeybees, have an amazing aroma and are edible as well. The wood makes great firewood, as the tree grows quickly.

▲ *Black cherry tree.*

Black Cherry or Wild Cherry (*Prunus serotina*)

The black cherry tree is native to the US, including the east and southwest, as well as Europe. It grows well in forest environments in full to medium sun and in many soil types, reaching 60 to 100 feet high. It provides food and habitat for a variety of wildlife. The black cherries are edible and can be made into jams, jellies, or delicious wine. The inner bark of the small branches has medicinal properties when harvested and used in the right way. Check out herbrally.com to learn more.

▲ *Hazelnut tree.*

Hazelnut (*Corylus americana*)

North American hazelnut is native to North America; other varieties are native to Europe. The Arbor Day Foundation offers hybrid hazelnuts that are hardy to zones 3 to 9. The Arbor

Day Farm Hazelnut (*Corylus spp.*), hybridized to cross the characteristics of the European, American, and beaked hazelnut varieties, produces sweet, delicious hazelnuts in about 5 years, yielding approximately 7 pounds per bush. They grow well in full sun and moist well-drained, acidic soil. Hazelnuts can be incorporated into a variety of ecological agricultural systems, including silvopasture and agroforestry.

▲ *Eastern Redbud tree.*

Eastern Redbud (*Cercis canadensis*)

The eastern redbud tree, native to North America, often grows as an understory tree in oak-hickory forests of the midwestern US. It grows well in full sun and partial shade, tolerates many well-drained soil types, reaches heights of 35 feet, and is hardy in zones 4 to 9. Its beautiful pink flowers that bloom in April are an excellent source of food for pollinators. They can be added to salads and as a garnish to cakes, cookies, and cupcakes.

▲ *Trifoliate orange tree.*

Trifoliate Orange (*Citrus trifoliata* or *Poncirus trifoliata*)

The trifoliate or hardy orange, native to northern and central China, is hardy in zones 5 to 9 and grows well in full sun and well-drained soils. This tree is drought tolerant, and grows up to 20 feet, and is covered in large, sharp thorns. The edible fruit, which resemble small-medium oranges, are very seedy and bitter and are best made into a marmalade or juiced. Hardy orange trees make a wonderful hedgerow or living fence line.

Pecan Tree (*Carya illinoinensis*)

The *Carya illinoinensis* pecan grows up to 100 feet in full sun and a variety of well-drained soil

▲ *Pecan tree.*

types, hardy in zones 6 to 9. This tree starts producing delicious and nutritious nuts within 6 to 10 years, yielding up to 150 pounds per year.

Gingko (*Gingko biloba*)

The *Gingko biloba* tree, native to China, is hardy in zones 3 to 8. It grows well in full sun and moist well-drained sandy soils, reaching heights of 80 feet. The gingko tree is drought tolerant, adapts well to many different urban environments, and is resistant to most pests and diseases. Its leaves have been used historically as medicine.

▲ *Gingko tree.*

Kousa Dogwood (*Cornus kousa*)

The Kousa dogwood, native to China, Japan, and Taiwan, is hardy in zones 5 to 8. It grows well in full sun to partial shade and in well-drained rich soils, reaches heights of 10 to 30 feet, and is resistant to most pests and diseases. The large edible pink to red fruits ripen in early fall, are yellow or orange inside, and have an apricot-like texture with the flavor of an apple. The fruit can be eaten raw or made into jellies.

The following are not optimal for guild plantings but are otherwise great trees to plant.

Black Walnut (*Juglans nigra*)

The black walnut tree, native to large portions of the US and Canada, grows well in full or partial sun and prefers moist deep, rich soil, reaching heights of 120 feet. Young transplanted trees need to be subjected to cold temperatures for at least 90 days in order to produce nuts, which starts after 5 years. The highly nutritious

nuts are also an important food source for wildlife. These trees do produce a chemical called juglone that prohibits a lot of other plants from growing within 60 feet of the trunk. Annuals and vegetables are sensitive to black walnut toxicity, but variety of trees tolerate black walnut toxicity. Research all plants affected by black walnut toxicity before you place black walnuts in your yard or on your property.

▲ *Sugar maple tree.*

Sugar Maple (*Acer saccharum*)

The sugar maple tree, native in northeastern US and portions of Canada, can live over 400 years and typically reaches 80 to 110 feet or taller. It is hardy in zones 3 to 8a, grows well in full sun, and tolerates partial shade. It is well-known for the sap that can be boiled down into pure maple syrup. Leaves turn a striking golden and red in the fall.

▲ *Oak tree.*

Oak (*Quercus L.*)

The oak, a wonderful tree that grows very large, provides shade, food, and habitat for wildlife, and is excellent for large plots of land, specifically in savanna ecosystems. Edible acorns include those from the white oak (*Quercus alba*) and the bur oak, and chestnut groups including chestnut oak (*Quercus prinus*), swamp white oak (*Quercus bicolor*), and chinquapin oak (*Quercus muehlenbergii*). The bur oak produces very large tasty acorns and require the least processing. Leech out the bitter tannins by soaking acorns in salt water for a couple of days, changing it a few times daily. Another method is to add acorns to boiling water and simmer them for 15 to 20 minutes. They can be then ground and add to baked goods or oven roasted, dried, and ground into a flour. All oaks produce acorns. Caution: Do not use the acorns from the red oak, black oak, or pin oak as they are poisonous and contain phenolics.

▲ *Calamondin orange tree.*

Indoor Citrus (*Citrus L.*)

Kumquats, Meyer lemons, limes, and key limes can all be grown indoors in a sunny window in regions that experience harsh winters.

GROWING MUSHROOMS

Several varieties of mushrooms can be easily grown in your backyard.

▲ *Wine cap stropharia mushrooms.*

Wine cap stropharia mushrooms are among the easiest to grow. The fresh spawn, which is available through Field & Forest Products, can be sprinkled on a thick layer of chip mulch in a weed-free bed, preferably under the shade of a tree or perennial plants. Cover with 1 to 2 inches of mulch and then water. They grow to the size of small portabellas and can be cooked and sautéed just as you would those.

Mushroom Inoculation

Mushroom inoculation can be done easily at home. Several DIY tutorial videos are available online. We have successfully inoculated logs with shiitake, hen of the woods, lion's mane, oyster, and reishi mushrooms and grown lion's mane, pink and gold oyster, and shiitake in bags.

▲ *Mushroom harvest from Ozark Forest Mushrooms.*

Inoculating a Log with Mushroom Plug Spawn (Early to Late Spring)

This method, from a Field and Forest tutorial, works well for shiitake and reishi plug spawn.

You will need several logs, ideally red or white oak, but sugar maple and sweetgum would also work, preferably from healthy trees. We tend to go for live trees that have fallen from a storm or in an area that needs to be thinned to promote the growth of healthy native trees. The logs should be between 4 and 8 inches in diameter and nearly 3½ feet long.

Spawns come in different sizes. Use a cordless drill with a bit roughly the same size as your plug spawn or thimble spawn. Mark your bit at one inch with a piece of tape to drill holes that deep about 6 inches apart in 2 or 3 rows. Inoculate them with shiitake plugs with a foam seal or dowel plugs and brush melted

▲ *An example of inoculating on logs.*

beeswax over them. Be sure to label your logs with the date, type of spawn, and other pertinent information. Store them horizontally in a north-facing shady area of your yard. The ideal temperature range is 60°F to 85°F. Logs should be watered regularly to prevent them from drying out. Place them a couple of inches off the ground to permit air flow and to prevent them from being immersed in standing water.

It could be up to one year before the logs set fruit (produce mushrooms). Check them regularly and make a note of when they do. Mark your calendar for the following year so you will know when to expect them. The logs will continue to fruit from anywhere between 2 and 8 years.

Growing Oyster Mushrooms on a Stump Using the Totem Method

Using this method, adapted from a Field & Forest Products tutorial, you will need:

> 6 logs between 6 and 12 inches in diameter and 12 to 16 inches long
>
> 6 2-inch slices of the same stump (carefully cut with a chainsaw)
>
> 6 black plastic bags without fungicide
>
> Sawdust inoculated with mushrooms — 2½ pounds of sawdust spawn should inoculate roughly 6 logs
>
> 12 to 24 sheets of black-and-white newspaper
>
> 6 large heavy-duty rubber bands

Open the plastic bag and spread about 1 cup of sawdust spawn at the bottom until it is roughly an 8-inch circle. Place the large stump on top of the spawn in the bag. Spread about 2 cups of sawdust spawn evenly onto the top of the log (it should be about ¼" thick). Add the 2-inch slice of log. Spread 2 cups of sawdust spawn evenly on top of this layer. Cover with 2 or 3 sheets of newspaper and fasten with a rubber band.

There should be 3 total layers of sawdust inoculated with oyster spores between the components: in the bag underneath the stump, between the stump and the stump slice, and on the top of the stump slice.

Tie up the bag and place in a shady area of your basement for roughly 4 months. The ideal temperature for inoculation is between 60°F and 80°F. Move it outside into a shady location and remove from the bag. The log should fruit in late summer to early fall. Check logs regularly. They will continue to produce for 2 more years. Repeat the steps every 2 years to ensure a yearly mushroom harvest.

Tee Pee Oyster Kit

Another simple way to grow oyster mushrooms (especially with kids) is using the Tee Pee Oyster Kit from Field & Forest Products. Their 7-roll kit includes instructions as well as a 2-pound bag of oyster mushroom grain spawn, 7 filter bags, and 7 rubber bands.

Fill a large pot halfway with water and bring to a boil. Remove from heat. Clean work surface. Using a pair of tongs, dip the toilet paper rolls one at a time into the boiled water until they become fully saturated.

Place them on a rack to drain and cool. When cooled, transfer one to each filter bag. Shake the bag of spawn until the grains have separated. Cut a small opening in the corner of the spawn bag and carefully fill each of the inside tubes of the toilet paper rolls with the grain. Close each bag with a rubber band above the filter patch. Place the bags in a dark area where the temperature is between 65°F and 75°F. Within 3 weeks, a white coating, the mycelium, should appear. Let it grow for 1 to 3 more weeks. Four to 6 weeks after inoculation, place in the refrigerator for 48 hours. Then

remove and place in a sunny area at room temperature. Remove rubber bands and open the bags. Within 1 to 2 weeks, you should see the first mushrooms. Spray with water while they are developing. When they are about 2" wide, twist the base to harvest. Rinse well.

After you harvest, close the bag again, place in a dark area and repeat the process about 2 or 3 more times. Compost toilet paper rolls when no more mushrooms appear (after your third harvest).

To order mushroom inoculating supplies, visit fieldforest.net, mushroommountain.com, or fungi.com. Logs already inoculated with spores can be purchased and have good results, but with shorter periods of harvest time. Mushrooms can also be inoculated in straw and grown inside laundry baskets.

Ozark Forest Mushrooms, owned by Nicola and Dan MacPherson, is a farm in a Missouri Ozarks area that has been designated as one of the Last Great Places by the Nature Conservancy. It's a great example of how a business can be formed by growing and selling quality fresh mushrooms to restaurants, stores, and individuals at farmers markets. They practice healthy forest ecology while growing and harvesting a renewable supply of mushroom bed logs. Their draft horses naturally thin their forests under the Missouri Department of Conservation guidelines. This farm produces delicious mushrooms as well as value-added products. They have been advocates of the local foods movement for decades and continue to do their part in helping to create localized food systems.

▲ *Nicola McPherson of Ozark Forest Mushrooms.*

Chapter 7

Edible Landscaping Designs

WHEN PLANNING YOUR DESIGN, find out the plant's maximum height at maturity. Be sure to give the plant plenty of room to grow both in height and width. When locating it near a house, place it far enough away to not cause issues with the roots disturbing the foundation of the house. Be sure to not plant any larger tree species underneath a power line. Call DIG-RITE (or a local company that can give you information about buried utilities and sewer pipes) before planting any large tree.

Read the labels or research the different varieties before planting and be sure to place them according to height speci-fications. Plants that will reach tall heights should be located in the back

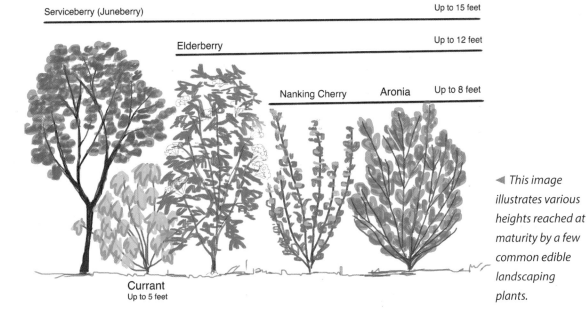

Serviceberry (Juneberry) — Up to 15 feet

Elderberry — Up to 12 feet

Nanking Cherry · Aronia — Up to 8 feet

Currant — Up to 5 feet

◄ *This image illustrates various heights reached at maturity by a few common edible landscaping plants.*

▲ *Container gardening can be a fun way to introduce the family to gardening. Container gardens minimize weed pressure. However, daily watering in periods of drought is necessary.*

of a landscape. Those that reach a medium height should go in front of the taller plants, with enough room for them to reach their full spanning potential. Smaller varieties could be placed in front of medium-sized ones. Finally, ground cover can be planted in the understory,

in front of small plants, and along the edges.

Below you will find some basic design ideas to use as a framework for choosing the design that works best for you.

SIMPLE FRONT YARD EDIBLE LANDSCAPE

A simple edible landscape design could start as small as 6 plants or be as extensive as you desire. Factors to consider are the amount of time you have to dedicate to weeding, watering, and general maintenance. This example shows roughly 30 plants in a small space. The back layer closest to the house could contain a variety of dwarf fruit trees, such as apple, pear, and peach. The next layer, which should be shorter, could contain fruit-producing shrubs, such as goumi, gooseberry, currant, honeyberry, raspberry, and Nanking cherry. The front and shortest layer could contain vegetables, strawberries, herbs, and flowers.

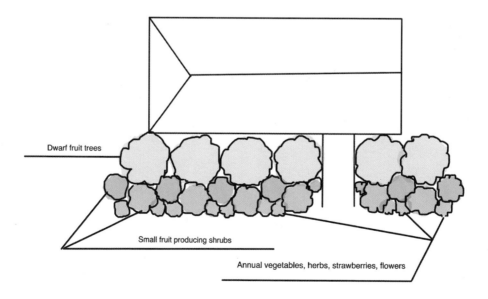

Dwarf fruit trees

Small fruit producing shrubs

Annual vegetables, herbs, strawberries, flowers

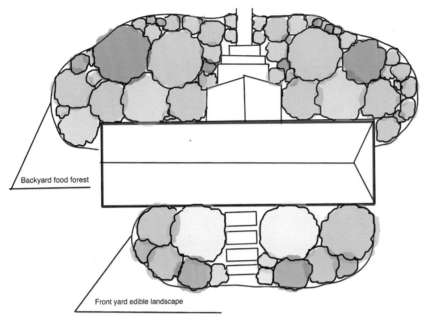

Backyard food forest

Front yard edible landscape

◀ *This image illustrates an extensive food forest planting in the backyard with various fruit trees, fruit-producing shrubs, perennial and annual vegetables, herbs, and pollinator-attracting flowers. The front landscape could contain dwarf fruit trees or fruit-bearing shrubs, perennial low-growing fruits such as strawberries, herbs, and flowers.*

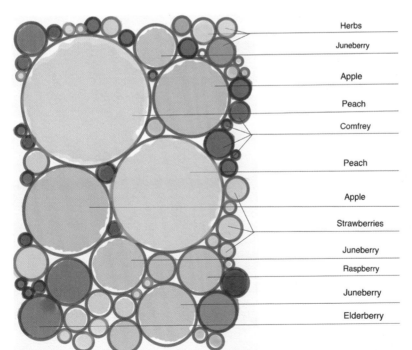

Herbs

Juneberry

Apple

Peach

Comfrey

Peach

Apple

Strawberries

Juneberry

Raspberry

Juneberry

Elderberry

◀ *This concept drawing illustrates the variety of fruit trees, fruit-producing shrubs, low-growing fruits, herbs, and comfrey. A path is not included in this example. The designer could create a path that allows easy access to water and equipment. It could be linear or meandering, but I would recommend creating multiple paths in a food forest to reach the various trees and shrubs. This food forest is planted in an organic fashion modeled after a forest.*

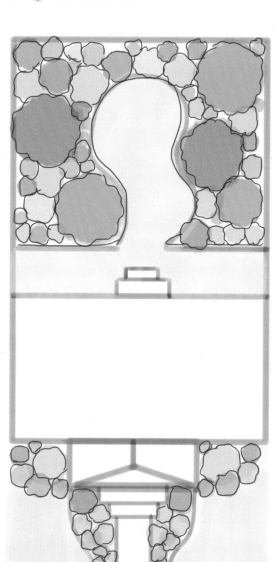

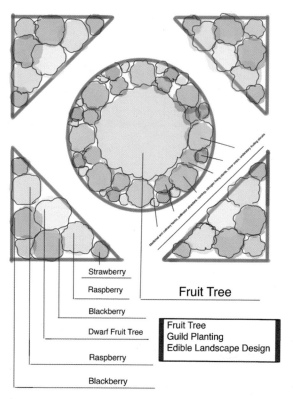

	Strawberry
	Raspberry
	Blackberry
	Dwarf Fruit Tree
	Raspberry
	Blackberry

Fruit Tree

Fruit Tree
Guild Planting
Edible Landscape Design

▲ This image illustrates a conceptual design that focuses on aesthetics and symmetry. A food forest can be contained within a central circle bordered by stone or rock edging and surrounded by gravel or mulched pathways. The corners contain small triangular beds filled with dwarf trees and smaller perennial fruits. Annual and perennial vegetables can be interplanted there as well.

▲ A keyhole design is an efficient design that helps to maximize space and promotes nutrient recycling. Soil can be built quickly in small spaces, therefore creating a healthy micro-ecosystem.

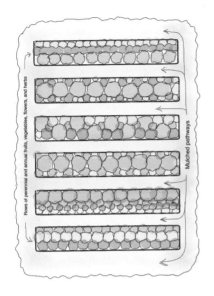

Rows of perennial and annual fruits, vegetables, flowers, and herbs

Mulched pathways

◀ *This farm-style backyard garden has mulched pathways and permanent raised beds for various fruits, vegetables, flowers, and herbs. Some can contain permanent perennial plantings while others beds grow annuals. Crop rotation can help increase soil fertility and reduce plant disease, pathogens, and pests. This cultivation style is easy to maintain and virtually weed-free if fresh soil is hauled in and there is enough mulch in the paths to suppress weeds.*

DESIGN IDEAS

Mapping out the layout of your farm, garden, or edible landscape before starting with planting will help you achieve the overall goals of the space. Mapping out the area after planting is complete will help to track and record information over time. Detailed maps can be very helpful for crop rotation, cover crop rotation, soil health, and future planting. A topographic map of your specific location can help assess terrain, slope, water flow, low spots where water could pool, etc.

◀ *This is a beautiful rendering of Matt Lebon's backyard food forest. In his backyard, pathways are mulched; beds are lined with stones; guilds are planted with fruit trees, pollinator attractors, perennial and annual vegetables, medicinal and culinary herbs, and understory fruit-producing shrubs.* Credit: Artwork by Eric Stevens.

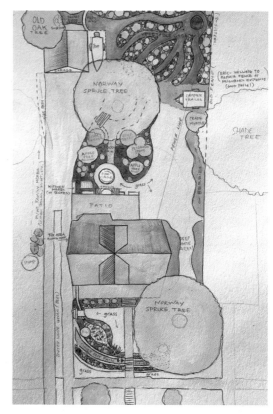

▲ *We designed and installed this front and backyard for a client. She and her partner wanted a front-yard rain garden, a pollinator garden, an edible landscape, a backyard food forest, a tea garden, a kitchen herb garden, and a backyard vegetable garden. The design focused on soil health, regenerative gardening, increasing biodiversity, and water retention.*

▲ ◄ Top and bottom left. *These images show an aerial view of EarthDance Organic Farm School. EarthDance is a 14-acre historic farm in Ferguson, MO. A linear permaculture orchard is planted on a berm and swale system. Between the rows are alley crops with annual vegetables.* Credit: Artwork by Eric Stevens.

As discussed in previous chapters, fruit tree guilds are a wonderful way to integrate biodiversity into your yard. Asian pear, Liberty apple, or tart cherry work well as the canopy layer (depending on your climate and zone). Serviceberry, elderberry, and aronia berry are good as the understory fruiting shrub layer. Sorrel and Egyptian walking onions are fine perennial vegetables, as is rhubarb, Turkish rocket broccoli, and sea kale (not pictured). Comfrey is an exceptional dynamic accumulator; blue false indigo helps to fix nitrogen, as does red clover, which also acts as a superb ground cover. Echinacea and yarrow are exceptional medicinal plants as well as pollinator attractors. Bee balm (not pictured) also fits in those categories.

◀ *This image illustrates an edible landscape design by Matt Lebon of Custom Foodscaping.* CREDIT: ARTWORK BY ERIC STEVENS.

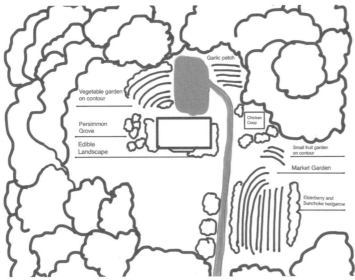

◀ *This is a basic drawing of our farm, which is surrounded by forest and woodland. We have planted several annual vegetable gardens, perennial fruit plots, a diversified vegetable market garden, a garlic patch, and an edible landscape.*

SORREL
Perennial
vegetable

ARONIA BERRY
Understory
fruit shrub

YARROW
Medicinal/
pollinator
attractor

**EGYPTIAN
WALKING ONIONS**
Allium family pest
deterrent/ perennial
vegetable

**BLUE
FALSE INDIGO**
Nitrogen fixer

**FRUIT
TREE**
Canopy
layer

RED CLOVER
Nitrogen fixer

COMFREY
Dynamic accumulator

ELDERBERRY
Understory fruit

RED CLOVER
Nitrogen fixer

ECHINACEA
Medicinal pollinator attractor

SERVICE BERRY
Understory fruit

SAGE OREGANO
Mediterranean perennial herbs

SMALL GARDENS

For beginning gardeners and budding green thumbs, it is best to start with small manageable spaces that focus on a small grouping of plants. For example, a kitchen garden, herb garden, tea garden, flower garden, or salsa garden could be installed and maintained easily with favorable conditions (water, sun, weed management plan).

A simple edible flower garden can be planted with nasturtium, calendula, and borage, all grown from seed in flats in early spring and transplanted in late spring. Nasturtium is a low-growing bushing plant that produces

gorgeous edible flowers and leaves that have a unique peppery flavor. They grow to about 2 feet tall; a climbing variety can reach up to 10 feet. Calendula plants grow to 3 feet tall and have gorgeous flowers that can be made into a tea or infused in oil for a moisturizing topical application. Borage plants, which can reach 4 feet tall, have small purple flowers and leaves that taste like cucumbers. Edible flower gardens would be a perfect niche garden or edible landscape garden for a baker who uses edible flowers to decorate sweet treats.

Medicinal and Culinary Herb Gardens

Medicinal herbs are easy to grow. Find out which native perennial medicinals are available as plant starts in your region. Some medicinal herbs are perennials and also attract pollinators. A medicinal herb garden or tea garden would be the perfect niche garden for a local tea shop, herbalist, or herb store.

Culinary herb gardens are fun and easy to grow in containers or garden beds and make a delightful addition to front or backyard edible landscapes. One would be the perfect niche

◀ *This image illustrates a simple medicinal herb garden.*

garden for a local restaurant that wants to use fresh herbs to garnish or enhance the flavors of their dishes.

No matter the design, your yard can act as the canvas and the plants as the paint. Have fun with designing the garden to match your needs. Choose your favorite plants, textures, colors, and design elements. The more you plant, the more you will learn. While there are so many guides and tutorials to help you along the way, learning by experiencing is inevitably often what makes the greatest impact and allows for the best lessons. As a designer, you get to transform your yard into an edible oasis, choosing the varieties that offer the most beauty and abundance for you.

▲ *This image illustrates a simple culinary herb garden planted with oregano, cilantro, basil, dill, common chives, and parsley.*

Chapter 8

Edible Landscape Showcase

I N THIS CHAPTER, you will find design inspiration, planting ideas, hardscaping suggestions, and a variety of images that illustrate designing for efficiency, interplanting, sheet mulching, weed suppression, maximizing bed square feet, and diverse plantings to increase yield.

START WITH A BLANK CANVAS OR PRE-EXISTING LANDSCAPE BED

▲ Starting with pre-formed beds and chip mulched pathways allows for a blank planting canvas.

▲ At the 13th Street Community Garden in North St. Louis, Jason Gerhardt has been building soil to increase organic matter with the help of community members. Because abandoned lots may contain heavy metals and toxins, Gerhardt practices extensive sheet mulching by adding several layers of straw and weed-free compost/topsoil blend. He lets the permanent raised beds age before planting in them.

Edging

▲ *Beds can be edged with a variety of materials including stone, brick, logs, or wood.*

▲ *Stones can be placed to border the edges of landscape beds.*

▲ *Larger flat landscape stones make a nice edging as well.*

◄ ▲ *Stone pathways allow easy access to crops. Flat landscape stones can be placed in pathways.*

▲ *Stacked bricks can be used to line herb or veggie beds.*

Weed Barriers

Using weed barriers is essential to low maintenance landscapes and foodscapes. As detailed in previous chapters, weed barriers include landscape fabric, plastic mulch, and sheet mulching.

▲ *At Flourish Farm, we build permanent raised beds. We line them with landscape fabric and sheet mulch the pathways with cardboard and chip mulch.*

▶ *This image illustrates stacking functions in permaculture. This chicken coop doubles as a tool shed and is located in close proximity to the house and main garden. It is adjacent to the outdoor dog pen, which helps to deter predators. The attached wire chicken run also acts as a trellis for cucumbers.*

▲ *At EarthDance Organic Farm School in Ferguson, fallen logs from the property are used to edge the herb beds. Pathways are sheet mulched using burlap sacks, cardboard, and chip mulch.*

▲ *This image illustrates multiple garden practices: weed barrier, interplanting, sheet mulching, and trellising.*

Trellising

Various trellising methods are used for growing food and specialty crops. Below are several examples of these methods.

▲ *The Florida weave method can also be used for peas in the spring. Pictured from left to right: Destinae, Jeremie, and Iris.*

▲ *At Flourish Farm, we use the string trellis method for tomatoes. To maximize space, we interplant squash, peppers, and herbs in our tomato patch. We use landscape fabric and mulch the pathways with chip mulch.*

▲ *The Florida weave method involves using twine or nylon trellis twine to contain plants between T-posts. Pictured here are tomatillos with the Florida weave method in the background and rows of rainbow chard in the foreground.*

▲ *This image illustrates a tall sturdy string trellis with hops vines growing. The trellis is fastened to the roof of the building as well as its base.*

▲ A treehouse can be adapted to add a trellis system for growing food. This treehouse was built out of reclaimed materials by my husband, Eric, and his friends, Michael and Jamie. Eric added a trellis system made out of slats of reclaimed wood. Planted at the base are gherkins.

▲ This gourd tunnel was built and planted with luffa (loofah) by Kaitie Adams at EarthDance Organic Farm School in Ferguson, MO. Tunnels made from PVC and fence paneling materials (or reclaimed materials) are a great way to grow vining crops.

▲ Cattle panel fencing can be used along with T-posts to create trellis for cucumbers or pole beans.

◀ Vining beans can be trellised along a stairwell.

◀ Iron fences can provide a trellis for grapes.

◀ This is a shaker-style trellis made from either long-fallen branches or bamboo. Poles, buried several inches beneath the soil surface for extra support, are placed like a teepee. A long horizontal post can rest between two or three teepees.

Raised Beds

▲ *Raised beds work especially well for school gardens. Beds can be made to the appropriate height depending on grade levels. They can also be built to be accessible and ADA compliant.*

▶ *Raised beds help keep crops contained. They make planting and harvesting easy.*

▶ *Planting herbs in raised beds are a great introduction for those new to gardening.*

◀ *Greenscape Gardens has a demonstration garden to show how many plants can fit in a few grow boxes.*

▲ *The Cowan family planted this raised bed garden in their front yard, which gets full sun. It contains beans, herbs, marigolds, cucumbers, and peppers. A lot of variety can fit into a small raised bed.*

▲ *Raised beds are perfect for small school gardens.*

Container Gardens

◄ *Balcony gardens work well for apartment dwellers. This is the St. Louis balcony of Connor and Jenna.*

▲ *A variety of herbs grow well together in containers.*

◄ *Several varieties of fruits and vegetables can grow together in one 8-gallon pot. In this container, there are berries, lettuce, and edible flowers.*

GUILDS

▲ *This is a 200-foot planting on a berm and swale system at EarthDance Organic Farm School in Ferguson, MO. The berm is covered with landscape fabric and a few inches of chip mulch. The guild contains several fruit trees, including paw paw, apple, Asian pear, peach, and cherry, as well as native pollinator-attracting plants such as yarrow, milkweed, golden Alexander, aster, and bee balm. Planted throughout the guild is comfrey, a dynamic accumulator; blue false indigo, a nitrogen fixer; a few dozen strawberry plants, as a perennial ground cover; gooseberries, Juneberries, and elderberries, to add continuous seasonal bounty.*

▲ *An example of a guild planting is a Three Sisters guild. Traditionally, tribes indigenous to North America and Mexico, specifically along the Mississippi River Valley, planted the Three Sisters (corn, beans, and squash) together as companion plants. Corn was planted near pole beans so that it could act as a trellis for the beans. The beans would vine up the corn stalks. Vining squash was planted around the corn and beans to act as a living mulch to suppress weeds, shade the soil, and preserve moisture. The vining squash also protects the crops from hungry predators.*

◀ *In this guild planting at EarthDance Organic Farm School, alley crops of annual vegetables grow between berm plantings. This berm is thriving with a variety of fruit trees, pollinator-attracting plants, understory shrubs, nitrogen-fixing plants, aromatic and medicinal herbs, and low-growing fruit.*

▲ *This is a closer look at a fruit tree guild planting at EarthDance Organic Farm School: several varieties of pear trees and paw paws, elderberries, gooseberries, saskatoon berries, dozens of species of native flowering pollinator-attracting plants, as well as aromatic herbs and culinary herbs.*

▲ *Here is a closer look at all of the biodiversity in the previous guild.*

▲ *This guild planting contains an Asian pear tree, milkweed, lemon balm, mint, and strawberries.*

▲ *This guild planting contains a paw paw tree, strawberries, lemon balm, elderberries, and yarrow.*

▲ *This guild at EarthDance Organic Farm School contains an Illinois everbearing mulberry, chocolate mint, lemon balm, milkweed, and yarrow.*

▲ *This guild planting at EarthDance Organic Farm School contains a Redhaven peach tree, elderberry, sage, mint, lemon balm, and a variety of native pollinator attractors.*

▲ *This guild contains an apple tree, comfrey, and anise hyssop.*

▲ *Cultivated paw paw trees require pollen from another tree that is genetically different in order for pollination and fruiting to occur. Farmers at EarthDance Organic Farm School use paint brushes to bring pollen from one flower to another. Paw paw trees are pollinated by several species of flies and beetles.*

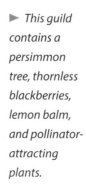

▶ *This guild contains a persimmon tree, thornless blackberries, lemon balm, and pollinator-attracting plants.*

▲ *This guild contains an Asian pear, comfrey, lemon balm, and common chives.*

▲ *This guild planting includes anise hyssop, paw paw, garlic chives, elderberry, and an Asian pear tree.*

◀ *This guild contains an elderberry shrub, an Asian pear, paw paw, anise hyssop, garlic chives, and a variety of native flowers.*

▲ *This guild contains comfrey, lemon balm, chives, yarrow, blackberries, thyme, strawberries, and a Cornelian cherry dogwood.*

GUILDS FOR SMALL SPACES

▲ *This small front-yard edible landscape guild includes a Nanking cherry, borage, scallions, comfrey, lemongrass, tulsi, hibiscus roselle, California poppies, moringa, and calendula.*

▲ *This front-yard edible landscape contains a goumi, a Chicago hardy fig, currants, josta berries, chives, herbs, and flowers.*

▲ *This small edible landscape includes josta berries, gooseberries, rhubarb, garlic chives, and common chives.*

▶ Center. *This small front-yard edible landscape guild includes a Nanking cherry, sage, rainbow chard, thyme, hibiscus roselle, California poppies, and lavender.*

▲ *This guild contains a Siberian pea shrub, yarrow, and elderberry.*

BIODIVERSITY

▲ Plant several species of fruits, vegetables, flowers, and herbs in multiple successions to increase biodiversity, attract pollinators, obtain a yield, and provide beauty.

▲ This butterfly garden designed by Elisa Thomas is at the Jaime Hines Children's Discovery Garden in Godfrey, IL. It is planted with dozens of species of pollinator-attracting native plants. Biodiversity promotes the attraction of beneficial insects. The beds are lined with rocks, and the pathways are sheet mulched with cardboard and chip mulch to suppress weeds.

◀ Integrating native pollinator-attracting perennial flowers increases biodiversity in landscapes.

FLOURISH FARM

At our small farm, we use various regenerative methods that focus on soil health, biodiversity, water retention, interplanting, companion planting, and succession planting.

- We compost all of our food scraps, duck, and chicken manure and integrate vermicompost.
- We use the finished compost to fertilize our veggie beds.
- We have created berms and swales to build soil and conserve water.
- We have over 300 varieties of fruits, vegetables, flowers, culinary, and medicinal herbs.

▲ *At Flourish Farm, we grow a variety of heirloom vegetables to sell at farmers markets and to local chefs.*

▲ *Sunflowers are fun and easy to grow with children. Pictured is our daughter, Iris, standing in front of the sunflowers with a basket full of bee balm.*

▲ *Zinnias are not edible, but they are a wonderful pollinator attractor and make a lovely addition to a flower garden.*

▲ *We like to make use of every bit of space at our farm. Pictured here are peas climbing up our wire compost bin.*

▲ *Pea flowers are gorgeous. We plant tons of pea seeds each year and cut some of the shoots and flowering tops to use in salads and sell to local chefs.*

▲ ▶ *Purple peas are fun to grow. They are prolific producers with beautiful purple flowers and stunning purple pea pods.*

▲ *Iris picking wild black raspberries.*

▲ *Eric created keyhole patterns in the wild blackberry patch next to our home. Because they are very thorny, he cleared out several sections and laid plastic and chip mulch so that we can pick and maintain them easily.*

▶ *We like to plant alliums (members of the onion family) throughout our gardens in order to help deter pests and predators. Throughout the years, we have noticed that they often attract beneficial insects and pollinators.*

▲ A garden gate can be easily built using a few tools and a pile of reclaimed wood. This gate was built by Eric Stevens.

▲ Certain types of bees are often attracted to allium flowers. Pictured here is a bee on a garlic chive bloom.

AMAZING YARDS AND FARMS

◄ *Tyrean Lewis is the founder of Heru Urban Farm in St. Louis, MO. He grows a variety of fruit trees, fruit-producing shrubs, flowers, medicinal herbs, culinary herbs, pollinator attractors, and vegetables on a city lot across the street from his home.*

▲ *Tyrean with his partner, Monique, and her two daughters, Myhyah and Sanayah.*

▲ *Tyrean's youngest daughter, Jada, who wants to be a farmer.*

◄ *Tyrean's son, TJ, who loves helping at the farm.*

▲ *Ronald L. Jones II of Blackberry Landscaping with his son in his urban oasis. Jones and his family grow hundreds of varieties of fruits, vegetables, flowers, and herbs in the JeffVanderLou neighborhood of St. Louis, MO. His backyard garden features a pollinator garden, a hummingbird garden, and a food forest.*

▲ *Ron uses reclaimed materials to build raised beds and trellises. He composts all of his food scraps, fallen leaves, and grass clippings. Pictured here is the abundance of biodiversity in Ron's garden: grapes, berries, flowers, herbs, and vegetables.*

▶ *Here is just one of the guild plantings in Ron's food forest.*

▲ *Ron Jones showcased his urban oasis at the 9th annual Sustainable Backyard Tour in St. Louis, MO.*

▶ *Ron grows a wonderful variety of unique fruits. Pictured here are josta berries.*

▶ *Ron interplants pollinator-attracting flowers and herbs with fruit-producing plants.*

▲ RA Ward has been adding plants to his urban food forest for nearly a decade in North St. Louis, MO. He grows a variety of fruit trees, fruit-producing shrubs and bushes, pollinator-attracting plants, and vegetables, as well as culinary and medicinal herbs.

▲ RA Ward's front yard is thriving with rose of Sharon, flowers, raspberries, and fruit trees including a cherry tree.

▲ RA keeps chickens in style with this chicken hotel.

▶ RA Ward grows several varieties of grapes along the iron fence at his urban food forest, using bamboo to trellis them as they grow.

▲ RA keeps geese to help control pests in the garden and provide fertilizer.

▶ RA grows a variety of tropical plants including moringa and citrus, starting them from seed in his basement under grow lights.

▲ *The gift garden in St. Louis, MO, donates all of their produce to local food pantries*

▲ *Rebecca Hankins loves maintaining her backyard rain garden/pollinator garden.*

Rebecca and David Hankins have transformed their yard into a thriving ecosystem for pollinators. They installed a rain garden with mostly native plants, a small food forest, and several raised beds full of vegetables.

▶ *Rebecca and David have planted a variety of fruiting shrubs including aronia berry, as pictured.*

▶ *They filled their raised beds with lots of different veggies and interplanted marigolds to maximize space.*

▲ *Rebecca and David have planted a variety of edibles and pollinator-attracting plants into their landscape, using reclaimed bricks to line their garden edges.*

◀ *They have built a small bridge over their rain garden bioswale.*

▲ *Shannon and AJ Thompson of Indie Eatery have a herb garden with dozens of herbs for tea and culinary use in their catering business.*

◀ ▲ *Cathy Moore and Steven McGehee grow a lot of food in a tiny space in their backyard garden. They fit 10 tomato plants, 6 pepper plants, corn, beans, squash, kale, chard, collards, celery, herbs, and flowers into a roughly 20' x 60' plot.*

▲ ► Ann and Barry Stevens have a variety of culinary herbs as well as cherry tomatoes growing among their front-yard ornamental landscape. They love the aesthetics of ornamental perennial flowers and shrubs but like the colors and textures of culinary herbs, which they use daily in their meals. In their backyard, they have created an oasis for pollinators, integrating hundreds of pollinator-attracting plants over the last decade. They are registered participants in the Monarch Flyway program. They have also created a riparian ecosystem with native shrubs, grasses, and flowers that help prevent erosion along the creek that runs along their property.

► Tiffanie Jones loves to integrate edibles into her backyard. She prefers a low-maintenance garden and grows all of her vegetables, flowers, and herbs in planter boxes and raised beds lined with stone.

▲ *Maginel Galt and Tom Grebel have transformed their yard into an edible oasis. They have a front-yard rain garden/pollinator garden that helps mitigate stormwater runoff. Their small but mighty food forest is filled with a persimmon, elderberry, aronia berry, service berry, perennial fruits and veggies, comfrey, and culinary and medicinal herbs. They also have a tea garden, a veggie garden, a shade garden, and a Three Sisters garden.*

▲ *Maginel's herb garden includes culinary herbs on one side and a tea garden featuring a variety of medicinal teas on the other side. Behind this is the start of the food forest with a dwarf apple tree, comfrey, garlic chives, edible flowers, and pollinator-attracting plants.*

◀ ▼

The transformation of Maginel and Tom's yard.

Matt and Deidre's Urban Food Forest

Matt Lebon, founder of Custom Foodscaping, and his partner, Deidre Frances, an educator, live in St. Louis, MO. Together, they have created an urban oasis with meandering mulched pathways, fruit trees, perennial fruits and vegetables, medicinal and culinary herbs, nitrogen-fixing plants, dynamic accumulators, and native flowers.

▲ *Matt and Deidre have a hardy kiwi growing up their stair rail and deck.*

▲ *Matt and Deidre use chip mulch to line the pathways of their backyard urban food forest.*

▲ *Matt and Deidre use chip mulch to line the pathways of their backyard urban food forest.*

▲ *Matt and Deidre have installed several guild plantings throughout their backyard. This guild includes a dwarf mulberry tree, Welsh onions, herbs, flowers, and chamomile planted along the edge.*

▲ *This guild is integrated into a rain garden bioswale. Its main feature is the goumi (a nitrogen-fixing fruiting shrub); it also includes comfrey, yarrow, native flowers, and grasses.*

▲ *Pawpaw tree up close.*

▲ *This guild contains a pawpaw tree, blue false indigo, comfrey, and a variety of herbs and flowers.*

◀ *Matt and Deidre love to grow unique varieties of fruits. This is a young jujubee, also known as the Chinese date. It is a nitrogen-fixing fruit tree native to China that can reach up to 40 feet tall. A mature jujubee can produce up to 100 pounds of delicious fruit per year.*

▲ *With limited space in his Urban Food Forest, Matt chose a plum tree grafted with multiple varieties.*

▲ *Matt and Deidre received a grant from the Metropolitan Sewer District to help mitigate stormwater runoff. They installed an 865-gallon Bushman Rain Harvesting Tank in their backyard that provides water for their duck pond and rain garden. The overflow waters other parts of the urban food forest. They also have a 265-gallon tank that collects rainwater from the roof and waters the front-yard edible landscape.*

▲ *Matt and Deidre built this cold frame that doubles as a grow box with a removable trellis. Cold frames offer a jumpstart to the season in late winter, as well as an option for season extension in the late fall. To start greens in late winter, they simply remove the trellis, plant seeds, and place upcycled windows of top of the cold frame. To keep greens growing through the winter, they plant seeds in late summer and place the windows on the cold frame once freezing temperatures are on the horizon in mid-late fall.*

▲ *Matt and Deidre's front yard is also planted with an abundance of fruits, vegetables, flowers, and herbs.*

 ▶ *Matt and Deidre have planted a guild in their front yard with an Asian pear tree, common chives, and Chinese pink celery.*

Ryan's Backyard

Ryan Young and his wife, Amy, have a backyard garden that is irrigated with rainwater they collect through barrels. They are recipients of Project Clear through the Metropolitan Sewer District. Their backyard includes paw paws, cherries, pears, aronia berries, veggies, and culinary and medicinal herbs. They are a compost drop-off site for friends and neighbors.

◄ *Ryan has interplanted comfrey with mullein as well as a variety of flowers, veggies, and herbs.*

▲ *Elderberries are lined against the garage along with a pawpaw tree.*

▲ *Ryan has planted dozens of pollinator-attracting plants in his backyard. Pictured here is a favorite of bees, Monarda didyma or scarlet bee balm.*

▲ *Ryan grows a variety of vegetables in a small space in his backyard. Pictured here are several varieties of tomatoes, garlic, fennel, and other vegetables and herbs.*

▲ *This front yard is packed with biodiversity, including fruit trees, fruit-producing shrubs, flowers, veggies, and several herbs.*

Farmers Inspiring Change

▼ ▶ *David Bohlen, pictured below, grows a variety of heirlooms including corn, peppers, squash, and greens. Gibron Jones, pictured right, has been growing microgreens for over a decade but is now transitioning to farming vegetables for the local school districts as well as pumpkins to produce high quality pumpkin seed oil. David and Gibron have teamed up and will be growing on a large scale for the St. Louis area.*

FRUITS, VEGETABLES, FLOWERS, HERBS, AND SPECIALTY PRODUCE

Fruits

▲ *Purple European pear fruit.*

▲ *There are many pear and apple varieties to choose from. Pear trees are prolific if the tree is well maintained. Most fruit trees need regular pruning, healthy well drained soil, adequate moisture, and full sun. Visit several local orchards to find out which varieties of fruit trees grow well in your region. Choose those that are disease- and pest-resistant and that can tolerate your local weather fluctuations.*

▲ *Liberty apple tree.*

▲ *Grapes are a lovely addition to an edible landscape, especially if you have an existing arbor to support them. Grapes do require trellising. Choose a variety that is acclimated to your zone and is both disease- and pest-resistant.*

▲ *Peach trees are a wonderful tree to grow in a guild planting. This Redhaven peach tree at EarthDance Organic Farm School started producing after just 4 years.*

▲ ▼ *Cherry plums, which resemble large cherries, can be eaten fresh; they have the texture of a plum and the sweet tartness of both a plum and a cherry. Cherry plums are native to western Asia and southeast Europe. Choose a variety that is on the sweeter side and hardy to your zone.*

▲ *Blueberries can often be challenging to grow organically due to a fair amount of pest pressure. I tried growing blueberries multiple years in a row and had no success due to swarms of Japanese beetles eating the foliage. Blueberries grow best in acidic soil, so the pH needs to be altered typically with peat moss.*

▶ *Strawberries, an easy perennial, make a nice border plant around vegetables.*

Vegetables

▲ *This colorful planting includes kale, rainbow chard, cabbage, and shiso.*

▲ *This edible design concept is interplanted with cabbage, tomatoes, and basil. Marigolds are a companion plant that help deter pests as well as attract beneficial pollinators.*

◀ *Multiple varieties of greens can be planted in a small area. Those with a shorter growing window, such as lettuce, can be planted in the shade of greens that grow throughout multiple seasons, such as kale.*

Tried and True Favorites

▲ *Basil can be planted at the base of tomato plants to maximize space.*

▲ *Sungold cherry tomatoes, a prolific producer, provide sweet, delicious bite-size tomatoes throughout the summer and early fall.*

▲ *At Flourish Farm, we grow a variety of cherry tomatoes. Some of our favorites are Sungold, Sweet 100s, chocolate cherry, Matt's wild cherry, and red and yellow pear.*

▲ *Roma tomatoes are a great variety to plant midsummer for a bountiful harvest through the fall.*

◀ *At Flourish Farm, we grow several varieties that are included in the Slow Food Presidia. The fish pepper (Capsicum annuum) is listed on the Slow Food Ark of Taste. According to Slow Food USA, "the fish pepper is an African-American heirloom that predates the 1870s. In the late 1800s, it was widely grown in the Philadelphia and Baltimore area." This small, sweet and spicy pepper makes a great addition to soups, stews, salads, and salsa. Traditionally, the fish pepper was used to flavor seafood in the Chesapeake Bay area. Both the leaves and the fruits of this pepper are variegated. The stripes change from light and dark green to orange and brown as they ripen and turn red.*

▲ *At Flourish Farm, we grow a variety of colorful peppers. Some of our favorites are California wonder, red knight, Carmen, lilac bell, purple beauty, and chocolate pepper.*

▲ ► *We also grow a variety of other colorful produce to maximize the palette at our farmers market booth. We experiment with different varieties of potatoes each year. Pictured here are Yukon gold, French fingerling, and All Blue, our favorite.*

▲ *We planted several rows of squash on contour on a hillside behind our home.*

◄ *A lovely addition to edible landscapes, beet greens grow about a foot tall and look vibrant until the beetroot is ready to harvest.*

▲ *Eggplant leaves have a nice silvery bluish appearance and can reach up to 4 feet. They provide nice color and texture in an edible landscape. The leaves are often prone to damage caused by flea beetles, but this usually can be treated with neem oil.*

Flowers

▲ *Calendula, a very attractive and aromatic flower, grows to about 3 feet tall at maturity. The flowers can be used to make tea or infused in oil to make topical herbal salves and lotions.*

▶ *Tradescantia flowers are edible. The plant gives color and texture to an edible landscape.*

▲ *Passionflower, a vining plant, has absolutely stunning flowers. While the bloom time is short, it truly makes a lasting impression. The vines look good for most of the year. Flowers are a natural sedative and should be used with caution.*

▲ *Bee balm is a lovely plant that has flowers that are edible and medicinal and leaves that attract a variety of pollinators. Bee balm does get rather large eventually, so it is best placed at the back of a landscape.*

◀ *Medical herbs make a lovely addition to an edible landscape.*

▲ *There are several varieties of basil, all which look great in an edible landscape. My favorite varieties are lettuce leaf basil and amethyst basil.*

▲ *Herb gardens look beautiful when they are well-maintained. To keep weeds at bay, we prepare the beds, cover them with landscape fabric, plant the transplants, and apply a heavy layer of mulch/compost blend around each plant and throughout the bed. This limits the amount of maintenance necessary. Pictured here is tulsi, oregano, moringa, and lovage.*

▲ *Lemon verbena makes a very attractive edible landscape. Young leaves can be added to salads. Leaves can be used to season fish and poultry or made into a lovely tea.*

▲ *Lemongrass is a gorgeous and fragrant addition to an edible landscape. The leaves can be used to season dishes or make a delicious tea.*

Specialty Greens

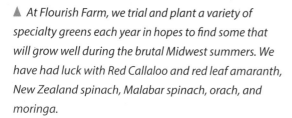

▲ *At Flourish Farm, we trial and plant a variety of specialty greens each year in hopes to find some that will grow well during the brutal Midwest summers. We have had luck with Red Callaloo and red leaf amaranth, New Zealand spinach, Malabar spinach, orach, and moringa.*

▲ *We love growing shiso, a beautiful herb that has a lovely flavor and makes an attractive addition to an edible landscape.*

Other Specialty Crops

◄ *Bok choi can provide unique color and texture to an edible landscape. It is best to start with established transplants rather than growing from seed. Some insect damage could occur. Bok choi would make an attractive border around edible landscapes if insect damage is controlled by using natural sprays such as pyganic or hot pepper spray. Bok choi is delicious in stir-fry or made into kimchi.*

▲ *Ginger and turmeric are fun and easy to grow. Seed tubers can be purchased from several companies and planted in spring for fall harvest. They grow best in a*

high tunnel or greenhouse. However, they both can be grown in pots outdoors. They need to be watered regularly.

Chapter 9

Yard-to-Table Recipes and Preserving the Harvest

I F WE REVISIT THE IDEA of the home system, let's start in the kitchen. What do you eat? How much money do you spend on food? What percentage of food do you grow and preserve? What changes would you like to make with the food you purchase and consume? What are the obstacles preventing you from moving toward a more self-reliant economics system?

It is best to grow our own food in our own backyard first. What we can't grow ourselves, we can acquire at local community gardens and small farms or by supporting local farmers markets. We can then support area businesses that are purveyors of local foods. Finally, only after we simply have utilized all of our local resources, we visit the chain supermarket to complete our food needs.

This mindset offers a creative insight into how our thoughts about food need to shift a little in order to truly be invested in the local food movement. Beyond food, permaculture offers a solution-based concept that examines the big picture in all aspects of life and how each of the basic human needs are all interconnected and how to attain these needs while considering sustainability.

There is value in home-cooked meals! Choosing to cook with food from your garden or a local farm significantly reduces the number of travel miles and resources needed. Growing your own food truly reduces your carbon footprint in a very significant way.

Below are some ways that you contribute positively to the environment through supporting local food:

- Reducing reliance on fossil fuels
- Localizing your food supply
- Supporting the local economy
- Reducing reliance on corporations
- Withdrawing support of pesticide and herbicide usage

HELPFUL SUPPLIES FOR PUTTING UP FOOD FOR THE WINTER

Things to acquire, combing Craigslist, bartering, or thrift stores:

- Wide-mouth Mason jars in all sizes
- Canning pot/canning basket
- Shelving for canned goods

    Things best when bought new:

- Pressure canner
- Standard Mason jar lids and rings (for canning)
- Plastic Mason jar lids (for freezing, reusing jars and fermentation)
- Freezer-safe bags
- Reusable freezer-safe containers with lids

RESOURCEFULNESS FROM THE GARDEN TO THE KITCHEN

I have enjoyed challenging myself to create beautiful gourmet meals without feeling the dire urge visit the grocery store, but instead just opening the pantry and the refrigerator to see what ingredients I already have on hand. This not only saves money but also frees up time to spend with my family.

For example, say the family is craving pasta. I open the pantry, and there is no pasta. I muster up the motivation and spend the gas money and the time to go to the grocery store and face the inevitable "went in for one thing, came out with a cartful" that we all have experienced. My alternative is to figure out a creative way to use what is on hand, like making a similar dish with a whole grain instead of pasta. Or slicing vegetables such as zucchini, squash, or even sweet potatoes to resemble pasta. It can be challenging but creative and rewarding.

Eating with the seasons requires dedication to the environment, commitment to

your health, and a newfound creativity in the kitchen. Trying new recipes is a classic way to conquer picky eating habits. A surefire way to get on board with the local food movement is to broaden your horizons by changing the way you see your food. The seasonal produce that grows throughout the world at specific seasons should be revered as foodshed miracles.

EAT WITH THE SEASONS: GET CREATIVE IN THE KITCHEN

When discovering the newfound excitement of eating with the seasons, we have the opportunity to get a little more creative in our own kitchens. I make most of our meals primarily from vegetables we grow ourselves, minus the occasional gourmet ingredients such as various cheeses and staples such as oils and vinegars. I used to carry around a mile-long grocery list with me. After living and working on a vegetable farm for so long, I have done without most of the items on that list. As it turns out, we are perfectly content with a primarily vegetarian diet prepared with farm-fresh seasonal veggies that are abundant, tasty, and beautiful.

Create beautiful home-cooked gourmet meals from seed to table. Create amazing new recipes by pairing the foods in your bountiful harvest.

YARD TO TABLE: QUICK AND DELICIOUS MEAL AND SNACK RECIPES

Before we delve into preserving the harvest, here are several quick and delicious beverage, meal, side, salad, and snack ideas that highlight seasonal veggies and fruits.

Breakfast Dishes

Seasonal Veggie Egg Bake

Farm-fresh eggs are the most amazing we have ever had. Egg bakes can be made quickly the night before using dinner leftovers.

1 dozen farm eggs

1 cup of bread cubes (could be day-old bread)

roasted veggies (leftovers from dinner)

handful of hardy greens, such as spinach, kale, or chard

¼ cup cream or milk (or substitute)

½ cup cheese (cut into small pieces)

pinch of salt (optional)

herbs (optional)

Grease a baking dish and preheat the oven to 400°F.

Whisk together eggs and cream. Add veggies, salt, bread cubes, and cheese. Stir well. Pour mixture into baking dish and cook for 25–30 minutes or until the eggs have set in the middle.

You can also make the mixture the night before but stir in bread cubes and refrigerate in a covered baking dish.

Chard and Kale Omelette

Chard and kale are so versatile: chop them up and throw them into any savory dish. One of my favorites is to cut leaves fine with scissors and whisk with 4 or 5 eggs, a splash of cream, goat cheese, minced garlic, roasted red peppers, and baby Swiss chard. Our kids clear their plates every time!

Use chard and kale like spinach, fresh or raw! Finely cut and add to stir-fries, soups, salad, pesto, pastas, spanakopita, and artichoke dip.

Sweet Potato Pancakes

Peel, boil, and mash 3 medium sweet potatoes. Add them to your favorite pancake recipe (decreasing wet ingredients by one-quarter). They turn out best when cooked in butter on a cast-iron griddle.

Summer Breakfast Hash

3 potatoes, chopped into small cubes

3 sweet potatoes, chopped into small cubes

2 sweet peppers, chopped

2 onions, chopped

1 tomato, diced

sprigs of fresh basil and parsley, chopped for garnish

Sauté finely chopped potatoes, sweet potatoes, and onions in olive oil for 15 minutes. Add finely chopped squash and peppers. Sauté for 10 minutes. Top with diced tomato, fresh basil, and parsley. Add a farm egg for extra protein. Optional: garnish with shredded cheese, hot sauce, and a dollop of vegan mayo.

Hearty Salads: Nutritious. Delicious. Hundreds of Ways to Prepare!

Vegan Caesar Salad

4 handfuls of spring greens, washed and spun

1 avocado, finely chopped

2 cloves of garlic, minced

5 tablespoons vegan mayo

pinch of Celtic sea salt

dash of freshly ground black pepper

1 cup homemade croutons

3 tablespoons hemp seeds

3 tablespoons nutritional yeast

Toss first six ingredients together in a large bowl. Top with with croutons, seeds, and yeast.

Spring Detox Salad and Dressing

4 handfuls spring greens, washed and spun

1 handful raw pumpkin seeds

¼ cup shredded red cabbage

¼ cup chopped raw cauliflower

1 chopped avocado

¼ cup apple cider vinegar

¼ cup flax oil

2 tablespoons dill weed

1 tablespoon raw honey

1 lemon, juiced

Toss all ingredients together in a large bowl. For best results, use all organic ingredients.

Fruits and Blooms

Nothing says welcome to summer like fresh-picked strawberries! Add strawberries to a refreshing spinach salad with sliced crisp apples, dandelion flowers, candied or raw walnuts and cashews, and homemade strawberry poppy-seed dressing. Our kids can never get enough "Strawberry Fields Forever"!

Beautiful brunch salads are a scrumptious way to devour the delicate blossoms of spring alongside the fruits of a farmer's labor. Fresh, gourmet mixed greens, which are available locally in the summer, provide a neutral base for a flavorful salad topped with sweet and sophisticated fruit, blossoms, nuts and cheeses. The following two recipes were originally published in *Feast* magazine.

Dandelion and Violet Brunch Salad with
Maple Fig Balsamic Dressing

1 pound fresh salad greens, washed and spun
10–15 fresh-picked dandelion flowers, washed and
    dried
1 cup of violet flowers
½ cup pecan halves (candied optional)
3 ounces fresh goat chèvre, separated into small
    pieces (or crumbled goat or feta cheese)
15 strawberries, sliced lengthways (optional)

This salad is best served on a large shallow
platter to showcase its beauty. Arrange the
greens evenly. Layer the pecans, strawberries,
and goat cheese and top with maple fig dressing. Garnish with dandelion and violet flowers.
Organic ingredients are the best.

Creamy Maple Fig Balsamic Dressing

1 cup extra virgin olive oil
¾ cup balsamic vinegar
¼ cup pure maple syrup (local syrup is available at
    farmers markets)
12 dried figs, hard tips removed

In a blender, combine all ingredients, processing 1 minute or until completely smooth and
creamy. Add more olive oil and blend again if necessary. Taste to assure desired flavor is achieved,
equal parts sweet and slightly sour, and adjust
accordingly. Refrigerate any extra in a Mason jar
with a tightly fitting lid for up to 3 weeks.

Spinach and Strawberry Salad with Edible Flowers

4 cups spinach
4 cups salad greens
12 strawberries, sliced
1 cup pecans
½ cup edible flowers

Add spinach to salad greens and top with
sliced strawberries, pecans, and edible flowers
such as nasturtiums. Serve with strawberry pop-
pyseed dressing or balsamic vinaigrette.

Strawberry Poppyseed Vinaigrette

1 cup fresh strawberries, tops removed, washed, and
    cut in half
1 cup extra virgin olive oil
½ cup white balsamic vinegar
2 tablespoons honey or maple syrup
6 tablespoons poppy seeds

In a blender or food processor, blend strawberries until they are smashed. Slowly add oil, vinegar, and honey or maple syrup. Process until smooth and creamy. Add poppy seeds and blend again. Refrigerate in Mason jars for up to 1 week or freeze. If freezing, thaw and blend again before serving.

Liz's Seasonal Fruit Salad with Honey Mint Dressing

Chop 2 sprigs of fresh mint (apple mint is best). Add ¼ cup of honey and stir well. Mix into any fruit salad. Seasonal fruits are great. I like to combine peaches with cantaloupe and watermelon because I can buy them locally in the summer. I do enjoy bananas in a fruit salad though, so I buy organic bananas. Edible flowers make a beautiful garnish.

Artichoke and Arugula Salad with Lemon White Balsamic Vinaigrette

4 cups arugula
1 bunch scallions
1 small bunch chives, cut thin with scissors
1 cucumber, sliced
1 bunch radishes, sliced thin
1 jar marinated grilled artichokes
small handful of chive blossoms (optional)

Arrange greens in a large bowl. Top with remaining ingredients.

Lemon White Balsamic Vinaigrette

1 cup extra virgin olive oil
½ cup white balsamic vinegar
pinch of sea salt and pepper
1 teaspoon dill
1 teaspoon mustard seed
1 lemon, juiced

Whisk ingredients together in a bowl. Enjoy!

Grilled Radicchio and Napa Cabbage Salad

2 heads of radicchio
1 large head of Napa cabbage
½ cup extra virgin olive oil
¼ cup apple cider vinegar
1 teaspoon sea salt
1 teaspoon freshly cracked pepper
1 teaspoon natural sugar

Cut radicchio and cabbage in half. Brush with olive oil. Grill for a few minutes on each side. Cut into thin strips and toss in oil, vinegar, salt, pepper, and sugar. Add sriracha if you like a little spice.

Salad in a Jar: A Simple On-the-go Meal!

Pour salad dressing into a Mason jar. Layer greens, red cabbage, carrots, sunflower seeds, and whatever else you wish. Squeeze fresh lemon over greens to preserve freshness. Shake before eating.

Golden Zucchini, Cucumber, and Basil Salad

2 medium zucchini, cut into matchsticks
2 medium cucumber, cut into matchsticks
24 fresh basil leaves
1 cup cherry tomatoes, cut in half
¼ cup white balsamic vinegar
¼ cup extra virgin olive oil
pinch of sea salt
pinch of fresh cracked black pepper

Combine all ingredients in a bowl and serve with fried green tomatoes or baked and breaded zucchini.

Slaws

Zucchini and Carrot Slaw

½ green cabbage
1 medium zucchini
3 carrots
¼ cup apple cider vinegar
2 tablespoons olive oil
½ tablespoon honey
1 teaspoon cumin
pinch of salt
½ bunch of scallions, chopped
handful of chopped almonds

Shred vegetables and toss with remaining ingredients in a bowl.

Spicy Kale Chips

2 cups raw cashews
1 cup raw sunflower seeds
¾ cup raw sesame seeds
½ cup sun-dried tomatoes
6 figs
¼ cup raw pumpkin seeds
6 cloves garlic
2 stalks celery
2 carrots
½ cup melted coconut oil or avocado oil
4 tablespoons Bragg's apple cider vinegar
4 tablespoons Bragg's liquid aminos
1 tablespoon ground red pepper
1 lemon, juiced
2 cups nutritional yeast
2 tablespoons poppy seeds
water, as needed
6 heads curly kale

Soak first six ingredients in distilled water for about 1 hour. Blend them and the water they were soaking in with garlic, celery, and carrots in a food processor until smooth. Add remaining ingredients, except kale. Add extra water if you need to. The mixture should be a thick paste.

Remove stems and tear kale into large pieces. Wash well and dry with a large towel. In a large bowl, combine with the paste. Place the coated kale on food dehydrator layers. Dehydrate for at least 6 hours. The kale chips should be crispy. Bake any extra coated kale (leftover), after filling the dehydrator on the lowest setting in an oven for 1 hour or until crispy.

Starters

Farmer Eric's Radish Dip

Farmer Eric loves radishes… especially when minced and mixed with soft cheese! We grow the bright pink ones called red meat or watermelon radishes.

8-ounce package of goat cheese, softened
6 radishes, minced
2 scallions, sliced thin
1 small bunch of chives, chopped
2 teaspoons poppy seeds
pinch of salt

Combine all ingredients and serve on crackers, Melba toast, or with cucumber tea sandwiches.

Vegetarian Buffalo Chicken Dip

4 cups sautéed squash and onions
1 cup shredded cheddar cheese
¼ cup Buffalo-style hot sauce (such as Frank's)

Combine all ingredients in a baking dish and cook for 20 minutes at 425°F.

Vegan Sweet Potato Pub Cheese

Sweet potatoes are a very versatile vegetable. They can be sliced with a spiral slicer to make noodles and are actually amazing when eaten raw with the right spices. Cook them whole, roasted, baked, boiled, fried, sautéed, steamed, and shredded. This was originally published in *Feast* magazine.

Chips and rarebit is one of my weaknesses, but only in moderation since it isn't exactly a health food. Luckily, boiled sweet potatoes when blended with a few ingredients can taste so much like a bar cheese or rarebit, you may forget it's a healthy alternative. Served with baked Yukon gold potato rounds, they make a perfect pair when starch is what you crave.

6 medium-large sweet potatoes, peeled
1 cup hemp milk or other milk/milk substitute
1 tablespoon sea salt
1 teaspoon black pepper
1 tablespoon smoked paprika
½ cup dark beer
1 teaspoon Bragg's liquid aminos or tamari soy sauce
   (for a richer flavor)

Cut sweet potatoes into 1-inch cubes and boil until slightly soft (about 25 minutes).

Drain, keeping the broth to add later or as a broth for other recipes. Place potatoes and remaining ingredients (except the beer) into a food processor. Pulse until smooth. Process on high for 2 minutes, adding a little more of the sweet potato water to thin if necessary.

In a medium saucepan on low, slowly add the beer to the sweet potato "cheese," stirring regularly for about 5 minutes. While the sweet potatoes boil, create your chips.

Baked Yukon Gold Potato Rounds

6 Yukon gold potatoes
1 teaspoon sea salt
extra virgin olive oil
fresh sage, pan-fried (optional)

Preheat oven to 425°F. Wash the potatoes and cut into ¼-inch slices. Toss in a large bowl with sea salt and enough olive oil to evenly coat them. Place in a single layer on a baking sheet. Bake for about 25 minutes or until tender and slightly crispy on the edges. Broil for 1 to 2 minutes until golden and a little crisper. Top with pan-fried sage.

Farm Fresh Pico de Gallo

1 jalapeño pepper
1 cucumber
1 tomato
12 cherry tomatoes
1 cucumber, minced
small bunch of cilantro (stems removed)
½ red onion
½ lime
salt, to taste
pinch of smoked paprika (optional)

Finely chop vegetables. Add seasonings. Toss with a splash of olive oil. This recipe is delightful!

Light Meals

Chard Rolls with Nutty Ranch Dipping Sauce

12 large chard leaves

2 cups fresh greens of your choice

1 cup local mushrooms

2 cloves garlic, minced

½ cup sliced colorful peppers

½ cup sprouts or microgreens

½ cup chopped vegetables of your choice

Rinse and dry chard leaves. Cut the tip of the stem adjoining the leaf in an upside-down V (you don't want the stem in your rolls because it might rip the leaf, causing the wrap to fall apart). Lay the chard leaves (shiny side down) side by side on a large flat surface.

Combine remaining ingredients in a large mixing bowl. Place 4 large spoonfuls of the mixture onto each leaf (toward the end where you cut a V). Roll up like a burrito and use a toothpick to hold each one in place.

Chard can be a substitute for a tortilla or bread and tastes great with any savory filling. I like to serve omelettes on a chard roll and let the whole family roll their own breakfast burritos. Chard is beautifully matched with lemony flavors and neutralized by cream cheeses or soft cheeses such as goat chèvre or brie. It can also be sautéed with onions and garlic, chopped and added to soups, or chopped and served in a salad. Collards, kale, or cabbage leaves may also be used.

Nutty Ranch Dipping Sauce

1 cup raw cashews

¼ cup purified water

2 tablespoons dried or fresh herbs of your choice (I use a mixture of fresh dill, parsley, thyme, oregano and cilantro)

pinch of Celtic sea salt

In a food processor, blend the cashews until they are finely crumbled. Slowly add the remaining ingredients. Add a splash more water, if necessary, to make the mixture smooth and creamy but not too thin.

Raw Power Slaw

A great way to use your farm veggies is to make a delicious raw slaw. You can flavor it any way you'd like.

I start with thinly sliced or shaved veggies, oil, vinegar, sea salt and cracked pepper. I like to make a variety of slaws: curry raisin, Asian sesame, fresh herbs and apple cider vinegar, etc. Get creative! Be resourceful and challenge yourself to use what you have in your kitchen!

Sushi

Sushi is a great way to prepare a variety of veggies from your garden.

1 package nori sushi seaweed papers

3 cups assorted seasonal vegetables, sliced into thin strips or matchsticks

6 cups sushi rice (or cauliflower rice)

2 tablespoons rice vinegar

2 tablespoons sugar

Cook sushi rice according to package instructions, adding rice vinegar and sugar 10 minutes before rice is cooked. (Make it raw by substituting rice with cauliflower pulsed in the food processor — add a handful of cashews to make the mixture sticky.) Place nori sheet onto dry cutting board. Spread sushi rice evenly onto it with a spatula. Add veggies. Roll sushi using a bamboo sushi roller or simply use a large Ziploc bag. Cut with a sharp knife.

Zucchini Noodles

My favorite example of retraining yourself to eat with the seasons is zucchini noodles. When they are in season, I don't even keep pasta stocked in the pantry because zucchini noodles are delicious and healthy; my entire family loves them and asks for seconds. Getting kids to eat healthy can be a challenge, but it is always a little easier when they can be involved in the process. I love preparing raw food meals with farm-fresh produce during the summer to be sure we get the maximum nutrients and flavor. One of my favorites is a raw version of fettuccine Alfredo using thinly sliced zucchini as the noodles, topped with cashew and basil cream sauce.

Score large zucchini lengthwise with a paring knife all the way. Use a handheld vegetable peeler or julienne peeler to slice "noodles" from top to bottom.

A spiral slicer is a small investment. I have had mine for about 6 years, and it still works perfectly. Use them in place of noodles in any recipe.

Serve zucchini noodles hot or cold, with pesto or the sauce of your choice. My three favorites are pesto, a cashew-based Alfredo sauce, and a raw sun-dried tomato and date sauce.

Cashew Alfredo Sauce

2 cups raw cashews
pinch of Celtic sea salt
½ a lemon, juiced
2 cups purified water

In a food processor, blend cashews until finely crumbled. Slowly add salt, fresh lemon juice, and water until the mixture is smooth and creamy. Add a splash more water, if necessary, to achieve creaminess.

Pesto Cream Sauce

Make cashew Alfredo sauce from recipe above. Add 6 tablespoons of pesto and blend until smooth.

Sun-dried Tomato and Date Sauce

1 cup sun-dried tomatoes
¼ cup pitted dried dates
3 cloves garlic
pinch of Celtic sea salt
1 cup purified water

In a food processor, blend sun-dried tomatoes and dates until they are roughly chopped. Add garlic, salt, and water and blend until mixture resembles pasta sauce.

Sides

Kohlrabi Fries

Preheat oven to 425°F. Peel kohlrabi. Slice into fries. Toss in olive oil, sea salt, and black pepper, as well as any other desired seasonings. Bake for 20 minutes.

Roasted Veggies

A simple way to use your harvest! Preheat oven to 425°F. Cut your veggies into 1-inch pieces. Coat with extra virgin olive oil, a pinch of salt, and your favorite spices and herbs. Lay veggies in a single layer on a sheet pan. Bake for 25-30 minutes, flipping them halfway through.

Cook firm root veggies such as carrots and potatoes together and tender veggies such as peppers and squash together. Tender veggies may only need 15 minutes depending on the oven.

Roasted veggies make excellent additions to quesadillas, sandwiches, pizza, soups, and stews. Freeze leftovers for later use.

Turnip Mash and Braised Greens

6 turnips, boiled and mashed
2 onions, sliced thin
6 cloves garlic, minced
2 tablespoons balsamic vinegar
1 teaspoon salt
3 tablespoons extra virgin olive oil
6 cups of mixed greens (turnip, kale, chard, collards, and even radish tops work well)

Sauté greens in olive oil and simmer until tender. Add garlic, balsamic vinegar, and salt, and simmer a few more minutes. In a separate saucepan, caramelize onions until tender.

Replace boiled and mashed turnips for potatoes in your favorite mashed potato recipe. Add a few eggs and lots of cheddar cheese and bake for 20 minutes at 400°F. Serve on bed of braised greens and top with caramelized onions.

Honey-glazed Rosemary Turnips Sautéed in Brown Butter

6 turnips
½ stick butter
1 sprig fresh rosemary
6 tablespoons honey

Cut turnips into thin slices and then quarter the slices. In a large skillet, melt the butter. Sauté turnips until golden. Add fresh rosemary and honey. Sauté until the turnips are caramelized.

Pan-seared Turnip Greens and Onions with Red Wine Vinegar and Butter

1 medium onion
greens from 6 turnips
½ stick butter
4 garlic cloves, minced
⅛ cup red wine vinegar

Cut onion into thin slices. Chop turnip greens into small pieces. In a large skillet, melt butter. Add sliced onions and sauté until golden. Add minced garlic and turnip greens and sauté for 8–10 minutes. Add red wine vinegar and simmer on low for 2 minutes.

Garlic Scape Roasted Potatoes

12 potatoes
3 garlic scapes, minced
4 tablespoons extra virgin olive oil
pinch each salt and pepper

Preheat oven to 425°F. Cut potatoes into 1-inch cubes and toss in olive oil with garlic scapes. Roast for 20 to 25 minutes.

Main Dishes

Wild Greens Spanakopita with Wild Onion Dipping Sauce

This dish, originally published in *Feast* magazine, is sure to entice the beginning forager and get the taste buds accustomed to wild foods. Integrating them into your diet through tasty dishes and then slowly transitioning to the foods in their bare form is a way I have found to be enjoyable. Once a forager, always a forager.

Spanakopita — an authentic Greek pie that combines crispy layers of golden-brown phyllo dough with spinach, cheeses, and herbs — can be slightly altered to use wild greens. Often fibrous, they are easily cut with kitchen scissors.

½ cup extra virgin olive oil

16-ounce package phyllo dough

2 cups wild greens (¾ cup dandelion, ¾ cup plantain, ¼ cup chickweed, and ¼ cup red clover leaves), washed and chopped finely

2 cups spinach, washed and chopped finely

3 cloves garlic, minced

¼ cup chopped roasted red pepper

3 tablespoons minced wild onions (or cut finely with kitchen scissors)

1 cup feta cheese crumbles (optional)

pinch of sea salt

pinch of cracked black pepper

pinch each of thyme, dill, and parsley

1 stick butter

Preheat oven to 425°F. Grease bottom and sides of an 11"×17" glass baking dish with 1 to 2 tablespoons of olive oil. Remove phyllo dough from the package and unroll to thaw, covered with a damp towel to prevent drying. Heat 4 tablespoons olive oil in a large skillet. Add all greens, garlic, roasted red peppers, wild onions, herbs, salt, and pepper. Sauté for about 15 minutes on low-medium heat or until the greens are wilted and tender. Set mixture aside.

In a small saucepan, melt the butter. Add the remaining olive oil and stir well.

Assembling spanakopita is quite tedious and rather time-consuming, but the end result makes it worthwhile. Traditionally, spanakopitas are individually wrapped. However, the quicker method is to layer individual sheets with the greens mixture in a large baking dish. Place the first sheet of phyllo on the bottom. With a pastry brush, spread with the butter/oil mixture. Add another layer of phyllo and brush completely with the butter/oil mixture. Repeat until there are 12 sheets in the baking dish. Add half of the greens mixture and sprinkle half of the feta cheese crumbles evenly over it. Repeat the process: add 12 sheets of individually buttered phyllo sheets, followed by the remaining greens mixture and feta cheese. Add the last sheets of phyllo, individually buttering each layer.

Brush an extra coat of the butter/oil mixture to the top layer and bake for 15 minutes or until golden brown. Watch closely so that the spanakopita does not burn. Cut into eight squares or sixteen triangles.

Serve spanakopita as a side dish to a Greek-inspired meal or as the main attraction served with soup and salad.

Wild Onion Dipping Sauce

8-ounce package goat chèvre

½ cup plain yogurt

½ cucumber, chopped fine

⅛ cup minced wild onions

2 tablespoons dill, fresh or dry

1 teaspoon sea salt

Soften goat cheese in a bowl. Whip together with yogurt until smooth. Add the remaining ingredients and stir well.

Radicchio Ravioli with Walnut Sauce

Stuff individual radicchio leaves with your favorite ravioli filling. I use goat cheese, pesto, Parmesan cheese, sun-dried tomato pesto, caramelized onions, and fresh parsley. Fold them like packets, using the goat cheese to close them. Pan sear with olive oil and sliced onions. I like to top them with a white wine, butter, and walnut sauce with fresh parsley.

Radicchio is a specialty Italian vegetable in the chicory family. Peel back the outer leaves to view its vibrant and beautiful center. Radicchio is great mixed into salads, grilled, and sautéed. It has a unique bitter flavor so be sure to neutralize the intensity with something creamy. Radicchio is a nutrient-rich vegetable and a good source of dietary fiber, containing vitamins B6, C, E, and K, as well as iron, magnesium, phosphorus, zinc, copper, manganese, and potassium, among others.

Homemade Polenta with Fire-roasted Chilies

One of my favorite dishes to make from scratch is polenta with kale, chard, spring onions, and squash blossoms.

Preheat oven to 400°F. Follow a basic polenta recipe (corn grits) but add your preferred ingredients, such as sun-dried tomatoes, or ours, fire-roasted green chilies. Coat a glass pie pan with a small amount of olive oil. Put polenta mixture into it and bake for 15 minutes. Let cool and refrigerate. Place upside down on a large plate. Use a spatula to gently remove. Top with your favorite ingredients, such as salsa verde.

Spinach and Kale Polenta with Vegetarian Brown Gravy and Caramelized Onions

Follow basic polenta (corn grits) recipe. Add chopped kale, spinach, fresh herbs, salt, garlic, chives, and olive oil. Once polenta is cooked, pour into a greased glass pie pan and press down. Let it set for 30 minutes. Flip it upside down onto an oven-safe plate. Finish with gravy and caramelized onions and reheat in the oven for 10 minutes before serving. Enjoy!

Ratatouille

A family favorite, ratatouille is delicious and fun to make, taking about 1 hour from start to finish.

6 potatoes
3 small eggplant
2 zucchini
1 summer squash
1 onion
1 pepper
6 mushrooms
6 cloves garlic, minced
1 to 2 jars of pasta sauce

Preheat oven to 400°F. Slice veggies (I use a food processor to slice the potatoes, squash, and eggplant.). In the bottom of a lightly greased baking dish, add sauce, mushrooms, peppers, garlic, and onions.

Arrange ingredients, as pictured, in the following repeating order: potatoes, eggplant, squash. Drizzle with extra virgin olive oil. Sprinkle a generous pinch of sea salt and freshly cracked pepper over the top. Bake for 30 minutes.

Grilled Squash with BBQ Sauce

When it's in season, we like to use squash as a main course as much as possible. It's incredibly versatile. Serve it hot or cold, cooked or raw; it can be shredded, sliced, chopped, sautéed, boiled, broiled, steamed, puréed, and much more.

Grilling is one of our favorite ways to prepare squash. Simply slice lengthwise, brush with extra virgin olive oil, sea salt, pepper, and a pinch of Cajun seasoning if you like spicy. Grill for about 3 to 5 minutes on each side. Drizzle with organic BBQ sauce.

White "Chicken" Chili

6 large summer squash

2 onions, chopped

6 stalks celery, chopped

6 small colorful sweet peppers

1 pound white beans

1 pound kidney beans

salt, pepper, cumin, garlic powder, smoked paprika, and chili powder, to taste

½ cup coconut milk

1 jar of green salsa

1 cup shredded Monterey jack cheese

1 carton of vegetable stock

Preheat oven to 425°F. Cube squash, toss with olive oil, and roast for 20 minutes. Cook beans. Cut veggies, then sauté them in olive oil with spices in a skillet. Combine beans, squash, and veggies in a large pot and add coconut milk, vegetable stock, green salsa, and cheese. Simmer on low for 45 minutes to let flavors marry. Serve with blue corn tortilla chips, a dollop of sour cream, and scallions.

Farmer Eric's Veggie Samosas

3 cups garbanzo/fava flour (or gluten-free flour)

2 tablespoons baking soda

1 tablespoon sea salt

1 tablespoon flax meal (ground flax seeds)

½ cup water

½ cup extra virgin olive oil

Preheat oven to 400°F. Combine dry ingredients well. Pour in wet ingredients and mix well. Use your hands to knead the dough until wet and thoroughly mixed. Roll into a ball. With a rolling pin, roll into a rectangle, about ¼-inch thick, on a lightly floured surface. Cut into 12 to 24 even squares (depending on desired samosa size).

Fill squares with 2 tablespoons of veggies (roasted, grilled, or sautéed), leftover curry, mashed potatoes, and peas, or whatever your heart desires!

With your finger, brush the edges of each square with a little water. Fold into a triangle, pressing the edges firmly together to seal. Bake for 15 to 20 minutes or until golden.

Roasted Butternut Squash with Lemon Butter Sauce

Preheat oven to 425°F. Cut butternut squash in half lengthwise. Remove seeds (save to plant in your garden). Brush both sides with olive oil. Roast on a sheet pan for 15–20 minutes on each side until golden brown and semi-soft. Melt 1 stick of butter in a saucepan. Squeeze 1 lemon into the butter. Add a pinch of salt and stir well. Pour the lemon butter over the squash and serve hot.

Spicy Sweet Potato Latkes

2 cups shredded sweet potatoes

1 onion

2 poblano peppers, thinly sliced

½ cup panko crumbs

2 eggs

salt to taste

Combine all ingredients in a bowl. Drop spoonfuls into hot oil and cook on each side for 2 minutes or until golden brown.

Kale, Roasted Red Pepper, and Goat Cheese Popovers

1 package of puff pastry sheets

1 large bunch of kale, chopped fine

3 tablespoons extra virgin olive oil

1 jar of roasted red peppers, cut into thin strips

1 tablespoon sea salt

1 package of goat cheese crumbles

Thaw puff pastry and cut into squares. Massage kale with oil and salt. Preheat oven to 400°F. Place kale, red peppers, and goat cheese on squares. Fold into a triangle and pinch closed with your fingertips, sealing with a little water. Brush with olive oil and place on a greased cookie sheet. Bake for 10 minutes on each side or until golden brown.

Soups and Stews

Dad's Delicious Vegetable Soup

My father made the most amazing vegetable soup. I've tried many times and have come close but not once mastered his recipe, which was never written down. Here is my attempt.

10 cups water or broth

4 potatoes, cut into small cubes

4 carrots, sliced

1 onion, diced

4 stalks of celery, diced

1 pound fresh green beans, cut into thirds

3 beets, cubed

greens from 3 beets, chopped

6 garlic cloves, minced

4 tomatoes, chopped

Bring water or broth to a boil. Add potatoes, carrots, and onions. Cook for 10 minutes on medium heat. Add the remaining ingredients and simmer for 2 hours or until veggies are tender.

Potato Leek and Artichoke Soup

Chefs go crazy over bunching leeks, which grow in a clump like scallions, because of their delicate texture and elegant allium flavor. We grow them because we have not had success with large leeks. Cook them just as you would leeks or onions. I like to cut them into thin slices, using sharp kitchen scissors, to use raw in salads and receive their wonderful nutrients. They are rich in iron and vitamins K, A, and C, and a plethora of other nutrients.

I balance our healthy eating habits with a little gourmet foodie fun: I also like to flash-fry them in olive oil to garnish soups, pastas, and pizzas.

16 potatoes, washed and sliced thin
1 large leek or 6 bunching leeks
1 large onion, sliced thin
6 garlic cloves, sliced thin
6 cups vegetable broth
2 jars marinated artichokes
1 cup roasted red peppers
2 tablespoons smoked paprika
2 tablespoons sea salt
2 tablespoons cracked black pepper
6 tablespoons fresh or dried herbs (I like to use a
    combination of dill, oregano, and parsley)

Boil potatoes in a large pot of water for 15 minutes or until tender. Cut leeks with scissors and dip in cold water to remove silt. In a large skillet, sauté leeks for 5 minutes. Add onions and garlic and sauté for another 5 to 10 minutes or until tender. Fill a large pot with 6 cups of vegetable broth or water. Add the remaining ingredients and simmer on low for 10 to 15 minutes or until the flavors have married.

Autumn Stew

1 gallon of water

¼ cup hard cider or white wine

salt and pepper to taste

pinch of pumpkin pie spice

pinch of ground cloves

pinch of cumin (optional)

3 large sweet potatoes, sliced or cubed

3 large tomatoes, sliced and cut in half

4 medium peppers, sliced

Boil water, cider, and seasonings in a large saucepan. Add sweet potatoes. Cook for 10 minutes over medium heat. Add remaining ingredients and cook on low for 45 minutes.

Specialty Dishes

Stuffed Squash Blossoms

Squash blossoms are not only beautiful and vibrant but they are also edible, nutrient-rich, and delicious! They are high in iron, calcium, and vitamins A and C.

A timeless way to use squash blossoms is to stuff them with goat chèvre and lightly fry them in a drizzle of olive oil in a cast-iron skillet. The Zephyr squash is one of my top five all-time favorite vegetables! Its painted elegant appearance is striking… one of Nature's masterpieces.

Zucchini squash blossoms are regarded as a delicacy by chefs for their stunning appearance, unique flavor, and incomparable texture. The blossom melts in your mouth, leaving undertones of sweet nuttiness. Zucchini, also known as courgettes, are gorgeous when prepared with the flower still intact. The most dramatic appearance can be achieved by using baby zucchini (less than 3 inches long) with blossoms attached. Lightly sauté them in olive oil. Their natural beauty speaks for itself plated next to any main dish.

The squash blossoms of both zucchini and summer squash are edible; however, zucchini blossoms are preferred because they are a little stouter and they last longer. The blossoms are highly perishable and should be prepared within a few hours of harvest. It is best to cut about ¼ inch of zucchini end with the blossom so that it remains intact and easy to use. They have such a unique and delightful flavor that they are best prepared with just one or two simple ingredients. They are excellent stuffed with any cheese, but my favorite is the simple delicate flavor of goat chèvre.

This recipe was previously published in *Feast* magazine.

12 freshly harvested squash blossoms (optional: include the 3- to 5-inch zucchini)
4-ounce package of goat chèvre
4 tablespoons extra virgin olive oil

Prehcat the oven to 350°F. Coat a sheet pan with a thin layer of olive oil. Gently wash the squash blossoms and place them on a towel to dry. Remove the pistils with a sharp knife (be careful not to damage the flower). Place all the goat chèvre into a small Ziploc or sandwich bag. Press it into one corner and tie the opening off tightly with a twist tie or a rubber band. Cut off the tip of the corner with scissors. Place the opening directly into each squash blossom and squeeze until half-filled with cheese. Place the stuffed squash blossoms on the sheet pan and lightly drizzle with olive oil. Bake for about 10 minutes. Goat chèvre may be substituted with vegan soft cheese.

Scallion Pancakes

2 bunches of scallions, sliced thin
2 cups flour
4 eggs
½ cups fresh herbs (parsley and cilantro)
1 tablespoon salt
1 teaspoon freshly cracked pepper
¼ cup extra virgin olive oil

Combine all ingredients in a large bowl. Preheat and grease a large skillet. Add a large spoonful of scallion pancake mixture to the hot skillet. Cook for 4 minutes on each side or until golden brown.

Desserts

Raw Chocolate Fudge with Local Berries

2 cups coconut oil (melted)

1 cup raw cacao powder

4 tablespoons of raw honey or pure maple syrup

In a mixing bowl, combine the coconut oil, raw cacao, and honey or maple syrup until smooth. Pour into a freezer-safe glass dish and freeze for at least an hour. Serve immediately topped with seasonal local berries. Keep refrigerated.

Raw Foods Pie Crust

2 cups almonds

1 cup pitted dates, chopped

3 tablespoons pure maple syrup

In a food processor, blend almonds on high until they resemble flour. Add dates and maple syrup and blend until it forms a sticky ball. Grease a pie pan with coconut oil. Press the mixture into the pie pan to form a crust.

Raw Chocolate Mousse

4 avocados

4 tablespoons cacao powder

3 tablespoons pure maple syrup

Blend in a blender or a food processor until smooth and creamy.

Mulberry Cashew Crème Cheesecake

Crust

2 cups raw almonds

1½ cups dried mission figs (stems removed), chopped

1 cup almond flour

1 teaspoon coconut oil

In a food processor, blend almonds on high until they resemble flour. Add chopped dried figs and almond flour and blend until the mixture has formed a sticky ball.

Use about a teaspoon of coconut oil to grease a glass pie dish. Press the crust mixture firmly down until it is evenly spread to form a crust. This was originally published in *Feast* magazine.

Filling

5 cups raw cashews

1 lemon, juiced

12 tablespoons honey or pure maple syrup (set 2 tablespoons aside to drizzle over the finished cheesecake)

3 tablespoons pure vanilla extract

1½ cups coconut milk or water

3 cups mulberries

1 tablespoon coconut oil

In a food processor, blend the cashews until they resemble a fine powder. Add the remaining filling ingredients (except mulberries and coconut oil) and blend on high until smooth and creamy. Set aside half of the filling in a small bowl. Add 2 cups of mulberries to the remaining filling mixture and continue to blend on high until creamy and colorful. Pour the mulberry-tinted filling over the crust and spread evenly, saving about ½ cup of for topping.

Spread the cashew crème filling evenly over the colored filling. Add the remaining ½ cup of mulberry-tinted filling on top in the center. Using a toothpick, slowly move it from center to edge using a swirling motion. Be creative. There is no right or wrong way to do this. Drizzle the cheesecake with honey or maple syrup. Finally, arrange the remaining mulberries on top. I like to line them around the outside edge with a few in the center. Cover and refrigerate for at least an hour. Serve chilled.

Raw Juneberry (or Blueberry) Macaroons
(Makes 12 macaroons)

2 cups unsweetened shredded coconut
½ cup raisins or pitted dates
1 cup nuts
⅛ cup maple syrup or honey
1 cup of frozen or fresh wild blueberries or
    Juneberries

In a food processor, blend all ingredients except berries until fine. Add berries and blend until smooth, or you are able to form balls. Make 12 balls, roll them in shredded coconut and refrigerate for 1 hour… or devour immediately if you can't wait.

Three-tiered Carrot Calendula Cake with Honey Cream Cheese & 4 Hands Cast Iron Oatmeal Brown Frosting

4 cups all-purpose flour

1 tablespoon baking soda

2½ tablespoons baking powder

3 tablespoons ground cinnamon

1 teaspoon allspice

½ teaspoon ground cloves

1 tablespoon ground nutmeg

1 teaspoon ground ginger

1 teaspoon salt

1 cup of applesauce

1 stick of butter, softened

1 cup of coconut oil, softened

1 cup coconut sugar

1 cup of honey

2 cups shredded carrots

¼ cup calendula petals, fresh or dried

1 cup of raisins soaked in mixture of ¼ cup Irish
    whiskey, ¾ cup milk, 1 tablespoon honey

1 teaspoon hot pepper flakes

1 tablespoon sriracha hot sauce

5 eggs

1 cup vanilla almond milk

2 tablespoons pure vanilla extract

1 tablespoon apple cider vinegar

Preheat oven to 375°F. In a large mixing bowl, whisk together the flour, baking soda, baking powder, cinnamon, allspice, ground cloves, ground nutmeg, ground ginger, and salt. In a medium bowl, combine the coconut sugar, applesauce, honey, butter, and coconut oil. Blend together using an electric mixer. Add the eggs, one at a time, just until the mixture is whipped together.

In a small bowl, beat the apple cider vinegar and the vanilla extract into the almond milk. Add this to the sugar and egg mixture and stir well. Add the shredded carrots, calendula petals, raisins (with the soaking mixture), the hot pepper flakes, and the sriracha and stir well. Fold the wet ingredients into the dry ingredients.

Lightly grease 3 pie pans one slightly larger than the other (glass Pyrex bowls work well; aluminum cake pans will work, just as long as you have three tiers). Bake for 30 minutes or until a toothpick poked into the middle of the cake comes out clean.

The following is a gluten-free option:

1 package of Namaste Foods Gluten-free Spice Cake Mix (26 ounces)

2 cups of shredded carrots

1 cup of applesauce

1 cup of raisins soaked in mixture of ¼ cup Irish whiskey, ¾ cup milk, 1 tablespoon honey

2 tablespoons of cinnamon

1 teaspoon of hot pepper flakes

1 squirt of sriracha hot sauce

Follow package instructions and fold in the remaining ingredients. Bake according to package directions.

Honey Cream Cheese & 4 Hands Cast Iron Oatmeal Brown Frosting

Cast Iron Oatmeal Brown Beer: Using chocolate malt and roasted barley to give this beer a cast iron backbone, 4 Hands Oatmeal Brown pours a dark mahogany with aromas of dark chocolate and coffee.

8 ounces organic cream cheese (softened)

½ cup honey

1 tablespoon cinnamon

¼ cup 4 Hands Cast Iron Oatmeal Brown Beer (and stout will work)

Mix frosting ingredients in a food processor until smooth. Assemble cake with largest tier on the bottom. Stack the remaining tiers and glaze cake by pouring frosting in a spiral motion over the three tiers. Decorate cake with edible calendula flowers.

PRESERVING THE HARVEST

Growing and preserving your own food is an important component in the home system. Check out this article on the age-old art of hot water bath canning:

https://permaculturemag.org/2016/08/canning/

Here are some additional methods of preserving the harvest:

http://thehealthyplanet.com/2013/08/eat-with-the-seasons-preserving-autumns-garden-bounty/

When it comes to preserving the harvest, having a plan in place is helpful. Make a chart of the items you want to can, pickle, ferment, and preserve. This gives you a framework for the supplies you will need to gather in order to start the process.

With your harvest, cook large batches of soups or stews and freeze in freezer bags to thaw and heat in any amount you desire. Try new seasonal recipes such as hearty autumn stew, sweet potato pancakes, roasted butternut squash with lemon butter sauce, roasted butternut squash bisque topped with pan-fried sage, sweet apple and wild rice-stuffed acorn squash, and any other fall-inspired dishes that you have been eager to make. Make double or triple batches at a time. Freeze the leftovers for future ready-made meals. Be sure to date and label the bags.

Create your own value-added products, including pestos, jams, jellies, preserves, sauces, and salsas.

Spring Preserving Checklist

Strawberry jam
Mulberry jam
Pickled carrots
Wild greens pesto
First aid salve
Batch freeze berries
Lacto-fermented spring veggies
Kimchi

Summer Preserving Checklist

Salsa
Marinara
Bloody Mary mix
Garlic salt
Zucchini relish
Pickles
Pickled beets
Pesto
Large batches of grilled vegetables
Batch freeze cherry tomatoes, peppers, onions, squash
Sun-dried tomatoes

Fall Preserving Checklist

Large batches of butternut squash soup
Butternut squash "cheesy sauce"
Chowchow
Herb salts
Pesto
Batch freeze grilled veggies
Veggie pâté

Preserving the Harvest Supply List

Mason jars and lids
Labels
Large and medium freezer bags
Parchment paper
Muslin or cheesecloth
Plenty of freezer space
Pressure canner or hot water bath canner
Canning tongs

In the garden, one of the biggest perks is abundance. In a good year, there will be daily bounty to use in meals and often a surplus. Preserving and putting up food for the winter becomes second nature, knowing that, within just a small window of time, the garden will once again become dormant and barren, giving the soil time to rest.

For the Love of Fermentation

Lacto-fermentation is the process of fermenting veggies in lactic acid–forming bacteria that are beneficial to the body and help build the immune system. Fermentation is a wonderful way to preserve abundance from your garden.

Preserved Veggies in Brine

Sterilize Mason jars. Chop veggies and herbs of your choice and add to jars. Dissolve 1½ tablespoons of Celtic sea salt in 2 cups of purified water. Pour the brine over your chopped veggies in the jars. Leave ½ inch of space at the top. Put a cabbage leaf on top to help with the fermentation process. Cover with a plastic lid. Leave on the counter for 1 week. Remove cabbage leaf and refrigerate for up to 2 months. Be sure to label.

Sauerkraut in Mason Jars

3 large heads of green cabbage

4 tablespoons sea salt or kosher salt

1 tablespoon freshly cracked black pepper

4 tablespoons caraway seeds

2 dried cayenne peppers, seeds removed, and cut into strips with scissors (optional)

Have the following on hand before you begin:

Large cutting board

Large sharp knife (I find a nice large serrated knife works best for cutting thin strips of cabbage)

A giant mixing bowl

Measuring spoons/measuring cup

Canning funnel

6 large sterilized one-quart wide-mouth Mason jars and plastic lids

Muslin or butter muslin cheesecloth

6 large rubber bands

6 sterilized jelly jars that can fit into a wide-mouth Mason jar

Marbles (used to keep the cabbage beneath its own juices)

Wash everything you will be using very well. Sterilize jars. Cut the ends off the heads of cabbage. Slice very thin and place it in the large bowl. Add the salt evenly over it and mix by hand for at least 8 minutes. The desired result is slightly wilted and juicy cabbage in a fair amount of liquid.

Put the cabbage into the Mason jars, using the canning funnel, filling about ¾ full. Evenly pour the remaining liquid from the mixing bowl into each jar. Place a folded cabbage leaf over the surface of the shredded cabbage. It should be completely immersed in its own liquid.

Divide the marbles equally between the six jelly jars. Place them inside of each of the jars with cabbage. Use a wooden spoon to press the jelly jar down firmly, watching the liquid level rise.

Cut muslin or cheesecloth into 6 squares (4"× 4"), cover the jars, and secure with a rubber band.

Over the next few days, every couple of hours, or whenever you remember, press the smaller jar firmly down, allowing the juices to rise above the cabbage. If the liquid levels are not above the cabbage after 2 days, mix 1 tablespoon of salt with 1 cup of distilled water and pour it into each Mason jar, making sure the liquid covers the cabbage.

Ferment the cabbage for 7–12 days, keeping it out of direct sunlight and at a temperature that is between 60° and 75°F.

Check to make sure the liquid level stays above the cabbage. This is very important for fermentation and preventing slime mold. Once fermentation has occurred to your desired taste, remove smaller jars of marbles and the large folded leaves. Transfer the sauerkraut to smaller containers and add the plastic caps. Refrigerate and enjoy. Use within 4 to 6 months.

This is adapted from a recipe by Emma Christensen of Kitchn.

Integrating Probiotics into Your Kids' Diet

Add kefir grains to juice (kefir grains eat the sugar and leave behind bubbles)

Make homemade ketchup using tomatoes and dates. Add probiotics to it and let it sit on the counter for two days. Probiotics from whey eat all of the sugar.

Let them help you make lacto-fermented vegetables. Allow them to choose their favorite vegetables to add to the jars.

• Use organic sourdough bread

• Raw organic cheese and probiotic pretzels make excellent snacks
• Probiotic pickles
• Cultured carrots
• Smoothies with kefir
• Cultured fruits and fruit leathers, cultured applesauce
• Kombucha in small amounts
• Probiotic supplements
• Homemade probiotic yogurt

Fire Roasting

A simple way to build your own camp stove is with stones or fire bricks stacked in a ring about a foot high. Be sure you build it so your grill can rest securely on top. For example, if your grill top is 24 inches in diameter, build a ring with fire bricks that is 23 inches in diameter.

We built a multi-functioning firepit/outdoor wood-fired barbeque grill using large found stones and a circular grill from an old BBQ pit. We use our wood-fired grill regularly throughout spring, summer, and fall. That fire-roasted flavor enhances any dish. Compared to charcoal grilling, cooking with wood may just be a lost art, but the robust flavors attained by it are enhanced tenfold. Oak, cedar, and cherry woods all have great flavor. If you're not worried about the "campfire flavor," simply BBQ the veggies.

Wood-fired veggies are a great way to use seasonal bounty and make an excellent addition to soups, stews, pasta salads, and sides. Preserve them by freezing in freezer-safe bags. Cooking with fire is a great way to use up any produce with blemishes. We simply cut off the blemished parts, toss the rest in olive oil and a little sea salt, and throw them on the grill. Eat them immediately or chop and freeze them to add to hearty soups, stews, chili, or pasta.

Peppers are among our favorite vegetables to grill during the late summer months, when they are at their peak flavor and ripeness. We use these three methods:

- Fire-roasted on the wood-fired grill (4 minutes on each side)
- Fire-roasted on the charcoal grill (4 minutes on each side)
- Roasted in the oven (toss in extra virgin olive oil and a pinch of salt and bake at 425°F for 20 minutes)

We prefer to use jalapeño, poblano, and Anaheim peppers. It is best to leave them whole, toss them in olive oil and sea salt, and grill on each side for about 4 minutes, until they have slightly flattened, are tender, and have nice charred grill marks. Remove from grill and let cool for at least 30 minutes. Cut off the stems and remove seeds. Rinse slightly.

Fire-roasted Hot Pepper Paste

24 fire-roasted jalapeños (preferably red)
6 fire-roasted poblano peppers
2 tablespoons red wine vinegar
1 teaspoon Celtic sea salt

In a food processor, combine all ingredients and process for 1 minute or until smooth and creamy. The paste will keep refrigerated in a tightly sealed jar for up to 2 weeks. It freezes well in freezer-safe bags.

Spicy Chowchow with Fire-roasted Hot Peppers

2 large onions, diced
4 cloves of garlic, minced
1 green cabbage, cut in half lengthwise and grilled
3 small summer squash, cut in half lengthwise and grilled
3 fire-roasted poblano peppers, diced
5 fire-roasted jalapeño peppers, diced
2 fire-roasted bell peppers, diced
1 tablespoon Celtic sea salt
1 teaspoon cracked black pepper
1 tablespoon sugar (I prefer coconut sugar)

In a large pot, sauté onions and garlic in oil for 2 minutes. Chop grilled cabbage and squash and add to the pot. Cook on medium heat for 2 minutes. Add diced fire-roasted hot and bell peppers, salt, pepper, and sugar. Cook on medium heat for 5 minutes or until all ingredients are tender. Chowchow will keep refrigerated for 1 week in a tightly sealed jar. It freezes well in freezer-safe bags.

Farmer's Favorite Fire-roasted Hot Pepper and Tomatillo Salsa

36 fire-roasted tomatillos

6 fire-roasted jalapeño peppers

3 fire-roasted poblano peppers

1 fresh lime, squeezed

1 bunch fresh cilantro

1 teaspoon red wine vinegar

1 teaspoon Celtic sea salt

1 teaspoon sugar (I prefer coconut sugar)

1 teaspoon cracked black pepper

2 small red onions, diced

4 garlic cloves, minced

Blend everything, except for the onions and garlic, in a food processor on high for 1 minute or until thoroughly processed. Pour mixture into a large bowl. Add chopped onions and minced garlic. This salsa will keep refrigerated for roughly 1 week in a tightly sealed jar. It also freezes well in freezer-safe bags.

Batch Freezing

Freezing is an underutilized and excellent way to preserve your garden bounty. For squash, potatoes, sweet potatoes, or eggplant, chop and then fully cook or blanch them and freeze in a freezer bag for quick meal additions. For peppers, corn, or onions, just chop and freeze them to later add to omelettes, quiches, stir-fries or other meals. This will make meal preparation more convenient too!

Don't forget about your freezer. Make batches of sauces or salsas and freeze in labeled freezer bags. Grill a large quantity of veggies, cut into strips, and freeze in labeled freezer bags to have the taste of summer any time of the year.

Gourmet Pasta Sauce

(makes 6 batches)

4 onions, chopped

24 cloves of garlic, minced

15–20 peppers, chopped

¼ cup extra virgin olive oil

¼ cup red wine

¼ cup red wine vinegar

1 small bunch of each of these fresh herbs: parsley,
    oregano, thyme, basil and sage, chopped

4 tablespoons Celtic sea salt

½ cup brown sugar or coconut sugar

70–100 tomatoes (peeled using the hot water
    method) OR

3–5 gallons of Sungold cherry tomatoes (no need to
    peel)

Sauté onions, garlic, and peppers in olive oil.
Add red wine and red wine vinegar and simmer
for 5 minutes. Add chopped fresh herbs, salt,
and sugar and simmer for 5 minutes. Add this
mixture to tomatoes in a large stockpot. Bring
to a boil. Cook on medium heat for about 25
minutes or until everything is tender. Simmer
for 10 minutes on low heat. Let mixture cool
to room temperature. You may process this
mixture in the blender to achieve the desired
consistency. Separate into Ziploc bags, label the
contents, and date.

Canning

An avid gardener's greatest bounty occurs
in the late summer and early fall. The seasoned
homesteaders and canners have it down to a
science, putting up multiple jars of tomatoes,
sauces, salsas, fruits, vegetables, jams, and jellies.

Hats off to those folks. Becoming skilled in
this age-old hobby requires knowledge of safety
measures and temperature regulation to prevent
risks of botulism and temperamental pressure
canners. I would recommend taking a few classes through your local Extension office before
delving into the art of pressure canning.

For beginners, it is best to stick to the hot
water bath canning, an art passed down from
generation to generation. I was taught by
Colleen Smith, my homesteading hero friend.
Colleen, her husband, and their three beautiful
daughters live in the two-room schoolhouse
her grandparents both attended decades ago.
Colleen is a master herbalist and avid gardener
who has been canning tomatoes since she was

a teenager. Her father is the king of tomatoes, winning many blue ribbons. Colleen uses a portable propane cooker or turkey fryer to can like a rock star.

It is best to take a class in your local community before canning at home. There are many important things to know such as sterilization techniques, proper temperatures, and safety methods and just good general tips.

Canned Vegetables

(makes 3 to 6 quarts)

Place a large canning pot on a propane cooker or on your stovetop. Place a canning rack inside the pot and add 6 to 8 jars. Fill pot with water about ¾ full, making sure the jars are fully submerged to sterilize them. Turn heat to medium high. Bring water to a boil. Use canning tongs to remove jars and lay them right side up on a towel to air dry. Sterilize lids and ring in a separate small saucepan of boiling water.

Fill a separate large stainless steel pot with boiling water. Add 6 quarts of vegetables. Boil vegetables for about 3 to 5 minutes and strain.

Reboil the pot used to sterilize jars (you will use this to can the vegetables).

Fill sterilized jars with vegetables. Boil about 8 quarts of water. Sprinkle ½ tablespoon of canning salt over the vegetables in the jars. Pour boiled water over vegetables in each jar, leaving about one inch of head space. Using a clean cloth, dip an end into boiled water to wipe the rims of the jars before placing the lids on. Once they are securely fastened, arrange jars of vegetables on the canning rack. Carefully place it into the large pot of boiling water and process for about 45 minutes.

Using canning tongs, remove jars from the hot water bath. Place them on a towel to dry. Be sure that the lid sinks down, becoming concave. Listen for the popping sound that occurs once the jar has sealed. If you can push the lid down like a button, it has not sealed. Jars need to be sealed completely. If you have trouble getting them to seal all the way, you can always pour the contents into a freezer-safe Ziploc bag and freeze them. Don't forget to label your jars and your freezer bags with the contents and the date.

For more homesteading ideas and tips on canning, preserving, and foraging wild edibles, visit Colleen and Jamie's blog at Wildstead. wordpress.com.

Pickling

Pickled Taqueria-style Carrots

4 pounds carrots, cut into 3-inch pieces

6 cups water

6 cups vinegar

3 tablespoons salt

1 tablespoon sugar (optional)

sprig of each oregano and thyme

1 tablespoon peppercorn

1 tablespoon toasted cumin seeds

6 cloves garlic

1 hot pepper for each jar

Sterilize jars and lids. Make a simple pickling brine by combining water, vinegar, salt, and sugar. Bring to a boil. Simmer for 5–10 minutes. Fill jars with garlic, hot pepper, then carrots. Cover with hot brine. Wipe rims of jars with cloth dipped in hot water. Place lids on jars. Hot water bath process (boil jars for five minutes). Remove with canning tongs.

Pickled Vegetables

4 pounds vegetables, sliced

6 cups water

6 cups vinegar

4 tablespoons salt

1 bunch fresh dill or 2 tablespoons dried dill

6 cloves garlic (one for each jar)

1 hot pepper per jar

Sterilize jars and lids. Make brine. Fill jars with garlic, hot pepper, garlic, then veggies. Cover with hot brine. Wipe rims of jars with cloth dipped in hot water. Place lids on jars. Hot water bath process (boil jars for five minutes). Remove with canning tongs.

Here is a partial list of some common home-grown fruits and veggies to dehydrate:

Apples	Mushrooms
Pears	Peppers
Peaches	Onions
Apricots	Chives
Figs	Tomatoes
Nectarines	Zucchini
Berries	Squash
Ginger	Peas
Kale	Runner beans
Chard	Bush beans

Dehydrating

Veggies and fruits can be preserved using a dehydrator. Simply cut thin slices of fruit and vegetables and lay them out in a single layer with plenty of space between each piece. Follow the specific settings on your dehydrator to achieve the proper dried texture.

Dehydrating Herbs

Most dehydrators have a "dried herbs" setting. Leafy herbs can be dried on the lowest setting overnight.

Hang Drying Herbs

String bundled herbs upside down in a dry place. To avoid dust or insects landing on the herbs, place them in brown paper bags. When the leaves are crisp, remove from stems and store in labeled and dated glass jars. Once you have multiple dried herbs, you can create custom spice blends. Create a handmade label and give as gifts to friends and family.

Freezing Herbs

One of the easiest ways to capture their essence is to simply cut fresh herbs with a pair of scissors and freeze them in ice cube trays. Cut the leaves from stems. Fill ice cube trays with water, and then firmly place herbs (roughly 1 teaspoon) into each cube. Freeze overnight. Place frozen herb ice cubes in labeled freezer bags. These work well added to soups, stews, or sauces.

Herbal Vinegars and Olive Oils

Simply place a small handful or a few sprigs of fresh (rinsed and dried) herbs into an 8-ounce jar of apple cider vinegar, white wine vinegar, white balsamic vinegar, or extra virgin olive oil. Store in airtight jars, labeled for contents and date. Hardy herbs such as rosemary and thyme may stay in the jars. Remove leafy herbs such as basil and parsley after 1 to 2 weeks. No need to refrigerate. Use within 6 months.

Herb Butters

Experiment with different herb combinations and create butters from your favorites. Remove leaves from stems, keeping the stems for later use in a broth. Chop herbs finely.

Melt a stick of butter in a saucepan over medium heat. Sauté herbs gently over low heat for a few minutes, then remove from heat. Pour the melted butter and herbs into a large glass mixing bowl and whisk for 1 minute. Pour the mixture into labeled baby food jars. Stir while the jar is cooling. Refrigerate once the butter has cooled. If you desire whipped butter, simply whip the melted herb butter in a food processor and refrigerate in baby food jars.

Pestos

Pesto is a simple way to prolong the freshness of herbs. According to the *Etymology Dictionary*, pesto got its name from *pestato*, past participle of *pestare* "to pound, to crush" (from the Latin root of "pestle"), in reference to the crushed herbs and garlic ingredients. It can be made from basil, parsley, cilantro, chervil, dill, mint, or lemon balm. During the winter, when basil is not available by the armful, take any pesto recipe and replace it with spinach, kale, chard, lettuce, and even wild greens such as lamb's quarters and chickweed!

Our kids love pesto and can eat it by the spoonful. After trying Colleen's delicious lamb's quarters pesto, I started throwing all kinds of greens into my pesto, such as spinach, chard, kale, and even gourmet salad mix to sneak those nutrient-packed greens into the kid's daily meals.

Basic Pesto

6 cups fresh herbs (leaves only)

1 cup nuts (pine nuts are standard, but use any nuts or sunflower or pumpkin seeds)

1 cup extra virgin olive oil

2 cloves garlic

pinch of salt

1 tablespoon lemon juice, to preserve freshness

Combine ingredients in a food processor until desired consistency. Adjust to your personal taste and desired texture. Adding more oil and lemon juice, for instance, will make the pesto runnier; using less will make it more spreadable for sandwiches or bagels. Freeze excess pesto in labeled freezer bags or ice cube trays. Place the frozen cubes in a labeled freezer bag. Thaw and use as needed.

Try the following recipes, inspired by herbalist Colleen Smith's lamb's quarters pesto. (Previously published in *Mother Earth News*.)

Wild and Gourmet Greens Pesto

4 cups wild and gourmet greens (equal amounts of chickweed, lamb's quarters, spinach, and leaf lettuce)

pinch of Celtic sea salt

1 cup extra virgin olive oil

½ cup toasted nuts

6 cloves garlic, toasted

Blend the greens and salt in a food processor, then slowly add the remaining ingredients. Purée until the desired consistency is reached.

Peppermint Pesto

4 cups peppermint leaves (any mint will do)
½ teaspoon organic sugar or honey
1 cup extra virgin olive oil

Blend the mint and sugar in a food processor, then slowly add the remaining ingredients. Purée until the desired consistency is reached. Peppermint pesto is excellent served on homemade brownies or natural vanilla ice cream.

If you have mint growing in your yard, take advantage of it! Peppermint has a cooling effect on the body, is great for the digestive system, and helps to soothe fevers. It is also great with lemon balm in herb-infused water.

Arugula, Lemon, and Artichoke Pesto

6 cups arugula
½ cup extra virgin olive oil
½ cup toasted nuts
6 cloves garlic, toasted
1 jar of artichoke hearts packed in oil (don't throw out the oil)
1 lemon, juiced
pinch of Celtic sea salt

Blend the greens and salt in a food processor, then slowly add the remaining ingredients. Purée until the desired consistency is reached.

Garlic Chive & Kale Pesto

1 bunch of garlic chives
6 leaves of kale
2 cups extra virgin olive oil
pinch of sea salt
handful of fresh herbs (basil and parsley work well)
handful of pine nuts (optional)

Combine in a food processor or blender for 1 minute.

Garlic Scape Pesto

More Pesto Ideas!

Mix pesto with olive oil and vinegar for a delicious salad dressing.

Mix pesto with a cream sauce for a delicious pesto Alfredo.

Use pesto as a spread on sandwiches, bagels, and wraps. Mix pesto with sun-dried tomatoes to make sun-dried tomato pesto.

Add pesto to macaroni and cheese or lasagna.

10 garlic scapes
1 cup extra virgin olive oil
pinch of sea salt
handful of fresh herbs (basil and parsley work well)
handful of pine nuts (optional)
¼ cup Asiago or Parmesan cheese (optional)

Combine in a food processor or blender for 1 minute.

Use garlic scapes just as you would use garlic. Chop, dice, blend, roast, or cook them whole in soups and stews. Blend with olive oil, vinegar, and fresh herbs for a tangy salad dressing!

Chapter 10

DIY Herbal Remedies and Recipes

HOME APOTHECARY

M OST OF THE HERBS needed for your home apothecary can be grown in your herb garden. Bulk dried herbs can also be purchased online through Mountain Rose Herbs or Starwest Botanicals, or at your local herb or natural foods store.

Helpful items to have on hand for starting your own herbal apothecary include:

- Mason jars with lids or recycled jars of all sizes with lids
- Baby food jars for making salves and lotions
- String or twine for hanging herbs to dry

- Food dehydrator
- Extra virgin olive oil
- Vodka or brandy for tincture making
- Vegetable glycerine for tincture making
- Aloe vera juice/gel
- Essential oils
- Beeswax
- Shelf to store apothecary items

TEA

From its humble beginnings in the Himalayan foothills of Southeast Asia, the salubrious tea plant has been traded

by humans to every nook and cranny of the globe, and adopted by every people under the sun. Long before igniting the American War of Independence, it abetted the poets of China in their greatest achievements. It has burrowed itself to the core of the Japanese soul, solaced many a weary Tibetan yak herder, fueled the midnight cogitations of Britain's great inventors, and offered untold numbers of Russian peasants with a path to sobriety. Through the centuries, it has provided a safe, stimulating beverage that played a crucial role in reducing human epidemics and making habitation in crowded, bustling cities possible. In the modern world, it marks the day's rhythm for hundreds and millions of people, from the Koryaks of the Kamchatka Peninsula in Russia to the Samburu pastoralists in Northern Kenya. It is precisely the epic nature of tea's odyssey that has always made its history so difficult to write. With its botanical, medical, religious, cultural, economic, anthropological, social and political dimensions, with its roots in antiquity and utter unconcern for distances and linguistic divides, the task of gathering its many strands into a single story for the general reader has always proved daunting for authors, whether from the West or the East.

The True History of Tea by Victor H. Mair
and Erling Hoh

Botanical Tea Blends for Health and Immunity

This is my article published in Issue 25 HEARTH of *Taproot* magazine, October 4, 2018.

Tea has been long revered by cultures around the globe for its medicinal healing properties. It has been highly valued and traded throughout civilization. Tea has been at the crux of ritual throughout history. It has been and still is in certain parts of the world in religious and sacred ceremonies that span the globe. From holy basil in India to green tea leaves in China, tea is a recognized symbol of warmth, hearth, and healing. Wrapping one's hands around a warm ceramic mug evokes visceral comfort. The steam appears to dance as it rises past the rim of the mug. The lore of growing tea herbs, harvesting and drying them, and the soothing effects of drinking a warm cup of herbal tea have been written in ancient texts, passed down from generation to generation through oral tradition, and are alive and well today. Tea is traditionally a hot water infusion of herbs. Typically, water is brought to a boil and poured over herbs which are then left to steep for a few minutes. Cold water infusions generally involve fresh herbs or plant material. I like to allow the herbs to remain in a cold-water infusion for several hours to draw out the medicinal properties and flavor. A decoction is made using roots, stems, and bark. It is a process of extracting the plants active constituents, oils, and volatile organic compounds.

Over the years, I have grown hundreds of varieties of medicinal and culinary herbs. Each year, I add 10–20 new herbs to our ever-expanding herb garden. Some of my favorites to grow and use are echinacea, stinging nettles, motherwort, tulsi, lavender, St. John's wort, lemon balm, lemon verbena, New England aster, horehound, thyme, sage, parsley, dill, mint, oregano, papalo, cilantro, anise hyssop, and rosemary. Ethical foraging is very dear to my heart. I love to walk through prairies and savannas, along creeks and rivers, through forests, woodlands, and glades in search of wild edibles and medicinals. I love to sit by plants in the beautiful ecosystems they grow in with my sketchbook and study them during all of the seasons. I take note of their life cycles, their appearance as young seedlings, what time of year they flower and bear fruit, when they go to seed. I collect specimens for my pressed plant journal. I spend time tasting, smelling, and feeling the herbs as well as connecting with them on the hillsides and in the valleys where they dance. Some of my favorite herbs to forage in the wild are goldenrod, mullein, red clover, dandelion, plantain, chicory, and purslane. Plants are such an important part of human history; they have played tremendous roles in civilizations for food, medicine, fiber, shelter, and lore. The anecdotes of herbs make my heart sing. I especially feel connected to herbs and

their healing abilities when I am feeling under the weather in the winter. Winter can be harsh. The trees are barren; the frost is heavy on the ground; dormant life rests beneath our feet; icicles hang from front porches; long nights are followed by short days; unshakable chill is in the air despite the knitted wool sweaters. With a bleak ambiance such as this, a hot cup of spicy chai tea couldn't be more welcoming. Herbs have become such an integral part of healing for my family and me over the last 2 decades. When a member of our family starts to show cold symptoms, I head to my homegrown apothecary shelf and choose from the dozens of Mason jars of dried herbs. Herbalists all over the globe have their go-to herbs to help alleviate cold and flu symptoms. My first-choice herbs may be different from other herbalists, but I have had tremendous success with fighting off the winter blues and recovering from sickness quickly with the following herbs. When I present Introduction to Herbalism classes in my community, I encourage the participants to seek from their spice cabinet when they feel the onset of cold symptoms. Culinary herbs are highly medicinal. Ground cinnamon, ginger, and turmeric can be mixed with honey or maple syrup for a soothing cough syrup. Sage, rosemary, thyme, parsley, mint, and oregano can be made into a simple tea to help alleviate symptoms of respiratory upsets such as coughing.

Culinary Herbal Tea

This tea blend prepared with equal parts of common herbs helps to alleviate respiratory upsets and soothes a sore throat.

2 tablespoons parsley
2 tablespoons sage
2 tablespoons dill
2 tablespoons rosemary
2 tablespoons oregano
2 tablespoons thyme
2 tablespoons mint

   Place 1 gallon of water in a large pot and bring to a boil. Add parsley, sage, dill, rosemary, oregano, thyme, and mint. Remove from heat. Allow tea to steep for 10 to 15 minutes. Add honey if you wish.

Immune Boost Tea

This tea blend prepared with equal parts echinacea root, slippery elm bark (ethically harvested), New England aster flowers, and tulsi not only is soothing and delicious but also helps to boost the immune system.

2 tablespoons echinacea root
2 tablespoons slippery elm bark
2 tablespoons New England aster flower
2 tablespoons tulsi

   Place 1 gallon of water, echinacea root, and slippery elm bark in a large pot. Bring to a boil. Add New England aster flower. Remove from heat. Allow tea to steep for 10 to 15 minutes.

Dandelion and Chicory Root Tea

Dandelion and chicory roots can be dug in the fall from areas that do not spray pesticides. The roots should be washed and scrubbed thoroughly. This tea has a remarkable flavor, and it makes a wonderful coffee substitute.

several dandelion roots
several chicory roots
honey (optional)

Harvest the roots and spray them with a hose to remove mud. Cut the top ½ inch of the root off with the greens attached. (The greens can be used in a separate tonic tea. They are very bitter.) Chop the roots into ¼-inch sections. Preheat the oven to 400°F. Dry roast them on a sheet pan in the oven for 15 to 20 minutes or until they are golden brown. They can also be dehydrated.

Bring 1 gallon of water to a boil. Add roasted roots and simmer on medium for 15 to 20 minutes. Serve hot with almond milk and honey (optional).

Golden Chai Tea

Chai often takes a backseat for coffee lovers such as myself, but in winter, I can't get enough chai. Perhaps it's me waxing nostalgic to the smells, tastes, and sights of the holidays. Some of my favorite memories from childhood are the scent of cinnamon and pumpkin spice candles, the pot of cinnamon sticks, and orange peels that my mother simmered on the stove for hours to make the house smell nice. The tastes of chai are warm and welcoming. What the spices do to the taste buds this time of year can be compared to the comfort brought about by being wrapped in a quilt grandmother made or being fireside with a favorite book. Hearth. Warming. Spiced. Layered. Complex. Sweet. All words I would use to describe the fiery body of chai tea.

The origin of chai tea dates over 5,000 years ago to India. Legend has it that a king created a healing tea, and it has since been used as a quintessential blend in Ayurvedic medicine. When I think of chai, I can't help but remember those cold winter mornings when it turned a gloomy day into a bright one. When I make chai tea now, I have a little more intention behind it. As a farmer and a herbalist, I recognize the medicinal properties of the food we put into our bodies, and I now know the amazing active constituents that spices and herbs contain and make up their healing qualities.

Chai is a warm soothing cup of immunity. Cinnamon contains antibacterial, antiviral, and immune-building properties. Ginger strengthens the immune system and aids in digestion. Cloves have antioxidant, antiseptic, and anti-inflammatory properties. Chinese star anise has antifungal and antibacterial properties.

The secret ingredient in the chai I brew at home is dried cayenne pepper. My husband and I receive so much joy from growing food and herbs that have medicinal properties. We pick as many sun-ripened fire red cayennes from the bright green plants as we can throughout the season and dehydrate them to use all winter long. Cayenne peppers, revered as containing some of the most healing properties in the world, are used to treat a plethora of ailments throughout many cultures. They boost the immune system, provide relief from cold and flu symptoms, migraines and headaches, and help to detoxify the body and improve circulation and overall heart health. Nothing pleases me more than sipping on hot chai tea on a cold winter day with my family.

1 gallon of purified or distilled water

3 tablespoons freshly grated ginger

1 tablespoon whole cloves

1 dried vanilla bean pod

2 whole nutmeg seeds, cut in half

6 whole cinnamon sticks

1 dried or fresh cayenne pepper (seeds removed and cut into strips)

1 cup vanilla almond milk (per 4 servings of chai tea)

4 tablespoons local honey (per 4 servings of chai tea)

In a large pot, bring water to a boil. Remove from heat. Add all the tea herbs and steep for 5 to 10 minutes.

To make chai latte, blend 1 cup of vanilla almond milk (or milk of your choice) with 4 tablespoons local honey for 1 minute or until milk is frothy. Pour 8 ounces of piping hot chai tea into each of the four mugs. Top them with equal amounts of milk and honey.

Making Your Own Herbal Tea

Preparing your own herbal tea is fun and cost-effective. You can grow most of the tea plants yourself. Keep your dried tea blends in a Mason jar. Buy tea bags and fill them with the blend of your choice. Iron the tea bags shut and store them in a jar or decorative tin. You may purchase dried stevia leaf and add it to your tea blend to naturally sweeten it. Teas make excellent gifts. Package them beautifully with a small jar of local honey. If it is for a very special person, include a tea set.

Herbal Tea Blends

- **Cold and flu support tea:** thyme, oregano, sage, rosemary, clove, cinnamon bark, ginger, mullein, stevia leaf, lemon, and honey
- **Floral energy tea:** red clover flowers, calendula flowers, chrysanthemum flowers, echinacea petals, rose hips, lemon balm, red raspberry leaf, nettles
- **Digestion tea:** ginger root, peppermint leaf, basil leaf, and chamomile flowers
- **Rest and relax tea:** chamomile and valerian root
- **Stress relief tea:** kava kava, chamomile flowers, spearmint, passionflower herb, rose petals, lavender flowers, and cinnamon bark
- **Immune builder tea:** echinacea, goldenseal, red clover blossoms, nettle

leaf, pau d'arco bark, sage leaf, St. John's wort, and ginger root
- **Headache relief tea:** peppermint leaves and lavender flowers

Each of these tea recipes can be made into popsicles, using a mold, to soothe a sore throat. These recipes are not intended to treat or cure. They are provided for educational purposes. Keep a journal of the herbs that work for your body.

Many herbs are contraindicated during pregnancy or while using prescription drugs. Herbs should be used with caution and under the supervision of a doctor or herbalist when major illness or disease is present. Consult with a physician or a naturopathic doctor when using herbs.

Hot infusions are soothing, warming, and comforting during winter months. Herbs can be steeped for 10 to 40 minutes to extract the active constituents and the medicinal benefits from the herb. Leaves and flowers require less time to steep than roots and bark. Often, I bring water to a boil, add herbs, turn off the heat, and let the herbs steep overnight.

I make roughly 6 cups of tea at a time in a large glass Pyrex measuring cup. It can also be made in a medium pot. I boil the water and remove from heat. I place my herbs in a glass measuring cup and cover with the hot water for 5 to 10 minutes. After straining the herbs in a fine-mesh stainless steel strainer, I add honey. What my family doesn't drink, I refrigerate for later use. For individual servings, use a tea ball, a stainless steel ball that opens and latches and is used to steep herbs.

Spring Tonic Tea Blend

¼ cup burdock root, fresh or dried
¼ cup dandelion leaves, fresh
⅛ cup dandelion root, fresh or dried
⅛ cup echinacea root, fresh or dried
⅛ cup ginger root, fresh or dried
¼ cup nettle leaf
⅛ cup red clover blossoms
2 gallons water

Boil water and pour over herbs. Let steep for 5 minutes and cool. Strain herbs. Store in the refrigerator up to 4 days. Drink a cup in the morning, one in the afternoon, and another in the evening.

OXYMELS

Oxymels, herbal-infused vinegar mixed with honey, were traditionally prepared to help boost immunity, fight infections, or soothe the symptoms of respiratory ailments. The standard preparation is to use 1 part herb-infused vinegar to 5 parts honey.

There are several ways of making an oxymel. A simple one starts with preparing a herb-infused vinegar. After 1 or 2 weeks, strain the herbs and add the vinegar to equal parts honey. The following recipe is adapted from Mountain Rose Herbs and the Herbal Academy.

Basic Oxymel

1 part dried herbs
1 part honey (raw honey is best)
1 part apple cider vinegar

Fill a 1-quart Mason jar about ⅓ full with dried herbs. Cover with 1 part apple cider vinegar and 1 part honey to try to achieve a 1:3 ratio. Stir the mixture well and cover with a plastic lid. Be sure to label as to contents and date.

Store the jar in a dark cabinet. Shake it vigorously daily. After 2 weeks, use a mesh strainer and cheesecloth to strain into a clean jar. Be sure to label. This preparation should stay good for up to 6 months if stored in a cool, dark place free of moisture. Take a few tablespoons as needed.

Rosemary Gladstar's Fire Cider Recipe

Sourced from Gladstar's book, *Winter Recipes for Health & Well Being*

Fire cider, an oxymel combining spicy herbs and veggies, helps to boost immunity and offer support to the circulatory system.

½ cup freshly grated ginger
½ cup freshly grated horseradish
1 onion, chopped
10 cloves of garlic, minced
2 jalapeño peppers, chopped
1 lemon (juice and zest)
2 tablespoons rosemary, dried; or several sprigs of
    fresh
1 tablespoon turmeric, ground or freshly grated
apple cider vinegar (enough to fill jar)
¼ cup honey (plus more to taste)

Place ginger, horseradish, onion, garlic, peppers, lemon zest, lemon juice, rosemary, and turmeric in a 1-quart canning jar. Cover with apple cider vinegar by about 2 inches. Place natural parchment or wax paper under the lid to keep the vinegar from touching the metal. Shake well. Store in a cool, dark place for 1 month and shake daily.

Use cheesecloth to strain out the pulp, pouring the vinegar into a clean jar. Be sure to squeeze as much of the liquid goodness as you can from the pulp while straining. Add ¼ cup of honey and stir until incorporated. Taste your cider and add another ¼ cup until you reach desired sweetness. Fire cider should taste hot, spicy, and sweet. It is great as a winter tonic and as a remedy for colds and coughs. Often people use it as salad dressing or sauce on rice or steamed vegetables.

Fire cider is the people's medicine. Visit http://freefirecider.com/ to learn about the mission to help keep fire cider trademark-free.

Elderflower Cordial with Coconut Sugar and Lemon Verbena

20 elderflower umbels (flowering tops)

3 cups of coconut sugar (or organic cane sugar)

6 to 8 cups of water

4 lemons, sliced

3 sprigs of lemon verbena

2 tablespoons of citric acid

Snip the flowers into a large crock or pot with a lid. Add the sliced lemons and lemon verbena. In a separate large pot, bring the sugar and water to a light boil, stirring frequently until the sugar is dissolved. Allow the mixture to cool a little. Add this mixture to the elderflowers and lemons in the crock, making sure they are submerged. Cover with plastic wrap, tightly sealed, and add the lid.

Allow the pot to sit in a cool, dry location for 2 hours. Strain the mixture into a separate pot using a mesh strainer lined with cheesecloth. Add citric acid, bring to a boil, and then remove from heat. Pour the hot liquid into clean sterilized jars. Label and store in a cool, dark location for up to 6 months. Refrigerate if you wish. This cordial is lovely when mixed with sparkling water. Add gin, vodka, or brandy if you wish.

Elderberry Syrup

▲ *Elderberries growing in the Midwest.*

Adapted from Mountain Rose Herbs.

3 cups of elderberries, dried; or 6 cups of fresh

5 cups of purified water

4 tablespoons freshly grated ginger root

4 tablespoons dried echinacea root

4 cinnamon sticks

1 teaspoon cardamom

6 cloves

2 cups raw honey or maple syrup

In a large pot, combine elderberries, water, ginger, echinacea, cinnamon, cardamom, and cloves. Bring to a boil. Reduce heat to low and simmer for 40 minutes. Remove from heat and allow to cool and steep for 1 to 2 hours. Strain into a separate pot using a mesh strainer lined with cheesecloth. Once the liquid has cooled completely, add honey and stir well.

For a longer shelf life, add 1 to 2 cups of brandy or vodka and stir well. For a version safe for kids, omit the alcohol. For toddlers, omit the honey and use maple syrup. Bottle in sterilized glass jars by boiling glass in water for 5 minutes in a canning pot.

After straining the mixture, I like to use the remaining berries and herbs to do a second steep. Once cooled and honey is added, I place the syrup in ice cube trays and freeze for later use. I also mix some with water or juice and add to popsicle molds and freeze for use during cold and flu season.

TINCTURE MAKING

Tincture making is an ancient art that has been passed down through generations, usually from mother to daughter, around the globe. Tinctures involve soaking herbs in a liquid — typically vodka, brandy, apple cider vinegar, or vegetable glycerin — to extract their medicinal properties. Alcohol tends to have a long shelf life, so the tincture will last up to a year. For advanced tincture making, 190-proof organic alcohol works best. Different herbs require varying concentrations of alcohol. Vinegar and glycerin tinctures have a shorter shelf life and may need to be refrigerated. The liquid used in tincture making is known as the menstruum.

The standard ratio for fresh herbs in tincture making is 1 part fresh herb to 2 parts menstruum. A single herb St. John's wort tincture, for example, uses 1 ounce of fresh St. John's wort, so you would need 2 ounces of menstruum. The standard ratio for dried herbs is 1 part dried herbs to 5 parts menstruum.

Typically the herb will rise to the top of the jar, above the liquid surface. To prevent this, weight down your herbs with a crystal (be sure to sanitize the crystal first).

Simple Tincture

herbs and flowers of your choice
Mason jar with lid
alcohol (organic vodka or brandy)

Label your jar with contents and date. Fill jar ¾ of the way full with herbs. Fill jar halfway with alcohol. Add water, leaving 1 inch at the top of the jar. Be sure your herbs are covered. If they are not, tamp them down with a spoon. Shake vigorously for 1 to 2 minutes. Store in a dark, cool, dry place. Shake daily. Medicine will be ready in 2 weeks and will last up to 1 year.

HERBAL ELIXIRS

Elixirs, one of my favorite ways to use herbs, really embody the essence of a herb through flavor, aroma, energetics, and its effects on the mind, body, and spirit. Historically, herbal elixirs were used medicinally, as a pleasant way to treat a variety of ailments.

Essentially, elixirs involve steeping medicinal herbs in honey or maple syrup, sometimes combining them with brandy or other alcohol, or fermenting them, such as with medicinal meads.

Basic Herbal Elixir

Simply combine equal parts of herbal honey and herbal tincture. Fill a pint jar with medicinal herbs of your choice. Pour ⅓ pint of honey over the herbs, covering them completely. Pour brandy over herbs and honey to fill the jar. Place a plastic lid on the jar and shake well. Place on a small plate to prevent leakage. Store in a dark cupboard for about 1 month. Strain the herbs. Enjoy the elixir 2 ounces at a time. Keep refrigerated to preserve longevity.

TOPICAL HERBAL RECIPES
Herbal-Infused Oils or Herbal Oil Infusion

Making a herbal oil infusion simply involves soaking herbs or flowers in a jar of oil, then straining the herb to use the oil. These infusions are used topically for dry skin or to heal blemishes. They can also be used to make lip balm, first-aid salve, or other healing salves.

1 cup dried herbs, or 3 cups fresh herbs (comfrey, dandelion, calendula, echinacea, plantain, and lemon balm)
2 cups carrier oil (grapeseed oil, extra virgin olive oil, sunflower oil, sweet almond oil, or apricot oil)
3 capsules of vitamin E oil

Pack herbs in a large Mason jar, cover with oil, and add vitamin E capsules, leaving 1 inch at the top. Shake vigorously. Seal the jar and leave it in a warm, slightly sunny place for 2 weeks, shaking daily.

Pour into a clean glass jar, straining through cheesecloth. Squeeze as much oil as possible through the bag, and pour into clean dark glass bottles. Seal, label, and store in the refrigerator for up to 3 months.

Healing Salve

This makes about 10 ounces of a great general-purpose healing salve.

2 cups of your herbal-infused oil (comfrey, chickweed, calendula, echinacea, plantain, lemon balm, dandelion)
1 ounce grated or chopped beeswax (beeswax pellets work well)
3 vitamin E capsules of at least 400 units (this is your preservative)
10 drops of lavender essential oil
cheesecloth to strain herbs
double boiler, or 2 pots (one that fits inside of the other)
glass measuring cup
large spoon
stainless steel container with a narrow pouring spout
baby food jars or tins

Place your herbal oil infusion in the top pot of your double boiler on a burner or on the stovetop. Very gently heat the oil mix on low.

Puncture and add vitamin E capsules and then add beeswax. Stir until it's completely melted and blended. Remove from heat and let cool just 1 or 2 minutes. Add 10 drops of lavender essential oil and stir. Pour into a wide-mouth jar or several small jars. As it cools, the mixture will become semi-solid, the perfect salve consistency. Label your jar with contents and date.

First-aid salve may be used in place of double or triple antibiotic ointment. It helps to heal minor cuts, scrapes, and burns. It also helps with bruises, dry skin, joint and muscle pain, and even arthritis pain.

Lip Balm

1 cup coconut oil, or other solid carrier oil
½ cup hemp seed oil, or extra virgin olive oil (infused with fresh mint if you wish)
2 tablespoons vitamin E oil
1½ ounces beeswax (or ¾ ounce candelilla wax and ½ ounce soy wax for vegan lip balm)

¼ ounce cocoa butter
pure essential oils
double boiler or 2 pots, one smaller than the other
small stainless steel pitcher with spout
approximately 50 lip balm tubes or tins (available online under the title "eco-friendly lip balm tubes")
heating element (stovetop, double burner, etc.)

Have all ingredients available and ready. Set up lip balm tubes upright with enough space between each to grab and fill.

Pour about 2 to 3 inches of water into the bottom pot of a double boiler. Once it boils, turn heat to low. Place beeswax (or alternatives) and cocoa butter into the smaller stainless steel pot and stir frequently until completely melted. Add coconut oil, hemp seed oil, and vitamin E oil. Stir well until mixture is liquid again. Turn heat off. With a potholder, remove the pot with the mixture and pour it into the small stainless steel pitcher with the narrow spout. Stir in 10 to 15 drops of essential oils. Immediately pour mixture into the lip balm tubes. A pitcher with a narrow pour spout works fairly well if you pour slowly. Otherwise, use a stainless steel funnel. Let the tubes sit until they harden. Once they harden, put the caps on, wipe them with a clean damp cloth, and label.

For an extra fresh flavor, infuse fresh mint from your garden into the hemp oil for 1 week prior to making the lip balm. Strain and use in the lip balm.

Lotion

½ cup coconut oil

¼ cup shea butter

¼ cup cocoa butter

1 cup emulsifying wax

2 tablespoons vitamin E oil

4 cups hot water

¼ teaspoons citric acid

pure essential oils (pick gentle ones such as lavender)

Melt oils, butter, and wax together in the top of a double boiler on low. Put mixture and hot water into large stainless steel bowl. Mix for one minute using an electric mixer, or whip by hand. Add essential oil drops and then blend or whip for an additional 30 seconds. Store in a baby food jar with tight-fitting lid. Label your jar with contents and date.

Poison Ivy Relief

Jewelweed is a natural antidote to poison ivy. It works well to alleviate pain, itching, and burning caused by poison ivy rash.

1 large handful of fresh or dried jewelweed

Use a mortar and pestle or food processor to crush jewelweed. Place equal amounts in each section of an ice cube tray. Carefully fill the tray with water and freeze. After it is frozen, empty into a freezer bag and label. As needed, pull one or two cubes out at a time. Wrap them in a fine muslin fabric and place on affected area for relief.

Sunburn Relief Spray

½ cup aloe vera juice
10 drops lavender essential oil
¼ cup pure witch hazel hydrosol

Combine all ingredients and, using a funnel, pour into spray bottles. Label with contents and date. Store in refrigerator.

A herbalist friend, Rebekah Dawn, uses wild rose-infused apple cider vinegar to help alleviate the heat and redness from sunburn.

Natural Insect Repellent

5 cups of distilled water (optional: infuse with fresh
      rosemary, cedar leaves, and eucalyptus overnight
      prior to making the insect repellent)
20 drops of lavender essential oil
20 drops of lemongrass essential oil
15 drops of citronella essential oil
15 drops of cedarwood essential oil
10 drops of eucalyptus essential oil
20 drops of geranium essential oil
1 tablespoon castor oil
1 tablespoon pure vanilla extract

Mix all ingredients in a large jar with lid. Shake well. Pour mixture into spray bottles. Label with contents and date.

Notes

Introduction

1. "Africa: Environmental Atlas," 06/17/08. Archived January 5, 2012, Wayback Machine African Studies Center, University of Pennsylvania. Accessed June 2011.
2. https://www.environment.gov.au/biodiversity/conservation/hotspots
3. "What If the World's Soil Runs Out?" *TIME* magazine, December 14, 2012.
4. Ibid.

Chapter 1

1. C. Milesi. "A Strategy for Mapping and Modeling the Ecological Effects of US Lawns," International Society for Photogrammetry and Remote Sensing. Supported by the NASA Earth System Science Fellowship program and the NASA Land Cover Land Use Change Research Program. https://www.isprs.org/proceedings/XXXVI/8-W27/milesi.pdf
2. UC Santa Barbara, Department of Geography. https://geog.ucsb.edu/the-lawn-is-the-largest-irrigated-crop-in-the-usa/
3. *State of the Industry Report. Lawn & Landscape.* Sponsored by John Deere. 2018.
4. Virginia Scott Jenkins. *Lawns: A History of an American Obsession.*

5. Ibid.
6. "The Life and Death of the American Lawn," August 28, 2015. https://www.theatlantic.com/entertainment/archive/2015/08/the-american-lawn-a-eulogy/402745/
7. "What Impact Does Your Lawn Have on Our Earth?" Michigan Engineering. Youtube.com
8. Moto-Mowers, ad. *House and Garden.* May 1959, 198.
9. William Grimes. "Why Grass Really Is Greener on the Other Side," *New York Times.* 2006. https://www.nytimes.com/2006/03/10/books/why-grass-really-is-always-greener-on-the-other-side.html?mtrref=undefined&gwh=A9ACE818FF5E62915293719AD145DBF7&gwt=pay)
10. Jane Clatworthy, Joe Hinds, and Paul M. Camic. "Gardening as a Mental Health Intervention: A Review," *Mental Health Review Journal*, Vol. 18, Issue 4, pp. 214–225, 2013.
11. Inhabit Film.
12. USGS. Estimate Annual Agricultural Pesticide Use. https://water.usgs.gov/nawqa/pnsp/usage/maps/show_map.php?-year=2012&map=GLYPHOSATE&hilo=L
13. https://www.epa.gov/pesticides

14. P.D. Capel, et al. *Agriculture: A River Runs Through It: The Connections Between Agriculture and Water Quality.* U.S. Geological Survey Circular 1433, 2018. https://doi.org/10.3133/cir1433

15. Ibid.

16. https://www.beyondpesticides.org/resources/pesticide-induced-diseases-database/overview

17. World Health Organization. International Agency for Research on Cancer. "IARC Monographs, Vol. 112: Evaluation of Five Organophosphate Insecticides and Herbicides," March 2015. https://www.iarc.fr/wp-content/uploads/2018/07/MonographVolume112-1.pdf

18. Brigitta Kurenbach, et al. "Sublethal Exposure to Commercial Formulations of the Herbicides Dicamba, 2,4-Dichlorophenoxyacetic Acid, and Glyphosate Cause Changes in Antibiotic Susceptibility in *Escherichia coli* and *Salmonella enterica* Serovar Typhimurium," *mBio.* American Society for Microbiology, March 24, 2015.

19. https://www.globalresearch.ca/monsanto-roundup-harms-human-endocrine-system-at-levels-allowed-in-drinking-water-study-shows/5441051

20. https://www.beyondpesticides.org/programs/lawns-and-landscapes/overview

21. D. Kriebel, et al. "The Precautionary Principle in Environmental Science," *Environmental Health Perspectives,* 109(9), 871–876, 2001, doi:10.1289/ehp.01109871

22. *Pollinator Partnership,* https://www.pollinator.org/pollinators

23. EPA WaterSense Program. "Water-Smart Landscapes: Start with Watersense," 2017, https://www.epa.gov/sites/production/files/2017-01/documents/ws-outdoor-water-efficient-landscaping.pdf

24. Pimentel, David. "Soil Erosion: A Food and Environmental Threat," *Environment, Development and Sustainability,* 8, no. 1, 2006, 119–137.

Chapter 2

1. https://www.treehugger.com/lawn-garden/gardener-sues-city-tulsa-cutting-down-her-edible-garden.html

2. https://www.huffpost.com/entry/julie-bass-jail-vegetable-garden_n_893436

3. https://www.miamiherald.com/news/local/community/miami-dade/miami-shores/article189273944.html

Chapter 3

1. "Nitrogen: The Double-Edged Sword," *Permaculture News,* October 29, 2014.

2. Personal communication.

3. "Inside NC Science: A World of Mystery Lives Underfoot in Soils," Newsobserver.com, May 17, 2015.

4. "Vermicomposting: Worm Your Way into Composting Heaven," *FIX,* fix.com/blog/composting-with-worms, December 12, 2014.

5. The book was self-published in 1982.

6. https://midwestpermaculture.com/2012/11/how-to-build-a-worm-tower/

7. https://www.sierra-worm-compost.com/storing-worm-castings.htm
8. The Grow Network, October 2, 2015.

Chapter 4

1. http://tobyhemenway.com
2. Crystal Stevens. *Grow Create Inspire: Crafting a Joyful Life of Beauty and Abundance.* New Society, 2016.
3. http://tobyhemenway.com/resources/ethics-and-principles/
4. PermaculturePrinciples.com
5. https://www.youtube.com/watch?v=crPfz52a32c
6. Rodale's *Organic Life* magazine, April/May2013, Vol. 60, Issue 3, p. 68.
7. https://www.nrcs.usda.gov/Internet/FSE_DOCUMENTS/stelprdb1263176.pdf

Chapter 5

1. "Crop Rotations," Rodale Institute. https://rodaleinstitute.org/why-organic/organic-farming-practices/crop-rotations/
2. "A Quick Guide to Crop Rotation & Vegetable Families," GrowOrganic.com. September 7, 2012.

3. "Vegetable Crop Rotation," https://harvesttotable.com/vegetable_crop_rotation/

Chapter 6

1. USDA, Agricultural Research Service. https://planthardiness.ars.usda.gov/PHZMWeb/
2. "Disease-Resistant Plants," January 13, 1995. https://hortnews.extension.iastate.edu/1995/1-13-1995/nodis.html
3. "What Is a Food Forest?" Permaculture Research Institute. April 16, 2019. https://permaculturenews.org/2019/04/16/what-is-a-food-forest/
4. Temperate Climate Permaculture, http://tcpermaculture.com/site/2013/05/27/nine-layers-of-the-edible-forest-garden/#prettyPhoto[gallery4607]/0/
5. https://foodforestsgrow.weebly.com/layers-of-a-food-forest.html

Index

About the Author

CRYSTAL STEVENS lives along the bluffs of the Mighty Mississippi River in Godfrey, Illinois, with her husband and 2 children. Stevens is an Author, an Artist/Art Teacher, a Folk Herbalist, a Regenerative Farmer, and a Permaculturist. Stevens has written 3 books: *Grow Create Inspire, Worms at Work,* and *Your Edible Yard.* Stevens speaks at conferences and *Mother Earth News* Fairs across the United States. She has been teaching a Resilient Living workshop series for over a decade. She and her husband, Eric Stevens, co-founded FLOURISH which encompasses a farm, a plant nursery, an apothecary, design services and educational programming including a Permaculture Design Course, and dozens of workshops throughout each season. They are both on the board of

PHOTO CREDIT: CANDICE PYLE

Slow Food St. Louis. Stevens co-founded Tend & Flourish School of Botanicals with Alex Queathem.

A Note about the Publisher

NEW SOCIETY PUBLISHERS is an activist, solutions-oriented publisher focused on publishing books for a world of change. Our books offer tips, tools, and insights from leading experts in sustainable building, homesteading, climate change, environment, conscientious commerce, renewable energy, and more — positive solutions for troubled times.

We're proud to hold to the highest environmental and social standards of any publisher in North America. This is why some of our books might cost a little more. We think it's worth it!

- We print all our books in North America, never overseas
- All our books are printed on **100% post-consumer recycled paper,** processed chlorine free, with low-VOC vegetable-based inks (since 2002)*
- Our corporate structure is an innovative employee shareholder agreement, so we're one-third employee-owned (since 2015)
- We're carbon-neutral (since 2006)
- We're certified as a B Corporation (since 2016)

At New Society Publishers, we care deeply about *what* we publish — but also about *how* we do business.

Download our catalogue at https://newsociety.com/Our-Catalog, or for a printed copy please email info@newsocietypub.com or call 1-800-567-6772 ext 111.

New Society Publishers
ENVIRONMENTAL BENEFITS STATEMENT

*By Using 100% post-consumer recycled paper vs virgin paper stock, New Society Publishers saves the following resources:[1] (per every 5,000 copies printed)

45	Trees
4,106	Pounds of Solid Waste
4,517	Gallons of Water
5,892	Kilowatt Hours of Electricity
7,463	Pounds of Greenhouse Gases
32	Pounds of HAPs, VOCs, and AOX Combined
11	Cubic Yards of Landfill Space

[1]Environmental benefits are calculated based on research done by the Environmental Defense Fund and other members of the Paper Task Force who study the environmental impacts of the paper industry.